MILTON'S SAMSON AGONISTES

Samson Agonistes

By
John Milton

WITH INTRODUCTION AND NOTES BY
H. M. Percival, M.A.
Professor of English Literature, Presidency College, Calcutta

LONDON
MACMILLAN & CO LTD
NEW YORK · ST MARTIN'S PRESS
1965

First Edition 1890
Reprinted 1891, 1895, 1896, 1900, 1902, 1906, 1912, 1916,
1923, 1930, 1933, 1947, 1949, 1950, 1951, 1958, 1960, 1964,
1965

MACMILLAN AND COMPANY LIMITED
St Martin's Street London WC2
also Bombay Calcutta Madras Melbourne

THE MACMILLAN COMPANY OF CANADA LIMITED
70 *Bond Street Toronto* 2

ST MARTIN'S PRESS INC
175 *Fifth Avenue New York* 10010 *NY*

PRINTED IN GREAT BRITAIN

CONTENTS

PREFACE

THE Text is substantially that of Masson's edition. In
the Notes I have tried to bring out the resemblance
between the Vocabulary and Phraseology of Elizabethan
literature and those of Milton's poetry. The resemblance between Shaksperian and Miltonic Grammar
needs no further proof or illustration after what Prof.
Masson and Dr. Abbott have written regarding this
point; but I was unprepared for the closeness and
extent of the resemblance in those two other points
that an actual comparison of words and phrases has
served to bring out. It has been my endeavour to
make this clear by means of quotations from Elizabethan
writers, specially Shakspere. A second object I have
had in view has been the study of words historically.
The valuable work done by the Early English Text
Society has furnished a rich storehouse of materials by
which this interesting study has been rendered more
accurate than it was only a few years ago, and has led
to results both simple and definite enough to be placed
within the reach of young students of English literature.
This I have tried to do in the quotations from Old
English. In a few passages, explanations or allusions
have been given for the first time, as far as I am aware.
Some of these (those in ll. 89, 91-93, 548, 1224, 37 and

1162) were communicated to the *Academy* by me, and appeared in the issue for 27th July last. The interesting allusions in l. 548 I owe to Mr. C. H. Tawney. In the case of those parallel passages that have been quoted by previous commentators, I have always, I trust, acknowledged the source whence they were obtained, except in the case of a few well-known passages, the right of quoting which may be looked upon as a sort of common property. In all other cases where no source is mentioned, the parallel passages are given for the first time. I am deeply indebted throughout to Todd's Variorum Edition, and to Prof. Masson's two standard works on Milton. In the grammatical and philological portion of the Notes, I owe much to the writings of Dr. Abbott, Mr. Oliphant, and Prof. Skeat. I have also found the editions of this drama by the Rev. J. Hunter and by Mr. J. C. Collins occasionally helpful.

H. M. P.

August, 1889.

In this issue, forty years after the first, besides the minor corrections now made, *one* correction—that of the *note* on l. 1519—I wish to mention here. The whole note has been revised.

H. M. P.

October, 1929.

INTRODUCTION.

SAMSON AGONISTES was licensed in July, 1670, and was Date and History of Composition. published, in the same volume with *Paradise Regained*, in 1671. The date of its composition is uncertain. From the general tone of the drama, and from particular allusions (such as those to the desecration of Cromwell's remains, ll. 368 *sq.*, in January, 1661, to the treatment of the remains of the other regicides at the same time, and to the trial of Vane, ll. 693 *sq.*, in July, 1662), it is almost certain that the work was not taken in hand before the Restoration. We know from Aubrey's *Memoir* that from 1658 to 1663, or perhaps 1665 (in which year the MS. was given to Ellwood), Milton was engaged upon *Paradise Lost;* and the well-known passage in Ellwood's *Autobiography* indicates that the years 1665 and 1666 were devoted to the writing of *Paradise Regained*. We are thus left to infer that the composition of *Samson Agonistes* proceeded side by side with that of one or the other of the two Epics, or that it was composed between 1666 and 1670. The choice between these two alternatives afforded by external evidence, is determined through evidence afforded by the drama itself. In simplicity of diction, in aphoristic condensation of thought, in chastened reserve of sentiment, in strength of didactic tone, in frequent recurrence of argument, in play of fancy habitually curbed and checked, in splendour of imagery rarely revealed, in subordination of action to speech, and lastly in a certain "homeliness of greatness," * *Samson Agonistes* resembles *Paradise Regained* more closely than it does *Paradise Lost*. But this resemblance does not necessarily imply that the two works were composed at about the same period of the author's life, since characteristics common to both may yet be the result of a different cause in each: namely, in the case of the epic, the result of a determination to present divine truth in all the simplicity of a Gospel narrative, supported by Milton's own theology, and, in the case of the drama, of a plan to reproduce the severity of its model, the Greek classical drama. But one strong circumstance—namely the transition from that tone of confidence in the future vindication of the Puritan cause, so clearly marked in the former (*P. R.* ii. 35-57), to the extinction of hope and the weariness of life most touchingly depicted in the latter (*S. A.* 594 *sq.*, and 1758)—indicates, as far as internal evidence can, that *Samson Agonistes* was a later utterance of Milton's spirit than *Paradise Regained*.

The exploits of Samson had, however, occurred to Milton long ago as subjects for dramas. In a list of Scripture subjects for tragedies drawn up in 1641, there occur the following:—"xvii. Samson marrying, or in Ramach-Lechi ; Judges xv. | xviii. Samson Pursophorus,† or Hybristes,‡ or Dagonalia, Judges xvi."

---

* Professor Seeley, *Lectures and Essays*.

† *i.e.* The Fire-brand Bringer.

‡ *i.e.* The Violent or the Insolent. This epithet is drawn, evidently, from Josephus (*Antiq.* v. 8, 10), who asserts that after the slaughter at Ramach-Lechi, Samson "held the Philistines in contempt."

This may point to as many as five distinct subjects (viz., the marriage with a Philistine woman, the slaughter of the Philistines at Ramach-Lechi, the burning of the standing corn of the Philistines, the carrying away of the gates of Gaza, or, perhaps, the bursting of the bonds with which Delilah had thrice bound him, and the revenge and death of Samson), or it may point to a projected *Trilogy*, after the manner of Æschylus, consisting of three dramas, each complete in itself, the actions of all three, however, tending to a common destiny. Thus Milton may have had in his mind the marriage of Samson as the *thesis*, by which he "sought an occasion against the Philistines" to deliver Israel from their hands; his temporary but dazzling success effected by means so ridiculously inadequate, as the *synthesis*, in which he would figure as "Pursophorus" or "Hybristes"; and lastly, his fall and revenge as the *antithesis*, of the Trilogy. If ever such a threefold drama had been in Milton's mind in 1641, it is not difficult to imagine how the downfall of Puritanism at the Restoration, his unhappy first marriage, and the loss of eyesight, would have made him realize with redoubled vividness the situations of the *last* drama of the Trilogy, while at the same time they would have untuned and unstrung his mind for the composition of the other two. How strongly the temper of his mind was influenced by these events, and how vividly that temper was reflected in the character of his compositions are, perhaps, sufficiently proved by the frequent political and personal allusions in *Samson Agonistes*.

The incidents of this drama are based upon the 13th, Source. 14th, 15th, and 16th chapters of the *Book of Judges*.

In some matters of detail (as in ll. 27, 325, 386, 1197), Milton follows Josephus (*Antiquities of the Jews*, v. 8). Attempts have been made to trace other possible sources to which Milton may have been indebted. Among such sources are, according to Todd, an Italian play of Samson by Roselli, 1554, a French tragedy of Samson, anonymous, 1622, and a *Historie of Samson* by Quarles, the Cavalier poet, 1632. Recent criticism fancies that it has discovered a source of Milton's drama in a play by the Dutch author Vondel. Milton very probably was acquainted with these works, but any claim on their behalf as having inspired him may be silently dismissed.

Structure. *Samson Agonistes* is written on the model of the classical Greek tragedy. As such it contains a Chorus, whose odes may serve to divide the piece into what correspond to Acts in modern drama. Such a division, however, is not, as Twining points out, in the notes to Aristotle's *Poetics*, always feasible, nor does it always give the number of Acts as five. In the following division I have preferred to make each Act commence with the entry of a personage, rather than with the announcement of his approach :—Lines 1-114 constitute the *Prologus* or portion that precedes the entry of the Chorus upon the stage. This Greek prologue is a part of the action of the play, and is therefore different from the prologues of Latin and modern plays. Ll. 115-175 are the *Parodos* (or first Ode), sung by the Chorus as they enter, and advance towards the or-chestra. Ll. 176-292 are the *first Epeisodion* (or Episode) which consists of dialogue between two choral odes. Ll. 293-325 are the *first Stasimon* (or second Ode), sung by the Chorus standing in its proper place in the orchestra. Ll. 326-651 are the *second Epeisodion*, of which ll. 326-331 announce, according to the custom of Greek tragedy, the approach of a personage on to the scene. Ll. 652-709 are the *second Stasimon.* Ll. 710-1009, the *third Epeisodion*, of which ll. 710-731 announce a personage. Ll. 1010-1060, *third Stasimon.* Ll. 1061-1267, *fourth Epeisodion* (ll. 1061-1075 announcing a personage). Ll. 1268-1300, *fourth Stasimon.* Ll. 1301-1426, *fifth Epeisodion* (ll. 1301-1307 announcing a personage). Ll. 1427-1440, *fifth Stasimon.* Ll. 1441 to the end constitute the *Exodus*, or "that part which has no Choral Ode after it," and which includes the *Kommos*, ll. 1660-1707, or "General Lamentation of the Chorus and the actors together." Milton therefore in concluding the Exodus with a Choral Ode (ll. 1745 *sq.*), and confining the dirge to the Chorus, follows the example of Greek tragedy, rather than the rule laid down by Aristotle. The modern division into Acts can be laid down from the above, thus:—Act I., ll. 1-331. Act II., ll. 332-731. Act III., ll. 732-1075. Act IV., Scene i., ll. 1076-1307 ; Scene ii., 1308-1444. Act V., ll. 1445 to the end.

Aristotle's brief sentence that the Chorus should be *The Chorus.* "a sharer in the action" (*Poet.* ii. 21) has been interpreted by Horace to mean that the Chorus should help on the action "by uttering words of encouragement and friendly counsel to the good, by rebuking the passionate, by loving the virtuous, by praising justice and peace, and obedience to the law, by recommending moderation in the appetites, and by praying to the gods to comfort the miserable, and humble the proud" (*De Art. Poet.* 193 *sq.*).

This has been summed up by Schlegel when he says that the Chorus is "the Spectator idealized," *i.e.* "is the universal voice of moral sympathy, instruction, and warning" (*Lecture* v.); and aptly figured by Schiller in his comparison of the lyric element in a drama with the rich and flowing drapery that softens the rigid outline of action and character (Introd. to *Bride of Messina*). How Milton's Chorus has fulfilled these functions may be seen by a short review of the motive ideas that successively prompt the odes :—In the Parodos the Chorus imparts to the audience the previous history of Samson, and expresses, with one skilful touch, all it feels at the contrast between what he is and what he once was. On eliciting from Samson the true object of his Philistine marriages, and the cause that led to its failure, it sees, in the one, an instance of the justice of God's ways, and, in the other, an instance of the blindness of the Jews; but in both cases it exonerates Samson from the charges that public opinion had been but too ready to bring against him. When Samson, in the bitterness of his self-accusations, refuses proposals of ransom made by Manoah, the Chorus seeks to cheer him, and, while seeming to assent to his despairing cry that God has cast him off, turns its assent into a source of consolation by pointing out that the hand of God has often rested heavily upon the chosen instruments of His glory. Passing over the ode in the scene with Delilah, where the Chorus distinctly deserts its functions, we find it again true to its character, when it endeavours to calm the indignation of Samson after the stormy scene with Harapha, by first drawing a picture of the triumphant deliverer of the oppressed, and then deliberately saying

that patience effects nobler triumphs, and that Samson
is one of those whom patience finally must crown. After
the scene with the Officer, the Chorus tries to persuade
Samson to obey the civil power, and when, at length, he
departs, its fervent prayer for his safety accompanies
him. When the catastrophe is announced, the Chorus
points out that Samson at his death has fulfilled the
work to which his life had been consecrated, and, in one
of the grandest similes to be found anywhere in literature, shows how unexpectedly this fulfilment has been
brought about. The concluding recitative (if the last
ode may be so called, to avoid clashing with Aristotle's
rule, quoted above) draws the moral—"All is best . . .
what the unsearchable dispose of Highest Wisdom brings
about"—and fulfils the end of tragedy by dismissing the
Chorus with "calm of mind, all passion spent." In the
ode passed over (ll. 1010-1060), the Chorus utter a series
of invectives against women, which Landor calls "hot
and corrosive," and compared with which the venom of
the "woman-hater," Euripides, whom Milton here resembles, is "as cold as hemlock." The latter further
errs in putting these sentiments of misogyny, not in the
mouth of the injured Samson, where they would be less
unjust, but in that of the Chorus, whose utterances are
expected to be the expression of dispassionate judgment
—a fault which not even Euripides commits.

Johnson based his depreciation of this drama chiefly The Action.
upon what he considered to be its defective action,
inasmuch as it had a *beginning* and an *end*, but wanted a
middle ; "since nothing passes between the first act and
the last, that either hastens or delays the death of Samson" (*Rambler*, iii. 139).   The reply to this criticism

was furnished by Cumberland, who pointed out three
passages (ll. 434-37, 468-71, 1250-52) that supply the
requisite "*middle*"—the first by announcing the festival
in honour of Dagon, the second by prophesying the
impending overthrow of this idol, and the confusion of
his worshippers, and the third by supplying an immediate
motive for the catastrophe in Harapha's malice (*Observer*,
iv. 111).   Thus the drama is not a mere string of scenes
as Johnson's remarks imply it to be, but develops an
"*entire action*" (Aristotle, *Poet.* ii. 4), having a *beginning*
—Samson overthrown, blind and in captivity,—an *end*
—Samson triumphant in death over his enemies,—and a
middle—the circumstances, namely, that lead from this
beginning to this end.

Is this transition effected without a surprise, or can
the reader all along foresee what is going to happen
next ?   The answer to this question will decide whether
the action of *Samson Agonistes* is "*simple*" or "*complex*"
(Aristotle, *Poet.* ii. 8).   The action of a tragedy is meant
to excite pity and terror, and these feelings are most
powerfully excited by events that happen unexpectedly.
The successive scenes in this drama are so arranged that
they bring expectation nearer and nearer to some catastrophe,—but *not* the one that actually happens:—Manoah
tells Samson of his purpose to ransom him, but though
Samson, weary of life and longing for his last rest, cares
little for his father's proposal, still Manoah's parting
words inspire us with some hope of Samson's deliverance :
Delilah offers to intercede for his release, but he repulses
her with savage scorn, and the indifference of her parting
words chills that hope, and makes us fear that Samson
is indeed "left to his lot."   Harapha's insolence, over-

matched by Samson's truculent aggressiveness, turns to malice, which threatens to make his lot worse than it is, by basely informing against him : and, lastly, the lords of the Philistines at whose mercy Samson entirely lies, are insulted by him through their officer.—Who would expect after all this that Samson would ever triumph over his foes? Who would not rather expect that these foes would heap still greater indignities and miseries on him? Yet this triumph is brought about; and ll. 1381-89 mark the point where our expectation is taken by surprise and turned back; and we begin now to look out for some great—some unexpected—event. These lines constitute the *revolution (peripeteia)*, that makes the action or fable of *Samson Agonistes, complex (peplegmenon)*. All that portion of the action that precedes the revolution, together with all that portion after it till the final catastrophe, is called the *desis* ('binding'), corresponding to the French *noeud* ('tying of the knot'). During the first of these portions the conviction of the spectator has been, "surely all this can end in only *one* way—more calamity to Samson, greater triumph to his enemies": during the second, the conviction has been replaced by a wondering doubt, "how *will* all this end?" Then comes the catastrophe, when that doubt is solved, and the answer given in Samson's triumph over his enemies. This catastrophe, then, is the *lusis* ('solution') (Aristotle, *Poet.* ii. 18), corresponding to the French *dénoûment* ('untying of the knot'). Throughout the latter portion of the *desis* there is an undertone of presage, becoming clearer as the action advances, and foreshadowing the catastrophe (see l. 1252 n. for the particular passages).

The remarkable *symmetry* of the plot is observable in

the very Argument, which falls into four parts:—
Samson as the Sufferer, bemoaning his lot: visits from
friends (the Chorus and Manoah), who comfort him, and
towards whom his manner and words are full of self-
accusation and penitence: then visits from foes (Delilah
and Harapha), who come to tempt and to insult him, and
towards whom his manner changes into anger and defiance: lastly, Samson as Agonistes, triumphing over his
foes and dying.

Of the three *Unities*, Milton himself notes the ob-
servance with regard to that of *time:* the events all
occurring within a day. The unity of *place* is as strictly
observed: every scene being placed before the prison at
Gaza; the catastrophe taking place *outside* (according to
a rule of the Greek drama, prohibiting the enactment of
violent deeds on the stage), and the Chorus never
leaving the stage during the whole of the action. With
regard to the unity of *action*, the scene with Delilah
contributes less directly to the catastrophe than any
other scene; but presents, next to Samson, the most
powerful study of character in the piece. Yet this
scene is not a mere episode: Delilah had been the instrument of Samson's fall, and she might again have
become the instrument of preventing his triumph, had
Samson yielded to her once again, and listened to her
entreaty to be allowed to intercede for him, and to be
the nurse and comforter of his old age and blindness.
How closely the other scenes are bound up with the
unity of the action has been already apparent in discus-
sing the question of a "middle."

Two other points, laid down in the *Poetics* of Aristotle, need mention. The action is *great* in a twofold

sense, both of which are not always present together, even in Greek tragedy. What may be called the "*physical* greatness" of the action, meaning the performance of deeds such as the gods and heroes of antiquity delighted in, is quite apparent in the catastrophe. But there is, besides, in the action of *Samson Agonistes*, a *moral* greatness,—namely, the sacrifice of one's own self for the sake of others—that ranks it with the greatest and noblest action in the entire range of Greek drama— that of the *Prometheus Bound* of Æschylus. In the case of Samson, the sacrifice is that of life itself, for the sake of God and country,—religion and patriotism; in the case of Prometheus, it consists in the endurance of unutterable torment for the sake of the whole human race,—universal philanthropy. It is hard to say which of the two sacrifices is the nobler. The other point is that the action should be *probable*. The bare fact that the deeds of Samson were recorded in Scripture would give them in Milton's eyes a degree of truth higher than probability. But this "absolute" probability apart, there is another that may be called "relative," which requires that the action should be such as the circumstances of the case, and the characters of the chief personages, would lead us to expect: in other words, which requires that the action should be *consistent*. The development of the plot, already traced, shows how well this requirement has been met.

Schlegel lays down "*Freedom within and Necessity without*" as the two governing principles in the action of a Greek drama. They operate in *Samson Agonistes* also. In the unconquerable spirit of Samson, rising, under divine inspiration, and asserting itself when his enemies believed it to have been crushed for ever under the load of his calamities, we recognize that freedom of the mind which the slavery of the body could not destroy; while in "dire Necessity" (l. 1666), as the Stoic philosopher would call it, or "Fate" as the Greek dramatist would term it, consists that other principle, which operates with inexorable uniformity, upon the good as upon the wicked.

In grandeur of action and loftiness of pathos, *Samson Agonistes* approaches the Æschylean drama, but does not share with it the artless simplicity of its plot, and the subordination of the dramatic to the lyrical element. In that lower order of pathos that physical suffering excites, and in its tone of bitter misogyny, it brings to mind similar traits in Euripides; but in the conduct of his Chorus, and in the justness of their remarks, always (with one exception) eminently suited to their character and to the occasion, Milton is superior to Euripides, whose Choruses indulge in sententious maxims and wordy declamations, too often irrelevant and wide of the mark. But in exquisite art and symmetry of con-struction, in complexity of plot, in skilful disposition of incidents so as to lead up to the catastrophe, in equally skilful concealment of this arrangement till the very last, so that the feeling of surprise may have its full share in intensifying those of terror and pity, and in that frequent "irony" which obscurely, nay, mislead-ingly, shadows forth the impending calamity—Milton's drama bears, in its action, a closer resemblance to the dramas of Sophocles, than to those of either Æschylus or Euripides. Particularly does the plot of *Samson Agonistes* bear a striking resemblance to that of the

Œdipus Coloneus of Sophocles, the work of his old age, as the other was of Milton's. This resemblance will be apparent from the sketch given under the character of Samson.

SAMSON possesses the essential characteristic of a Hero of tragedy as laid down by Aristotle. It is this:—he is not perfectly virtuous, for the tragic end of such a man would raise neither pity nor terror, but indignation; neither is he deliberately vicious, for the punishment of such a man would call forth approbation; but while possessing heroic virtues, he is, at the same time, subject to human frailty, and, yielding to it in a moment of weakness, he errs and falls. Presented to us in this fallen condition, blinded, enslaved, in chains, " ragged, unwashed, unshorn," his physical sufferings awaken the same kind of pity that we feel for Philoctetes, when he appears in front of his cave in the wilderness, banished from society, suffering from an incurable wound, amidst whose paroxysms he has dragged a solitary existence for ten long years. We next learn what Samson had once been:—a Nazarite from his birth; the consecrated deliverer of his people, a judge in Israel for twenty years, and, single-handed, the scourge and terror of the hosts of the Philistines. Alone, or in the sympathizing presence of friends, the fallen Samson yields to the weakness of lamenting his physical sufferings; but, quickly rising superior to that weakness, he acknowledges that his moral blindness in trusting a traitress was worse than loss of eyesight, and his yielding the freedom of his judgment to her artful tears, worse than chains and a prison. Then, forgetting self altogether, this deeply religious Hebrew nature

The Characters and the Sentiments.

finds in the dishonour he has brought upon the name of
Israel's God the deepest cause for lament and remorse.
It is in suffering of this kind, the noblest, because the
least selfish, that the character of Samson resembles that
of the Titan Prometheus. As Samson suffers most at
the thought that, through disobeying God, he had
failed to serve Him, so the thought that he had succeeded in conferring a benefit on the human race, comes
as a consolation to Prometheus in the midst of his
bodily torments. But in the case of neither can suffering overcome the lofty unconquerable spirit. Weary of
life and its ills, and longing for death as he is, the offer
of a ransom calls forth this spirit in Samson, and he
replies that liberty coming as a favour from his foes, and
life with dishonour, are not worth the having. So, to
the prudent Oceanus, who counsels submission to Zeus,
Prometheus firmly replies that he will continue defiant
and suffer in consequence, rather than submit and be
out of pain. When Samson's enemies stand in his
presence, a new side of his character is brought to light ;
the feelings of self-accusation and despair give way to
scorn, loathing, anger, and defiance, directed against the
insincere penitence of Delilah, and the cowardly insolence of Harapha. His fierce harshness towards the
former shows that shame for the fatal weakness so
terribly atoned for, has produced, in his strongly-
marked character, a reaction to the opposite pole, and
changed a too-confiding love into over-mistrustful hate.
Towards Harapha he is the Samson of old—hybristes,
contemptuous, aggressive, sarcastic, answering taunt
with taunt. Only once does he abandon this attitude.
when, touched to the quick, he eagerly clears his

character from the charge brought against it by the lying bully. It is in these traits that Samson resembles the fiery, impetuous, unyielding Ajax, as well as, it must be confessed, in the possession of strength without wisdom. He resembles him, too, in that sensitiveness to shame for an unworthy action, which drove the Greek to suicide, but which with the Hebrew stops at a prayer for speedy death. With the departure of his foes, this phase of Samson's character is withdrawn from us, and the deep religious spirit of the man reappears in the scene with the Officer. His refusal to obey the summons communicated by the latter, is based upon a fear of dishonouring God, and of incurring His displeasure anew, when the return of his strength makes him feel that He has forgiven him his former offence. Quick upon this follows the inspiration from heaven, as a confirmation of this feeling, and a sign that God deigns once more to employ him as the instrument of His choice against the heathen.

There is yet another hero in classical drama whom Samson resembles, not only in character, but in fate. A slight sketch of the story of the life of Œdipus, based upon the two plays of Sophocles bearing his name, may, perhaps, best explain this. Œdipus, like Samson, in the days of his prosperity, as king of Thebes, had been haughty and impetuous, but when a grievous pestilence afflicted his people, he, like Samson, worked with a noble zeal for their deliverance. He, like Samson, commits an error, which would have been a crime of the deepest dye, had it been committed knowingly ; and when it is revealed to him, in remorse he puts out his own eyes, and, shortly afterwards, is banished from

Thebes by his unnatural son Polynices. After years
of wandering and privations, his steps guided by his
daughter Antigone, yet a child, he takes shelter, at last,
in the grove of the Furies at Colonus. Here he is
visited by Theseus, king of Athens, who voluntarily
extends that protection which the exile had cared to
seek only from the gods; and by a friendly Chorus, at
whose advice he goes through a purification, depending
less upon ceremonial, and more, as with Samson, upon
the prayer and repentance of a contrite heart. Next
comes Creon, a cunning hypocrite, who, when unmasked
by Œdipus, becomes insolent, and threatens to drag him
away from the sanctuary of the altar; but he is cowed
by Œdipus, who answers him with his old impetuosity.
Œdipus then reluctantly consents to see his son Polynices, now touched with remorse at his father's pitiable
condition; but with Œdipus, as with Lear, filial ingratitude finds no forgiveness, and he heaps angry curses
on his undutiful child, and dismisses him from his
presence. Now come signs that the end is near: the
voice of Zeus calls mysteriously to the blind hero, who,
in obedience to it, retires to a lonely spot, where he is
left with none beside him except Theseus, who is shortly
afterwards discovered alone on the spot, veiling his
eyes as still in some awful presence. But Œdipus has
vanished. Here, in the midst of differences in details,
the resemblance between the characters of Samson and
Œdipus, and the similarity of their fate, are evident
enough. The imagination will readily discover some
degree of resemblance between the positions occupied by
Polynices, Creon, Theseus, and the Chorus of Athenians,
on the one hand, and Delilah, Harapha, Manoah, and the

Chorus of Danites, on the other, without, however, seeking to press the parallel too far.

But the most striking resemblance is that between Samson and Milton himself. Milton's blindness; his life of temperance and abstemiousness, like that of the Nazarites; his unhappy marriage with Mary Powell, the daughter of a Royalist; his championship of the Puritan cause, to which he had consecrated twenty years of the prime of life; the coldness with which his single-handed efforts in this cause were received by England; the unmerited neglect, bringing with it poverty and disease, into which he fell, when that cause was lost at the Restoration; England no longer to him the beloved land of his patriotism, but in the possession of the Philistines, and he a stranger in it, surrounded by foes; his hopes crushed, and his faculties drooping; his career ended, and his presentiment of approaching death, the deliverer:—all are referred to under the character of Samson, and find a counterpart in the incidents of his life, imparting to this character a most solemn and touching biographical interest, which the most skilfully constructed work of dramatic art could never command for itself. It is doubtful whether ever in the entire range of literature, fiction has owed to reality so much of its power to move human sympathy.

The Scripture character of Samson, upon which that of Milton is based, suggests a strong resemblance between the Jewish hero and the Greek Hercules. Like Samson, Hercules united superhuman strength to weak submission to the influence of women. He slew a lion (the Nemean), and his wife (Dejanira) was the cause of his death. Both were subject to human frailties, and to

the tyranny of strong passions ; both endured with
heroic fortitude the misfortunes that this subjection
brought upon them, and atoned, by a noble death, for
the error of their lives.   It has been conjectured that
the tradition regarding Samson was carried to Greece
by Phœnician merchants.   The conjecture becomes
probable when the coincidence is found to extend
from general traits of character to particular actions.
Thus, according to Herodotus, Hercules was once seized
by the Egyptians and carried in procession to be sacri-
ficed to Jupiter, but when he arrived at the altar, he
"put forth his strength, and slew them all."   A passage
in Lycophron says Hercules once lost all his hair, and
another in Ovid describes a custom of tying a torch
between two foxes in the circus, in memory of the
damage once done to the harvest by a contrivance
similar to that devised by Samson (*Judges*, xv. 3 *sq.*).

DALILA.   There is no mention in the *Book of Judges*
or in Josephus of any meeting between Samson and
Delilah since her betrayal of him.   Milton has made the
scene he invents the basis for a skilful delineation of
character, and, incidentally, of a bitter attack upon
women, put into the mouth of the Chorus, and therefore
meant to be a calm deliberate judgment passed on the
whole female sex, except the "virtuous rarely found."
The magnificence of Delilah's train, and the gaiety of her
personal adornment, tell a double story of wealth acquired as the price of a husband's betrayal, and enjoyed
by the wife in heartless impenitence.   True, she weeps,
but when she speaks, her lukewarm words belie her
tears, for they are not the language of true remorse.
Finding that the insincerity of her penitence does not

deceive Samson, she changes ground to sophistical justi-
fication of her conduct. Equally unsuccessful here, she
assumes a loftier tone, and speaks of religion and
patriotism as the motives that guided her action. But
when she fails to move Samson by this cunningly
planned appeal to the same two noble causes to which
his own life had been consecrated, and which, therefore,
she expected would go straight to his heart, Delilah
abandons her wiles, and displays, for a moment, a touch
of nature. She asks Samson's pardon, and offers a proof
of her sincerity. Though Samson but too naturally
suspects in this only a new snare, it is hard to think
that this offer concealed malice, and was not prompted
by a sincere, though fleeting, pity. Malice could scarcely
make Samson's condition worse than it already was, and
a touch of pity, even in the breast of Delilah, for one
whom she once called husband, finds a counterpart in
the mother's feeling that Clytaemnestra betrays when
she hears of the death of Orestes. Dramatists seldom
fail to bestow on their monsters some relieving touch,
to remind us that they are still human. But when
Delilah finds that her services are repulsed, as her arguments had been silenced, she completely recovers her
former evil self. She retracts her confession of guilt,
promises herself undying fame in her country's history,
and, well-satisfied with her lot, leaves Samson to his.

The sorcery of sensual beauty, the lust of sensual
pleasures, greed of gold, artful deception and treachery,
a hypocrisy that seeks a cloak for its actions in pretended love of country and zeal for religion, a faint
effort at reparation, ending in callous self-satisfaction,
and a glorying in her infamy—such are the traits in

this character, developed by Milton out of the bare
Scripture account, and reminding us, in some respects,
of the *Clytaemnestra* of Æschylus and Sophocles, of
Nimue in Malory's *Morte d'Arthur*, and of Vivien in
Tennyson's *Idylls of the King*. The revelation of true
and permanent traits of character, when freed from a
passing impulse that has for a moment concealed them,
is emphasized by the Chorus when they call Delilah a
"manifest serpent," and is called by Aristotle the
"*Discovery (anagnorisis) in character.*" Had these traits
been those commonly ascribed to many of her sex—to
Samson's first wife—"she of Timna,"—for instance,—
they might have been lightly visited as weaknesses. But
when to feminine curiosity and fickleness are added the
darker stains of avarice, artful dissimulation, unrelent-
ing perseverance in gaining an evil end, from which no
sentiment of wifely love and duty could turn her, and
which no feeling of shame or remorse could lead her to
regret, Delilah's character acquires a hatefulness that
seems to unsex her in our eyes.

Critics find an allusion in Samson's relation with
Delilah, to Milton's relation with Mary Powell, his first
wife. This is true, in so far as Mary Powell was a
Royalist, who had no sympathy for her husband's ways
of life and thought, and whose desertion of him had
affected his temper and his opinion of woman's character, for the worse. But the latter part of this relation
—his wife's penitence and their reconciliation—finds a
parallel rather in the scene referred to in the Notes
(ll. 732-765) between Adam and Eve (*P. L.* x.). But
even here the parallelism has been extended (perhaps,
strained), so as to find in Samson's repulse of Delilah,

an expression of Milton's own first impulse of resentment towards Mary Powell.

MANOA. The mention of the burying place of Manoah in *Judges*, xvi. 31, does not necessarily imply that he died before Samson. There is no mention in Scripture or in Josephus of any attempt at ransoming Samson made by him, or of any trait of his character, except his devout nature, and his social rank as the "principal person of his country" (Whiston). Milton's Manoah is presented to us for the first time when, broken down with age and grief, he advances with feeble, lagging steps, towards the prison of Gaza. At the sight of his son's condition, he cannot refrain from upbraiding Providence that had turned its special blessing into a curse, and allowed Samson's former deeds of glory to pass unrewarded. The father's grief seems to restore the son to self-possession, when, with the solemn rebuke, "appoint not heavenly disposition, father," he takes all the blame upon himself. But this burst of grief over, we find Manoah exercising a father's prerogative of gentle reproof to the son for his past errors —his two Philistine marriages, and the disgrace upon his house, and dishonour upon the name of Israel's God that they had brought. Just as the Chorus had not ventured beyond sympathy, where the father proceeds to reproof, so where the Chorus had limited itself to counsel, the father has brought something more substantial for his son—namely, a project for ransoming him. But now the respective moods of mind of Samson and Manoah are entirely reversed. The former reaches the lowest depths of despair, while the latter's hopefulness is correspondingly exalted. In this frame of mind

he departs to negotiate with the Philistine lords. When
he returns to announce the progress of his efforts, his
hopes seem to rise still higher, and he draws a loving
picture of his son, restored to his own house, tended by
his own fatherly care, and—such is the logic of affection
—restored to eyesight and the light of day, if God so
wills it. Then comes the announcement of Samson's
death to crush these hopes for ever; and as the artist is
said to have painted Agamemnon's grief at the sacrifice
of his daughter, by representing him with his face
veiled,* so has Milton depicted the grief of Manoah by
silence. During the long description of the death-
scene by the Messenger, and the lament of the Chorus,
a silent struggle is evidently going on in the father's
breast between grief and resignation, and when at
length he speaks, his first words show on which side the
victory has been: "no time for lamentation now, nor
much more cause," for his son has died as he should
have. Such is the character of Manoah: in the midst
of a father's anguish for a son's miseries, not forgetting
that son's transgressions; borne down by grief, yet
capable of carrying on difficult negotiations with
powerful enemies; resolved to succeed in them, though
it cost him all his wealth; hopeful of success as long as
his son was alive, and finding in his death both the
atonement for his error, and the fulfilment of his divine
mission; displaying a noble self-restraint over his own
grief, and recalling the Chorus from indulgence in
theirs; and while the latter seek, in the meditative
bent of their minds, for peace and consolation, his active

* The painter was Timanthes, and the story is told in Pliny,
Hist. Nat. xxxv. 36. 5.

and practical nature finds employment in attending to the last rites in honour of the dead, and planning a monument to his memory.

HARAPHA. As Samson represents might consecrated to the service of righteousness, so the character of Harapha supplies the foil of brute and boisterous force debased to the servitude of low passions. Boastful, for he proclaims his own descent from the giants of old; a coward, who declines Samson's repeated challenges; foul-mouthed, for he taunts Samson with his rags and misery, with being a murderer and a robber; blasphemous, when he declares Samson's strength to be due to magic and black enchantment, and his fall to the impotence of his God against the might of Dagon; full of malice, which he seeks to wreak on Samson; a vile informer, in order to gratify this malice: — such is Harapha.

The personage of Samson besides being a veiled presentment of the tragedy of Milton's own life, also allegorizes the ruin of the public cause to which that life had been devoted. *Political Significance and Allusions to the History of the Times.* Samson represents Puritanism fallen and captive, as the Philistines stand for the Royalists triumphant at the restoration; Delilah is that Restoration which had sought in vain to allure and win over Milton; the festivities held by the lords of the Philistines in the temple of Dagon typify the godless and dissolute manners prevalent at the court of Charles II.; and lastly, the freedom which Manoah predicts for Israel (l. 1719), and which they compassed under the prophet Samuel at the battle of Mizpeh, finds a distant parallel in the Revolution by which Stuart tyranny and licence were swept away.

Allusions to particular facts and events also occur. Besides those to the desecration of Cromwell's remains, the treatment of the bodies of the regicides, and the trial of Vane, already mentioned (p. ix), the following references have been traced :—to Cromwell as the deliverer of " the saints " from oppression (ll. 1270 *sq.*) ; to the favourable attitude of men in power, like Monk, towards the Restoration, and to Milton's single-handed efforts to oppose this event, and retrieve the Puritan cause (ll. 241 *sq.*) ; to General Lambert's efforts against Monk's designs, the want of support that these efforts met with at the hands of Parliament (1659), and his imprisonment (1662), (ll. 272 *sq.*) ; to the efforts made to secure Milton's safety at the Restoration by including his name in the Indemnity Bill of August, 1660, and to the varying degrees of favour with which these efforts were received by the different shades of political parties then in power (ll. 1457 *sq.*) ; to the degraded tastes of the English court and of the English stage (ll. 1323 *sq.*) ; and to the unbridled passions of the nobility and clergy, and of the common people (ll. 1418 *sq.*).

Place in Literature. The story of Samson's life is told by Boccaccio in Latin in his *Falls of Illustrious Men* (*De Casibus etc.*), translated into English by Lydgate under the title of *Tragedies*, as tragic tales were then called. Chaucer, in his *Monkes Tale*, written on the model of the same work of Boccaccio, gives a " tragedy " of Samson. The story of Samson, like that of Hercules among the Greek tragedians, formed the subject of a tragi-comedy in Spanish literature, of which a translation into Italian appeared in 1620 (Riccoboni, in Hallam, *Lit. of Eur.*, xxiii.). After Milton, we find Voltaire writing an opera of Samson (1732) full of conventional clap-trap. Handel composed his oratorio of Samson (1742), in which the words were adapted from Milton's tragedy, and a Chorus of the priests of Dagon was introduced. Still later, in German literature, three dramatists have written tragedies of Samson (or 'Simson' as the name is spelt in German, after the Hebrew) :—Gärtner (1849), Ed. Müller (1853), and Dulk (1859); the first in imitation of the old mysteries; the second making Samson not a free agent, but, in imitation of the spirit of Greek tragedy, the victim of Fate; the third ennobling the character of Delilah far above what the scripture account of her warrants, and seeking for theatrical effect by representing her as attending upon Samson in imprisonment, disguised as a boy (Kurz, *Geschichte der Deutschen Literatur*, iv.).

Instances of the use of a Chorus are numerous in the history of literature. But of these, some, like the Choruses of Shakspere (in *Henry V., A Winter's Tale,* and *Pericles*), and Marlowe (in *Faustus*), serve merely to continue the thread of the story between acts; others, though in the main fulfilling the purpose of the classical chorus, are based upon the declamatory models of the Italian school and of Seneca, the Roman tragic dramatist, both imitators, in their turn, of Euripides, in this respect. To this class belong the Choruses in Sackville and Norton's *Gorboduc* (1562), Gascoigne's *Jocasta* (1566), in *Tancred and Gismunda* (1568), *The Misfortunes of Arthur* (1587), and in Peele's *David and Bethsabe* (1599). Milton was the first to introduce, in *Samson Agonistes*, the true spirit of the classical Greek Chorus into English literature. The experiment, however, was not new in

European literature. Choruses, on the classical model, had existed in Italian plays long before, having been introduced by Politian in his pastoral tragedy of *Orpheus* (1483), and used by Rucellai in his *Rosmunda* (1515), by Trissino in *Sofonisba* (1524), and by Tasso in *Torrismondo* (1586). In Spanish, Sismondi gives an instance of the use of a Chorus by Lope de Vega in his *Arauco Domado*, though Schlegel notes, already in Cervantes, the substitution of allegorical figures for the Chorus, and Hallam says that, with the formation of the national school of Spanish drama, of which Calderon was the greatest ornament, the Greek Chorus was abandoned. In Dutch literature, Choruses occur in the almost contemporary dramas of *Palamedes* and *The Batavian Brothers* by Vondel. The classical Greek Chorus does not, however, occur in French literature till after Milton, in the *Esther* (1689) and *Athalie* (1691) of Racine, the Choruses in the *Cléopâtre* of Jodelle (1552) being, like *Gorboduc*, based rather on Seneca's. It appears still later in German literature, in the *Bride of Messina* of Schiller (1804), although other forms of the Chorus had existed in it before.

In England, Milton has had followers in the line which he was the first to strike out. The Choruses in most of the works of these dramatists are, like those of *Samson Agonistes*, not divided into strophes and anti-strophes The following may be mentioned : Mason's *Elfrida* (1753, chorus of British Virgins), and *Caractacus* (1759, chorus of Druids and Bards) ; Shelley's *Œdipus Tyrannus* (a burlesque, 1820, chorus of the Swinish Multitude), *Prometheus Unbound* (1821, choruses of Furies, Spirits, and Hours), and *Hellas* (1823, chorus of Greek captive Women); Byron's *Heaven and Earth* (a mystery, 1822, choruses of Earth Spirits and Mortals); Matthew Arnold's *Merope* (1858, chorus of Messenian Maidens, whose odes are strophic and antistrophic); Mrs. Browning's *Drama of Exile* (1844, choruses of Eden Spirits and Invisible Angels); Swinburne's *Atalanta in Calydon* (1864), and *Erechtheus* (1876, chorus of Athenian Elders, whose odes are strophic and antistrophic). There are, besides, numerous English translations or adaptations of classical dramas, that of course have Choruses.

The place occupied by *Samson Agonistes* in the contemporary dramatic literature of England is, perhaps, still more remarkable. Chronologically, this work belongs to the Restoration drama; but, in respect of form and treatment of plot, it is directly affiliated to the classical Greek drama, as shown above; and the assertion that, with regard to sentiment and treatment of character, it can be affiliated to the Elizabethan drama, requires some modification before it can be justified. The continuous line of the great Elizabethan dramatists, or more strictly speaking, of the Old drama, ended with Shirley, whose last important tragedy, the *Cardinal* (1641), may be taken as also the last unbroken link in the great chain. Literature, especially dramatic, received a check at the outbreak of the Civil War in September, 1642, and shortly afterwards, by Ordinance of Parliament, the theatres were closed, and continued so until 1656, when Davenant ingeniously obtained permission to bring out what was cautiously called an "entertainment" in scenery and music, "after the manner of the ancients"; but it was not till 1660 that plays began to be again openly acted. The end of the

Elizabethan, and the beginning of the Restoration, drama, would thus seem to be most definitely marked; but in reality the transition was not so abrupt. There had been in the former a long period of decay, which began when the portraiture of "passion" passed, as early as with Ben Jonson, into that of "humour," and a further lapse when, under the first two Stuart kings, there arose and flourished the "fantastic school," claiming Ben Jonson as their literary father. Split up as the old drama thus is into sections, Milton, as a dramatist, differs in varying degrees from them all, and there was one deep taint—that of immorality—infecting, more or less, each of these sections, and reappearing in a still more deplorable and offensive form in the drama of the Restoration, from which he is entirely free. In this respect *Samson Agonistes* deserves to be ranked as a Puritan poet's noble protest against the moral debasement of both these periods of the drama, against which the fantastic protest of a Puritan enthusiast (Prynne in his *Histriomastix*, 1632) had been directed in vain, and which was later on to call down on itself the more effective attack of a scholarly divine (Jeremy Collier, in his *Short View*, 1698). The purity of *Samson Agonistes* is, perhaps, the most prominent trait that makes this work stand out unique in the entire range of both Elizabethan and Restoration drama. But it is not the only one: in unyielding hostility to the reigning politics of his time, in deep settled religious belief, in a sublime spirit of self-sacrifice in the cause of patriotism and religion, in the bitterness of its scorn for the prevailing tone of social manners, and in the warning voice raised by its chorus against excess in

passion, *Samson Agonistes* differs widely from the Elizabethan drama, with its unquestioning obedience to
established state authority, its clear but cold reflection
of the ways of society—accurate but uncensuring—its
credulous superstition undermining religious faith, and
the unrestrained play it permitted to violent passion.
Milton himself, in condemning the introduction of a
comic element into tragedies, seems to emphasize his
dissent from the practice of Shakspere himself and his
school, on yet another point.   But these points of
difference eliminated, there remains one broad point of
resemblance, by virtue of which Shakspere may still
claim Milton among his sons : it is this—both have for
their subject the portraiture of human nature and
human passion.   Add to this the facts that Milton like
the Elizabethan dramatists since Marlowe, used blank
verse as the metre of his drama, and that his syntax
and idiom are largely, though not exclusively Elizabethan, and the points of resemblance are, perhaps,
exhausted.

But every trace of resemblance disappears when the
comparison is transferred to the contemporary Restoration dramas ; and *Samson Agonistes* stands out as solitary
in their midst, as Milton in the England of the Restoration, or Samson among the Philistines.   Shortly after
the reopening of the theatres the Earl of Orrery wrote
the tragedy of the *Black Prince,* (not acted till 1667) in
"the French manner," *because* the king approved of this
manner of writing, which consisted in the use of
rhymed heroic couplets.   This oft-told story significantly points out how much the Restoration drama
sought to accommodate itself to the tastes of the Court,

and to follow French models—two influences extending to far deeper matters than the innocent one of rhymes, and answerable for a great deal of the low tone of sentiment and morality pervading it. Dryden in his *Indian Queen* (1664) followed the example of Orrery, and continued it in later plays. In 1667 he defended the use of rhyme in plays, in his *Essay of Dramatic Poesy*, and in the very year in which *Samson Agonistes* was licensed, brought out his most extravagant effort in this line—his ranting play of *Almanzor and Almahide*. One cannot help exclaiming at the grotesque contrast, "Surely, this play is the very Harapha of the heroic drama, confronting Samson!" Next year appeared the *Rehearsal*, a burlesque upon rhymed heroic plays, and directed, among others, against Dryden's. Whatever the effect of this may have been upon Dryden's feelings, no change was visible in his method, till 1678, when he wrote *All for Love*, an imitation, in blank verse, of Shakspere's *Antony and Cleopatra*, in which, while observing the "Unities," he rejects the classical model, as unsuited to the spirit of English tragedy. So much for the contrast in form; still more striking is the contrast in subject-matter. In the Restoration drama the evidences are but too clear of a servile upholding of the divine right of kings, and of insults to the memory of the late Commonwealth; of the collapse of all religious belief, and the degradation of religion, as in the later days of the Roman Republic, into a mere tool of government; of the absence of any sentiment of patriotism, in which literature and court alike followed the example of the king; of the prevalence of gross immorality, traceable to the same source ; and of the influence (unhappily in its worst aspects) of foreign literatures, especially that of France. Instead of the model of the Attic drama, or of Shakspere, the Restoration playwrights delighted in seeking for inspiration in the alternate love-making and ranting of the heroes of the French romances of Calprenède and Scudéry, or in borrowing plot and character from the French dramatists of the 17th century, especially Molière, and spoiling what they borrowed. Thus while Dryden, the representative dramatist of the Restoration, is busy producing heroic plays in heroic couplets, Milton enters his practical protest against both, in the composition of *Samson Agonistes ;* and although, later on, this representative recants his views, and attempts to revive the school of Shakspere, the current of Restoration drama continued to flow in the channel once marked out for it, until it was checked by Collier's attack. Somewhat purified in tone, and with a newly acquired melancholy and pathos, Restoration tragedy ran a fresh course, till it may be said to have ended with Addison's *Cato* (1713). This work was meant to be a revival of the drama on a classical model, but Whigs and Tories only sought to find in it an instrument of political faction. So, too, Restoration comedy lost much in brilliance of wit, while it gained something in morality of tone, and soon passed in the *Lying Lover* of Steele (1704) into the Sentimental comedy. During the whole of this period, from the rise to the extinction of the drama of the Restoration, *Samson Agonistes* stands alone, having not a single feature in common with it, much that is directly antagonistic, and separated by a wide difference even from that work which may be

expected to have approached it, at least in form,—
namely, Addison's *Cato*.

Samson Agonistes possesses yet another interest in the
history of English literature—one that lies in the
history of Milton's own poetical writings.   It consists
in tracing the change from the joy and hope of youth,
to the sadness and disappointment of old age, in connection with his own life, and with the religious and
political causes to which that life had been devoted.   In
L'Allegro and *Il Penseroso*, Milton's mind is in suspense
between the two great parties that then divided England, Cavalier and Puritan, typified by Joy and Melancholy, whose claims are equally balanced.   In *Comus*
already this balance inclines, and Milton makes his
choice : Joy is now in his eyes associated with Vice and
Melancholy with Virtue.   *Comus* is the court of Charles
I., as Delilah is the court of the Restoration.   The
Lady is Virtue, and especially that particular virtue—
Chastity—which, more than any other, it was vain to
seek for in court life ; but she typifies Virtue relying
upon a spotless Conscience, looking forward in Faith
and Hope, resisting Temptation, unconquerable in
spirit, though her body is bound, and speedily released
from the snares of Vice by the grace of Heaven.   She
is the Puritan cause with a glorious future before it, as
Samson is that cause with nothing but a ruined past
behind.   He represents Virtue fallen, looking back with
a stricken Conscience upon the error that led him
astray, his future darkened with a struggle in which
Despair seems well nigh to overcome the Faith to which
he still clings.   But though fallen, he is not lost ; he
too resists Temptation when renewed, and displays

towards enemies the same unyielding spirit as in the days of his glory; and though no Sabrina rises to sweet music to release him from his bonds, that release is effected in a manner whose awful terror makes it, at the same time, a solemn expiation of his fault.

Critics have found a parallel between the attack upon the clergy of the Established Church so pronounced in *Lycidas*, and the savage, because powerless, hatred of the priests of Dagon, visible in *Samson Agonistes*. In the latter, however, there is no direct reference to the Restoration clergy as there is in *Lycidas*; except perhaps one in l. 857.

Milton's grammar and idiom have been characterized Grammar and as made up chiefly of two elements: Shaksperian and Diction. Classical. The following list of peculiarities under both these heads, is not meant to be exhaustive; but is sufficient to show the extent and nature of the affinity of Milton's English both to Shakspere's English and to classical Greek and Latin. Explanations, where necessary, have been given, either here or in the Notes; but discussion, even if my limits permitted it, is rendered superfluous by Dr. Masson's *General Essay on Milton's English* and Dr. Abbott's *Shaksperian Grammar*. To these two exhaustive works the student is referred for further information.

I. LATINISMS :—

The Gender of a word following that of the Latin word from which it is derived, or of the Latin equivalent for it :—ll. 71, 173, 612 (v. n.), 613.

The Participial construction, *i.e.* the use of a participle or a participial adjective, instead of a substantive followed by a preposition, commonly " of " :—ll. 28-29, 61, 515 ("against" is the prep. here), 1253, 1377-8, 1433, 1489.

The Interrogative used in a dependent clause or sentence :
—ll. 48, 167, 254-5, 604, 1361 (v. n.).

The Antecedent Substantive inferred from an adjective or
a possessive pronoun :—ll. 73, 377, 1000, 1134, 1267.

Omission of the Antecedent :—ll. 150, 295, 310, 1317.

Use of a Relative for a Demonstrative, and of a Relative
sentence for a Demonstrative sentence :—ll. 444, 482,
1635, 1718.

Omission of the Verb "to say" :—ll. 782, 836, 895, 1205.

The Ethical Dative :—ll. 439, 537.

Imitation of the Ablative Absolute :—l. 463.

"As ... so," used like the Lat. "*tum ... quum*" :—ll.
1550-51.

"All" used for "any," like the Lat. "*omnis*" :—l. 82.

II. GRÆCISMS :—

Verbum prægnans ; i.e. a word (usually a verb) that both
directly expresses an idea, and indirectly implies
another easily suggested by the first (*Jelf*, 895) :—ll.
139-40, 977, 1054-5, 1089-90, 1343.

The Participial construction :—l 1549.

Omission of the Substantive Verb "to be" after a verb of
thinking :—l. 295.

III. FIGURES (many of which are also classicisms) :—

Anacoluthon, or confusion of grammatical constructions :
—ll. 19-20, 180-3, 493-6, 516-8, 773-7, 1107, 1671.

Archaism, or the use of old grammatical forms :—l. 1025.
(Other instances occur under different figures.)

Asyndeton, or the omission of the connective conjunction :
—ll. 41, 365-6, 417, 563, 939, 1304.

Double Entendre, or a double meaning attached to a
single word :—ll. 102, 230, 394, 1645.

Enallage, or use of one part of speech for another :—
Noun for Verb :—ll. 27, 203, 267.
Verb for Noun :—ll. 257, 469, 556, 1223, 1746.
Noun for Adjective :—ll. 1284, 1641.
Adjective for Noun :—ll. 324, 484, 1048, 1153, 1211, 1302.
Noun for Adverb :—l. 1420.

Adjective for Adverb :—ll. 583, 944, 987, 1229, 1681.

Adverb for Adjective:—ll. 268, 382.

Latin Participle from Noun :—ll. 1754, 1755.

Double Enallage, or interchange of parts of speech :— l. 924.

Hendiadys, or the expression of a single complex idea by means of two nouns connected by a participle (" and " or " of ") instead of by a noun qualified by an adjective :—ll. 105, 159, 535, 1394, 1734-5.

Hypallage, or the attribution of an adjective to another than its natural noun, also called ' *Transferred Epithet' :*—ll. 536, 552.

Hyperbaton, or a displacing of the normal order of words in a sentence :—ll. 1238, 1505, 1623, 1647-8, 1726.

Litotes or Meiosis, i.e. stating less than is actually meant, or using two negatives as a feeble equivalent of an affirmative :—ll. 180, 970.

Metonymy, or the use of a related word for the proper one, *e.g.* Abstract for Concrete :—ll. 28, 635, 1512. Concrete for Abstract :—ll. 464, 899. Country for Inhabitants :—ll. 889, 891. Part for the Whole (*Synecdoche*), l. 677.

Oxymoron, or the joining together of apparent contraries :— ll. 75, 100.

Paronomasia, or play upon words having a similar sound, but different meanings :—ll. 588, 1117-8, 1134, 1278, 1529.

Pathetic Fallacy, or ascribing human feeling to inanimate objects :—l. 8.

Prolepsis, or the use of a predicative adjective or participle in a sentence when the action implied by the verb of the sentence takes place *before* that implied by the adjective or participle:—ll. 253, 439, 1134, 1241, 1430.

Synesis, or construction according to sense, rather than form :—ll. 424, 501, 645-6, 1408, 1604.

Zeugma, or " the connexion of one word with two words or clauses, to both of which it does not equally apply, so that for one of them, another word, to be gathered from the sense of the passage, must be mentally supplied " (Kennedy) :—ll. 139-40, 231-2, 568, 738, 1191, 1211-12, 1612.

IV. Many of the following constructions are SHAKS-PERIAN : which of them are so, can be determined by a reference to the Notes.

'*As*' used for '*that*' :—l. 354 ; used for '*so that*' :—l. 1397 ; omitted :—l. 931.

'*-ed*,' the sign of the passive participle, omitted after a dental sound :—ll. 31, 259, 1556 ; used for the active '*-ing*' :—ll. 119, 403, 1124 ; used for the adj. term : '*-able*' :—l. 915.

'*Had*,' used for '*would have*' :—ll. 1019, 1495.

Infinitive mood, used in a peculiar sense :—ll. 535, 1500, 1566.

'*It*,' impersonal, omitted :—ll. 63, 1455, 1498, 1600.

'*Mine*,' euphonic use of, for '*my*' :—ll. 45, 459.

Negatives, two, not amounting to an affirmative :—ll. 815.

Nominative, omitted :—ll. 906, 1046, 1344.

Nominative absolute, a quasi form of :—ll. 149, 1480.

Noun, omitted after an adj. pronoun :—ll. 266, 483.

Past tense, form of the, used for the past participle :—ll. 479, 629, 727.

Prefixes, unusual forms of :—ll. 282, 442, 1022.

Prepositions, omitted after verbs and adjectives, where they would now be expressed :—ll. 820, 838, 1202, 1346.

Prepositions, obsolete force of, thus :—*By*=through, ll. 188, 1582. *For*=through, l. 1027 ; =as, l. 1215. *Of*=by, ll. 530, 1046, 1582 ; =for, l. 1329 ; =from, ll. 188, 222, 889, 1367 ; =through, l. 1397. *To*=compared to, l. 950 ; =Fr. *à*, l. 1539. *With*=by, ll. 763, 1586 ; =in, l. 1112 ; =in the eyes of, l. 859.

Reflexive pronouns used without '*self*' :—ll. 241, 586, 1495.

'*There*,' omitted at the beginning of a sentence :—ll. 38, 1554, 1721.

'*To be*,' omission of various forms of the verb ; thus '*to be*' is omitted :—ll. 212, 300, 514, 554, 840, 1306 ;

'was' is omitted :—l. 165, 418 ; 'is there' omitted :
—l. 349.

Verbs of Motion, such as 'to go' or 'to come,' omitted :—
ll. 920, 1250, 1370, 1445, 1552.

'*Was*,' auxiliary used instead of 'had' :—l. 253.

The metre of *Samson Agonistes* is blank verse of five **Versification.**
feet in each line, and each foot consisting of two
syllables,—an unaccented followed by an accented.
This is known as *Heroic blank verse*, and each foot so
constituted is called an *Iambus*. There are many
variations, however, from this normal order, and two
views have been taken of them. The older view,
commonly adopted in grammars, is to explain these
variations according to rules of Greek and Latin pro-
sody. Thus, when three syllables occur in a foot, they
are reduced to two by processes called *crasis* or
synizesis or *elision* or *synalœpha, e.g.* "the Ocean stream"
becomes "th' Ocean stream." Such processes, however,
seem to be repugnant to the character of English pronunciation, as may be seen by simply writing the above
as it would be pronounced, if this system were
followed—"thocean stream." Dr. Masson, who rightly
calls such pronunciations "comicalities" when applied
to English, adopts a second view—namely, that of
having the number of syllables the same in scanning
as they are in actual pronunciation, and providing for
them as simple *trisyllabic variations* from the normal
order, *e.g.* :—"*Bùt próvì* | dènce ór | instínct | òf ná |
tùre seéms"; where the trisyllable is an *amphibrach ;*
"Àffórd | *mè àssáss* | ìná | tèd ánd | bètráy'd "; where
the trisyllable is an *anapaest* (the most common form of
this variation).

Another rule of classical prosody, by which no departure from the scheme of the verse is permitted, even when the number of syllables in a foot remains unaffected by the proposed change, is also disregarded by Milton. Thus, in his verse an *iambus* may be displaced by other two-syllabled feet. Such a displacement Dr. Masson calls a *dissyllabic variation, e.g.*—"Ó mád | nèss ! tò | thínk úse | òf stróng | èst winés," where there occur two dissyllabic variations :—a *pyrrhic* in the second, and a *spondee* in the third, foot : "*Fúll òf* | divíne | instínct | áftèr | sòme próof," where the first and fourth feet are *trochees.*

A third peculiarity, which, more than any other, has drawn upon *Samson Agonistes* the charge of harsh versification, is the use of a line with a *supernumerary final syllable.* This is due to the old English practice of ending a verse with a strong syllable followed by a weak one. The proportion of such extra-syllabled lines is larger in Milton's dramatic, than in his epic, poems; the proportion in *Samson Agonistes* being, according to Masson, one in every six lines of dialogue, while in *Paradise Regained* it is one in every thirty. See ll. 303, 306, 939 etc.

Milton uses *Alexandrines* or Iambic Hexameters in certain places where the length of the verse is meant to be an echo of the sense. See ll. 146, 149, 157, 497, 630, 1035, 1429 ; and the notes upon them.

In the following words the *accent* follows that of the word (Latin or French) from which each is derived :— *explóits,* ll. 32, 525 ; *captíved,* l. 33 ; *exíled,* l. 98 ; *transvérse,* l. 209 ; *contríte,* l. 502 ; *fermént,* l. 619 ; *irreparáble,* l. 644 ; *contést,* l. 865 ; *comrádes,* l. 1162 ; *instínct,* l. 1545.

Effective *Caesuras*, or a distinct stop in the middle of a foot, serving to emphasize the idea contained in the portion of the verse preceding the stop, occur in the following lines—101, 201, 375, 775, 944, 946, 1213, 1321, 1371, 1418. The effect is most striking when the caesura recurs in the middle of the first or second foot. Dr. Masson gives a more extended meaning to the Miltonic caesura (vol. i. p. cxxvii.).

A change of metre, meant to indicate contempt, occurs in ll. 298, 775, 1072 ; or to convey a repulsive idea, in ll. 621-622.

Lastly, Milton, in his prefatory note to *Paradise Lost*, gives his reasons for the low opinion he had of *rhyme* as an instrument of verse :—namely, that " it is the invention of a barbarous age, to set off wretched matter and lame metre "; and a thing " to all judicious ears, trivial and of no true musical delight." His theory receives practical illustration from the use to which he puts rhyme in *Samson Agonistes.* In a great number of instances where it occurs, it is meant to convey a feeling of contempt or disesteem for the person or thing referred to, or the thought or sentiment embodied, *e.g.* ll. 170-5, 297-8, 303-6, 658-9, 668-9, 672-3, 674-5, 688-91, 1010-17, 1031-2, 1841-2, 1053-60, 1525-6. In a few instances the use of rhymes seems to be accidental or, at least, of doubtful import, *e.g.* ll. 610-1, 615-6, 973-4, 1519-20.

SAMSON AGONISTES.

A DRAMATIC POEM.

THE AUTHOR

JOHN MILTON.

Aristot. Poet. cap. 6. Τραγῳδία μίμησις πράξεως σπουδαίας, etc.—
Tragœdia est imitatio actionis seriæ, etc., per misericordiam et
metum perficiens talium affectuum lustrationem.

OF THAT SORT OF DRAMATIC POEM
CALLED TRAGEDY.

TRAGEDY, as it was anciently composed, hath been ever held the gravest, moralest, and most profitable of all other poems ; therefore said by Aristotle to be of power, by raising pity and fear, or terror, to purge the mind of those and such-like passions,—that is, to temper and reduce them to just measure with a kind of delight, stirred up by reading or seeing those passions well imitated. Nor is Nature wanting in her own effects to make good his assertion ; for so, in physic, things of melancholic hue and quality are used against melancholy, sour against sour, salt to remove salt humours. Hence philosophers and other gravest writers, as Cicero, Plutarch, and others, frequently cite out of tragic poets, both to adorn and illustrate their discourse. The Apostle Paul himself thought it not unworthy to insert a verse of Euripides into the text of Holy Scripture, 1 *Cor.* xv. 33 ; and Paraeus, commenting on the *Revelation*, divides the whole book, as a tragedy, into acts, distinguished each by a Chorus of heavenly harpings and song between. Heretofore men in highest dignity have laboured not a little to be thought able to compose a tragedy. Of that honour Dionysius the elder was no less ambitious than before of his attaining to the tyranny. Augustus Caesar also had begun his *Ajax*, but, unable to please his own judgment with what he had begun, left it unfinished. Seneca, the philosopher, is by some thought the author of those tragedies (at least the best of them) that go under that name. Gregory Nazianzen, a Father of the Church, thought it not unbeseeming the sanctity of his person to write a tragedy, which he entitled *Christ Suffering*. This is mentioned to vindicate Tragedy from the small esteem, or rather infamy, which in the account of many it undergoes at this day, with other common interludes ;

happening through the poet's error of intermixing comic stuff with tragic sadness and gravity, or introducing trivial and vulgar persons: which by all judicious hath been counted absurd, and brought in without discretion, corruptly to gratify the people. And, though ancient Tragedy use no Prologue, yet using sometimes, in case of self-defence or explanation, that which Martial calls an Epistle, in behalf of this tragedy, coming forth after the ancient manner, much different from what among us passes for best, thus much beforehand may be *epistled*,—that Chorus is here introduced after the Greek manner, not ancient only, but modern, and still in use among the Italians. In the modelling therefore of this poem, with good reason, the Ancients and Italians are rather followed, as of much more authority and fame. The measure of verse used in the Chorus is of all sorts, called by the Greeks *Monostrophic*, or rather *Apolelymenon*, without regard had to Strophe, Antistrophe, or Epode,—which were a kind of stanzas framed only for the music, then used with the Chorus that sung; not essential to the poem, and therefore not material; or, being divided into stanzas or pauses, they may be called *Allœostropha*. Division into act and scene, referring chiefly to the stage (to which this work never was intended), is here omitted.

It suffices if the whole drama be found not produced beyond the fifth act. Of the style and uniformity, and that commonly called the plot, whether intricate or explicit,—which is nothing indeed but such economy, or disposition of the fable, as may stand best with verisimilitude and decorum,—they only will best judge who are not unacquainted with Æschylus, Sophocles, and Euripides, the three tragic poets unequalled yet by any, and the best rule to all who endeavour to write Tragedy. The circumscription of time, wherein the whole drama begins and ends, is, according to ancient rule and best example, within the space of twenty-four hours.

THE ARGUMENT.

SAMSON, made captive, blind, and now in the prison at Gaza, there to labour as in a common workhouse, on a festival day, in the general cessation from labour, comes forth into the open air, to a place nigh, somewhat retired, there to sit a while and bemoan his condition. Where he happens at length to be visited by certain friends and equals of his tribe, which make the Chorus, who seek to comfort him what they can; then by his old father, Manoa, who endeavours the like, and withal tells him his purpose to procure his liberty by ransom; lastly, that this feast was proclaimed by the Philistines as a day of thanksgiving for their deliverance from the hands of Samson—which yet more troubles him. Manoa then departs to prosecute his endeavour with the Philistian lords for Samson's redemption: who, in the meanwhile, is visited by other persons, and, lastly, by a public officer to require his coming to the feast before the lords and people, to play or show his strength in their presence. He at first refuses, dismissing the public officer with absolute denial to come; at length, persuaded inwardly that this was from God, he yields to go along with him, who came now the second time with great threatenings to fetch him. The Chorus yet remaining on the place, Manoa returns full of joyful hope to procure ere long his son's deliverance; in the midst of which discourse an Ebrew comes in haste, confusedly at first, and afterwards more distinctly, relating the catastrophe—what Samson had done to the Philistines, and by accident to himself; wherewith the Tragedy ends.

THE PERSONS.

SAMSON.

MANOA, the father of Samson.	Public Officer.
DALILA, his wife.	Messenger.
HARAPHA of Gath.	Chorus of Danites.

The Scene, before the Prison in Gaza.

SAMSON AGONISTES.

Sams. A little onward lend thy guiding hand
To these dark steps, a little further on ;
For yonder bank hath choice of sun or shade.
There I am wont to sit, when any chance
Relieves me from my task of servile toil,
Daily in the common prison else enjoined me,
Where I, a prisoner chained, scarce freely draw
The air, imprisoned also, close and damp,
Unwholesome draught.   But here I feel amends—
The breath of heaven fresh blowing, pure and sweet,   10
With day-spring born ; here leave me to respire.
This day a solemn feast the people hold
To Dagon, their sea-idol, and forbid
Laborious works.   Unwillingly this rest
Their superstition yields me ; hence, with leave
Retiring from the popular noise, I seek
This unfrequented place to find some ease—
Ease to the body some, none to the mind
From restless thoughts, that, like a deadly swarm
Of hornets armed, no sooner found alone   20
But rush upon me thronging, and present
Times past, what once I was, and what am now.
Oh, wherefore was my birth from Heaven foretold
Twice by an Angel, who at last, in sight
Of both my parents, all in flames ascended
From off the altar where an offering burned,

As in a fiery column charioting
His godlike presence, and from some great act
Or benefit revealed to Abraham's race?
Why was my breeding ordered and prescribed   30
As of a person separate to God,
Designed for great exploits, if I must die
Betrayed, captived, and both my eyes put out,
Made of my enemies the scorn and gaze,
To grind in brazen fetters under task
With this heaven-gifted strength?   O glorious strength,
Put to the labour of a beast, debased
Lower than bond-slave !   Promise was that I
Should Israel from Philistian yoke deliver !
Ask for this great deliverer now, and find him   40
Eyeless in Gaza, at the mill with slaves,
Himself in bonds under Philistian yoke.
Yet stay ; let me not rashly call in doubt
Divine prediction.   What if all foretold
Had been fulfilled but through mine own default?
Whom have I to complain of but myself,
Who this high gift of strength committed to me,
In what part lodged, how easily bereft me,
Under the seal of silence could not keep,
But weakly to a woman must reveal it,   50
O'ercome with importunity and tears?
O impotence of mind in body strong !
But what is strength without a double share
Of wisdom?   Vast, unwieldy, burdensome,
Proudly secure, yet liable to fall
By weakest subtleties ; not made to rule,
But to subserve where wisdom bears command.
God, when he gave me strength, to show withal
How slight the gift was, hung it in my hair.
But peace !   I must not quarrel with the will   60
Of highest dispensation, which herein
Haply had ends above my reach to know.

Suffices that to me strength is my bane,
And proves the source of all my miseries—
So many, and so huge, that each apart
Would ask a life to wail.   But, chief of all.
O loss of sight, of thee I most complain !
Blind among enemies !   O worse than chains,
Dungeon, or beggary. or decrepit age !
Light, the prime work of God, to me is extinct,   70
And all her various objects of delight
Annulled, which might in part my grief have eased.
Inferior to the vilest now become
Of man or worm, the vilest here excel me :
They creep, yet see ; I, dark in light, exposed
To daily fraud, contempt, abuse, and wrong,
Within doors, or without, still as a fool,
In power of others, never in my own—
Scarce half I seem to live, dead more than half.
O dark, dark, dark, amid the blaze of noon,   80
Irrecoverably dark, total eclipse
Without all hope of day !
O first-created beam, and thou great Word,
" Let there be light, and light was over all,"
Why am I thus bereaved thy prime decree ?
The Sun to me is dark
And silent as the Moon,
When she deserts the night,
Hid in her vacant interlunar cave.
Since light so necessary is to life,   90
And almost life itself, if it be true
That light is in the soul,
She all in every part, why was the sight
To such a tender ball as the eye confined,
So obvious and so easy to be quenched,
And not, as feeling, through all parts diffused,
That she might look at will through every pore ?
Then had I not been thus exiled from light,

As in the land of darkness, yet in light,
To live a life half dead, a living death,   100
And buried ; but, O yet more miserable !
Myself my sepulchre, a moving grave :
Buried, yet not exempt,
By privilege of death and burial,
From worst of other evils, pains, and wrongs ;
But made hereby obnoxious more
To all the miseries of life,
Life in captivity
Among inhuman foes.
But who are these ? for with joint pace I hear   110
The tread of many feet steering this way ;
Perhaps my enemies, who come to stare
At my affliction, and perhaps to insult—
Their daily practice to afflict me more.
          Chor. This, this is he ; softly a while ;
Let us not break in upon him.
O change beyond report, thought, or belief !
See how he lies at random, carelessly diffused,
With languished head unpropt,
As one past hope, abandoned,   120
And by himself given over,
In slavish habit, ill-fitted weeds
O'er-worn and soiled.
Or do my eyes misrepresent ?   Can this be he,
That heroic, that renowned,
Irresistible Samson ? whom, unarmed,
No strength of man, or fiercest wild beast, could withstand ;
Who tore the lion as the lion tears the kid ;
Ran on embattled armies clad in iron,
And, weaponless himself,   130
Made arms ridiculous, useless the forgery
Of brazen shield and spear, the hammered cuirass,
Chalybean-tempered steel, and frock of mail
Adamantean proof :

But safest he who stood aloof,
When insupportably his foot advanced,
In scorn of their proud arms and warlike tools,
Spurned them to death by troops. The bold Ascalonite
Fled from his lion ramp ; old warriors turned
Their plated backs under his heel,   140
Or grovelling soiled their crested helmets in the dust.
Then with what trivial weapon came to hand,
The jaw of a dead ass, his sword of bone,
A thousand foreskins fell, the flower of Palestine,
In Ramath-lechi, famous to this day :
Then by main force pulled up, and on his shoulders bore,
The gates of Azza, post and massy bar,
Up to the hill by Hebron, seat of giants old—
No journey of a Sabbath-day, and loaded so—
Like whom the Gentiles feign to bear up Heaven.   150
Which shall I first bewail——
Thy bondage or lost sight,
Prison within prison
Inseparably dark ?
Thou art become (O worst imprisonment !)
The dungeon of thyself ; thy soul
(Which men enjoying sight oft without cause complain)
Imprisoned now indeed,
In real darkness of the body dwells,
Shut up from outward light   160
To incorporate with gloomy night ;
For inward light, alas !
Puts forth no visual beam.
O mirror of our fickle state,
Since man on earth unparalleled !
The rarer thy example stands,
By how much from the top of wondrous glory,
Strongest of mortal men,
To lowest pitch of abject fortune thou art fallen.
For him I reckon not in high estate   170

Whom long descent of birth,
Or the sphere of fortune, raises ;
But thee, whose strength, while virtue was her mate,
Might have subdued the Earth,
Universally crowned with highest praises.

    Sams. I hear the sound of words ; their sense the air
Dissolves unjointed ere it reach my ear.

    Chor. He speaks : let us draw nigh.   Matchless in might,
The glory late of Israel, now the grief !
We come, thy friends and neighbours not unknown,   180
From Eshtaol and Zora's fruitful vale,
To visit or bewail thee ; or, if better,
Counsel or consolation we may bring,
Salve to thy sores : apt words have power to swage
The tumours of a troubled mind,
And are as balm to festered wounds.

    Sams. Your coming, friends, revives me ; for I learn
Now of my own experience, not by talk,
How counterfeit a coin they are who 'friends'
Bear in their superscription (of the most   190
I would be understood).   In prosperous days
They swarm, but in adverse withdraw their head,
Not to be found, though sought.   Ye see, O friends,
How many evils have enclosed me round ;
Yet that which was the worst now least afflicts me,
Blindness ; for, had I sight, confused with shame,
How could I once look up, or heave the head,
Who, like a foolish pilot, have shipwracked
My vessel trusted to me from above,
Gloriously rigged, and for a word, a tear,   200
Fool ! have divulged the secret gift of God
To a deceitful woman ?   Tell me, friends,
Am I not sung and proverbed for a fool
In every street ?   Do they not say, ' How well
Are come upon him his deserts ' ?   Yet why ?
Immeasurable strength they might behold

In me ; of wisdom nothing more than mean.
This with the other should at least have paired ;
These two, proportioned ill, drove me transverse.
    Chor. Tax not divine disposal. <u>Wisest men</u>   210
Have <u>erred, and by bad women been deceived</u> ;
And shall again, pretend they ne'er so wise.
Deject not, then, so overmuch thyself,
Who hast of sorrow thy full load besides.
Yet, truth to say, I oft have heard men wonder
Why thou should'st wed Philistian women rather
Than of thine own tribe fairer, or as fair,
At least of thy own nation, and as noble.
    Sams. The first I saw at Timna, and she pleased
Me, not my parents, that I sought to wed   220
The daughter of an infidel. They knew not
That what I motioned was of God ; I knew
From intimate impulse, and therefore urged
The marriage on, that, by occasion hence,
I might begin Israel's deliverance—
The work to which I was divinely called.
She proving false, the next I took to wife
(O that I never had ! fond wish too late !)
Was in the vale of Sorec, Dalila,
That specious monster, my accomplished snare.   230
I thought it lawful from my former act,
And the same end, still watching to oppress
Israel's oppressors. <u>Of what now I suffer</u>
She was not the <u>prime cause, but I myself,</u>
<u>Who, vanquished</u> with a peal of words, (O weakness !)
Gave up my fort of silence to a woman.
    Chor. In seeking just occasion to provoke
The Philistine, thy country's enemy,
Thou never wast remiss, I bear thee witness ;
Yet Israel still serves with all his sons.   240
    Sams. That fault I take not on me, but **transfer**
On Israel's governors and heads of tribes,

Who, seeing those great acts which God had done
Singly by me against their conquerors,
Acknowledged not, or not at all considered,
Deliverance offered.   I, on the other side,
Used no ambition to commend my deeds ;
The deeds themselves, though mute, spoke loud the doer.
But they persisted deaf, and would not seem
To count them things worth notice, till at length   250
Their lords, the Philistines, with gathered powers,
Entered Judea, seeking me, who then
Safe to the rock of Etham was retired—
Not flying, but forecasting in what place
To set upon them, what advantaged best.
Meanwhile the men of Judah, to prevent
The harass of their land, beset me round ;
I willingly on some conditions came
Into their hands, and they as gladly yield me
To the Uncircumcised a welcome prey,   260
Bound with two cords.   But cords to me were threads
Touched with the flame : on their whole host I flew
Unarmed, and with a trivial weapon felled
Their choicest youth ; they only lived who fled.
Had Judah that day joined, or one whole tribe,
They had by this possessed the towers of Gath,
And lorded over them whom now they serve.
But what more oft, in nations grown corrupt,
And by their vices brought to servitude,
Than to love bondage more than liberty—   270
Bondage with ease than strenuous liberty—
And to despise, or envy, or suspect,
Whom God hath of his special favour raised
As their deliverer ?   If he aught begin,
How frequent to desert him, and at last
To heap ingratitude on worthiest deeds !
    Chor. Thy words to my remembrance bring
How Succoth and the fort of Penuel

Their great deliverer contemned,
The matchless Gideon, in pursuit   280
Of Madian, and her vanquished kings ;
And how ingrateful Ephraim
Had dealt with Jephtha, who by argument,
Not worse than by his shield and spear,
Defended Israel from the Ammonite,
Had not his prowess quelled their pride
In that sore battle when so many died
Without reprieve, adjudged to death
For want of well pronouncing *Shibboleth.*
   Sams. Of such examples add me to the roll.   290
Me easily indeed mine may neglect,
But God's proposed deliverance not so.
   Chor. Just are the ways of God,
And justifiable to men,
Unless there be who think not God at all.
If any be, they walk obscure ;
For of such doctrine never was there school,
But the heart of the fool,
And no man therein doctor but himself.
   Yet more there be who doubt his ways not just,   300
As to his own edicts found contradicting ;
Then give the reins to wandering thought,
Regardless of his glory's diminution,
Till, by their own perplexities involved,
They ravel more, still less resolved,
But never find self-satisfying solution.
   As if they would confine the Interminable,
And tie him to his own prescript,
Who made our laws to bind us, not himself,
And hath full right to exempt   310
Whomso it pleases him by choice
From national obstriction, without taint
Of sin, or legal debt ;
For with his own laws he can best dispense.

He would not else, who never wanted means,
Nor in respect of the enemy just cause,
To set his people free,
Have prompted this heroic Nazarite,
Against his vow of strictest purity,
To seek in marriage that fallacious bride,   320
Unclean, unchaste.
     Down, Reason, then ; at least, vain reasonings down ;
Though Reason here aver
That moral verdit quits her of unclean :
Unchaste was subsequent ; her stain, not his.

FATHER.   But see ! here comes thy reverend sire,
With careful step, locks white as down,
Old Manoa : advise
Forthwith how thou ought'st to receive him.
     Sams. Ay me ! another inward grief, awaked   330
With mention of that name, renews the assault.
     Man. Brethren and men of Dan (for such ye seem
Though in this uncouth place), if old respect,
As I suppose, towards your once gloried friend,
My son, now captive, hither hath informed
Your younger feet, while mine, cast back with age,
Came lagging after, say if he be here.
     Chor. As signal now in low dejected state
As erst in highest, behold him where he lies.
     Man. O miserable change ! Is this the man,   340
That invincible Samson, far renowned,
The dread of Israel's foes, who with a strength
Equivalent to Angels' walked their streets,
None offering fight ; who, single combatant,
Duelled their armies ranked in proud array,
Himself an army—now unequal match
To save himself against a coward armed
At one spear's length ? O ever-failing trust
In mortal strength ! and, oh, what not in man
Deceivable and vain ? Nay, what thing good   350

Prayed for, but often proves our woe, our bane ?
I prayed for children, and thought barrenness
In wedlock a reproach ; I gained a son,
And such a son as all men hailed me happy :
Who would be now a father in my stead ?   TYPICAL REACTION.
Oh, wherefore did God grant me my request,
And as a blessing with such pomp adorned ?
Why are his gifts desirable, to tempt
Our earnest prayers, then, given with solemn hand
As graces, draw a scorpion's tail behind ?   360
For this did the Angel twice descend ? for this
Ordained thy nurture holy, as of a plant
Select and sacred ? glorious for a while,
The miracle of men ; then in an hour
Ensnared, assaulted, overcome, led bound,
Thy foes' derision, captive, poor and blind,
Into a dungeon thrust, to work with slaves !
Alas ! methinks whom God hath chosen once
To worthiest deeds, if he through frailty err,
He should not so o'erwhelm, and as a thrall   370
Subject him to so foul indignities,
Be it but for honour's sake of former deeds.
   Sams. Appoint not heavenly disposition, father.
Nothing of all these evils hath befallen me
But justly ; I myself have brought them on ;
Sole author I, sole cause.   If aught seem vile,
As vile hath been my folly, who have profaned
The mystery of God, given me under pledge
Of vow, and have betrayed it to a woman,
A Canaanite, my faithless enemy.   380
This well I knew, nor was at all surprised,
But warned by oft experience.   Did not she
Of Timna first betray me, and reveal
The secret wrested from me in her highth
Of nuptial love professed, carrying it straight
To them who had corrupted her, my spies

And rivals ?   In this other was there found
More faith, who, also in her prime of love,
Spousal embraces, vitiated with gold,
Though offered only, by the scent conceived,   390
Her spurious first-born, Treason against me ?
Thrice she assayed, with flattering prayers and sighs.
And amorous reproaches, to win from me
My capital secret, in what part my strength
Lay stored, in what part summed, that she might know ;
Thrice I deluded her, and turned to sport
Her importunity, each time perceiving
How openly and with what impudence
She purposed to betray me, and (which was worse
Than undissembled hate) with what contempt   400
She sought to make me traitor to myself.
Yet, the fourth time, when, mustering all her wiles,
With blandished parleys, feminine assaults,
Tongue-batteries, she surceased not day nor night
To storm me, over-watched and wearied out,
At times when men seek most repose and rest,
I yielded, and unlocked her all my heart,
Who, with a grain of manhood well resolved,
Might easily have shook off all her snares ;
But foul effeminacy held me yoked   410
Her bond-slave.   O indignity, O blot
To honour and religion ! servile mind
Rewarded well with servile punishment !
The base degree to which I now am fallen,
These rags, this grinding, is not yet so base
As was my former servitude, ignoble,
Unmanly, ignominious, infamous,
True slavery ; and that blindness worse than this,
That saw not how degenerately I served.

   Man. I cannot praise thy marriage-choices, son—   420
Rather approved them not ; but thou didst plead
Divine impulsion prompting how thou might'st

Find some occasion to infest our foes.
I state not that ; this I am sure—our foes
Found soon occasion thereby to make thee
Their captive, and their triumph ; thou the sooner
Temptation found'st, or over-potent charms,
To violate the sacred trust of silence
Deposited within thee—which to have kept
Tacit was in thy power.   True ; and thou bear'st   430
Enough, and more, the burden of that fault ;
Bitterly hast thou paid, and still art paying,
That rigid score.   A worse thing yet remains :—
This day the Philistines a popular feast
Here celebrate in Gaza, and proclaim
Great pomp, and sacrifice, and praises loud,
To Dagon, as their god who hath delivered
Thee, Samson, bound and blind, into their hands—
Them out of thine, who slew'st them many a slain.
So Dagon shall be magnified, and God,   440
Besides whom is no god, compared with idols,
Disglorified, blasphemed, and had in scorn
By the idolatrous rout amidst their wine ;
Which to have come to pass by means of thee,
Samson, of all thy sufferings think the heaviest,
Of all reproach the most with shame that ever
Could have befallen thee and thy father's house.
    Sams. Father, I do acknowledge and confess
That I this honour, I this pomp, have brought
To Dagon, and advanced his praises high   450
Among the Heathen round—to God have brought
Dishonour, obloquy, and oped the mouths
Of idolists and atheists ; have brought scandal
To Israel, diffidence of God, and doubt
In feeble hearts, propense enough before
To waver, or fall off and join with idols :
Which is my chief affliction, shame and sorrow,
The anguish of my soul, that suffers not

Mine eye to harbour sleep, or thoughts to rest.
This only hope relieves me, that the strife   460
With me hath end. All the contest is now
'Twixt God and Dagon. Dagon hath presumed,
Me overthrown, to enter lists with God,
His deity comparing and preferring
Before the God of Abraham. He, be sure,
Will not connive, or linger, thus provoked,
But will arise, and his great name assert.
Dagon must stoop, and shall ere long receive
Such a discomfit as shall quite despoil him
Of all these boasted trophies won on me,   470
And with confusion blank his worshipers.
   Man. With cause this hope relieves thee ; and these words
I as a prophecy receive ; for God
(Nothing more certain) will not long defer
To vindicate the glory of his name
Against all competition, nor will long
Endure it doubtful whether God be Lord
Or Dagon. But for thee what shall be done ?
Thou must not in the meanwhile, here forgot,
Lie in this miserable loathsome plight   480
Neglected. I already have made way
To some Philistian lords, with whom to treat
About thy ransom. Well they may by this
Have satisfied their utmost of revenge,
By pains and slaveries, worse than death, inflicted
On thee, who now no more canst do them harm.
   Sams. Spare that proposal, father ; spare the trouble
Of that solicitation. Let me here,
As I deserve, pay on my punishment,
And expiate, if possible, my crime,   490
Shameful garrulity. To have revealed
Secrets of *men*, the secrets of a friend,
How heinous had the fact been, how deserving
Contempt and scorn of all—to be excluded

All friendship, and avoided as a blab,
The mark of fool set on his front !
But I *God's* counsel have not kept, his holy secret
Presumptuously have published, impiously,
Weakly at least and shamefully—a sin
That Gentiles in their parables condemn   500
To their Abyss and horrid pains confined.
 Man. Be penitent, and for thy fault contrite ;
But act not in thy own affliction, son.
Repent the sin ; but, if the punishment
Thou canst avoid, self-preservation bids ;
Or the execution leave to high disposal,
And let another hand, not thine, exact
Thy penal forfeit from thyself.   Perhaps
God will relent, and quit thee all his debt ;
Who evermore approves and more accepts   510
(Best pleased with humble and filial submission)
Him who, imploring mercy, sues for life,
Than who, self-rigorous, chooses death as due ;
Which argues over-just, and self-displeased
For self-offence more than for God offended.
Reject not, then, what offered means who knows
But God hath set before us to return thee
Home to thy country and his sacred house,
Where thou may'st bring thy offerings, to avert
His further ire, with prayers and vows renewed.   520
 Sams. His pardon I implore ; but, as for life,
To what end should I seek it ?   When in strength
All mortals I excelled, and great in hopes,
With youthful courage, and magnanimous thoughts
Of birth from Heaven foretold and high exploits,
Full of divine instinct, after some proof
Of acts indeed heroic, far beyond
The sons of Anak, famous now and blazed,
Fearless of danger, like a petty god
I walked about, admired of all, and dreaded   530

On hostile ground, none daring my affront —
Then, swollen with pride, into the snare I fell
Of fair fallacious looks, venereal trains,
Softened with pleasure and voluptuous life,
At length to lay my head and hallowed pledge
Of all my strength in the lascivious lap
Of a deceitful concubine, who shore me,
Like a tame wether, all my precious fleece,
Then turned me out ridiculous, despoiled,
Shaven, and disarmed among my enemies.   540
    Chor. Desire of wine and all delicious drinks,
Which many a famous warrior overturns,
Thou could'st repress ; nor did the dancing ruby,
Sparkling out-poured, the flavour or the smell,
Or taste, that cheers the heart of gods and men,
Allure thee from the cool crystalline stream.
    Sams. Wherever fountain or fresh current flowed
Against the eastern ray, translucent, pure
With touch ethereal of Heaven's fiery rod,
I drank, from the clear milky juice allaying   550
Thirst, and refreshed ; nor envied them the grape
Whose heads that turbulent liquor fills with fumes.
    Chor. O madness ! to think use of strongest wines
And strongest drinks our chief support of health,
When God with these forbidden made choice to rear
His mighty champion, strong above compare,
Whose drink was only from the liquid brook !
    Sams. But what availed this temperance, not complete
Against another object more enticing ?
What boots it at one gate to make defence,   560
And at another to let in the foe,
Effeminately vanquished ? by which means,
Now blind, disheartened, shamed, dishonoured, quelled,
To what can I be useful ? wherein serve
My nation, and the work from Heaven imposed ?
But to sit idle on the household hearth,

A burdenous drone ; to visitants a gaze,
Or pitied object ; these redundant locks,
Robustious to no purpose, clustering down,
Vain monument of strength ; till length of years   570
And sedentary numbness craze my limbs
To a contemptible old age obscure.
Here rather let me drudge, and earn my bread,
Till vermin, or the draff of servile food,
Consume me, and oft-invocated death
Hasten the welcome end of all my pains.

   Man. Wilt thou then serve the Philistines with that gift
Which was expressly given thee to annoy them ?
Better at home lie bed-rid, not only idle,
Inglorious, unemployed, with age outworn.   580
But God, who caused a fountain at thy prayer
From the dry ground to spring, thy thirst to allay
After the brunt of battle, can as easy
Cause light again within thy eyes to spring,
Wherewith to serve him better than thou hast.
And I persuade me so.   Why else this strength
Miraculous yet remaining in those locks ?
His might continues in thee not for naught,
Nor shall his wondrous gifts be frustrate thus.

   Sams. All otherwise to me my thoughts portend—   590
That these dark orbs no more shall treat with light,
Nor the other light of life continue long,
But yield to double darkness nigh at hand ;
So much I feel my genial spirits droop,
My hopes all flat : Nature within me seems
In all her functions weary of herself ;
My race of glory run, and race of shame,
And I shall shortly be with them that rest.

   Man. Believe not these suggestions, which proceed
From anguish of the mind, and humours black   600
That mingle with thy fancy.   I, however,
Must not omit a father's timely care

To prosecute the means of thy deliverance
By ransom or how else : meanwhile be calm,
And healing words from these thy friends admit.
    Sams. Oh, that torment should not be confined
To the body's wounds and sores,
With maladies innumerable
In heart, head, breast, and reins,
But must secret passage find   610
To the inmost mind,
There exercise all his fierce accidents,
And on her purest spirits prey,
As on entrails, joints, and limbs,
With answerable pains, but more intense,
Though void of corporal sense !
    My griefs not only pain me
As a lingering disease,
But, finding no redress, ferment and rage ;
Nor less than wounds immedicable   620
Rankle, and fester, and gangrene,
To black mortification.
Thoughts, my tormentors, armed with deadly stings.
Mangle my apprehensive tenderest parts,
Exasperate, exulcerate, and raise
Dire inflammation, which no cooling herb
Or med'cinal liquor can assuage,
Nor breath of vernal air from snowy Alp.
Sleep hath forsook and given me o'er
To death's benumbing opium as my only cure ;   630
Thence faintings, swoonings of despair,
And sense of Heaven's desertion.
    I was his nursling once and choice delight,
His destined from the womb,
Promised by heavenly message twice descending.
Under his special eye
Abstemious I grew up and thrived amain ;
He led me on to mightiest deeds,

Above the nerve of mortal arm,
Against the Uncircumcised, our enemies :   640
But now hath cast me off as never known,
And to those cruel enemies,
Whom I by his appointment had provoked,
Left me all helpless, with the irreparable loss
Of sight, reserved alive to be repeated
The subject of their cruelty or scorn.
Nor am I in the list of them that hope ;
Hopeless are all my evils, all remediless.
This one prayer yet remains, might I be heard,
No long petition—speedy death,   650
The close of all my miseries and the balm.
   Chor. Many are the sayings of the wise,
In ancient and in modern books enrolled,
Extolling patience as the truest fortitude,
And to the bearing well of all calamities,
All chances incident to man's frail life,
Consolatories writ
With studied argument, and much persuasion sought,
Lenient of grief and anxious thought.
But with the afflicted in his pangs their sound   660
Little prevails, or rather seems a tune
Harsh, and of dissonant mood from his complaint,
Unless he feel within
Some source of consolation from above,
Secret refreshings that repair his strength
And fainting spirits uphold.
   God of our fathers ! what is Man,
That thou towards him with hand so various—
Or might I say contrarious ?—
Temper'st thy providence through his short course : 670
Not evenly, as thou rul'st
The angelic orders, and inferior creatures mute
Irrational and brute ?
Nor do I name of men the common rout,

c*

That, wandering loose about,
Grow up and perish as the summer fly,
Heads without name, no more remembered ;
But such as thou hast solemnly elected,
With gifts and graces eminently adorned,
To some great work, thy glory,   680
And people's safety, which in part they effect.
Yet towards these, thus dignified, thou oft,
Amidst their highth of noon,
Changest thy countenance and thy hand, with no regard
Of highest favours past
From thee on them, or them to thee of service.
    Nor only dost degrade them, or remit
To life obscured, which were a fair dismission,
But throw'st them lower than thou didst exalt them high—
Unseemly falls in human eye,   690
Too grievous for the trespass or omission ;
Oft leav'st them to the hostile sword
Of heathen and profane, their carcasses
To dogs and fowls a prey, or else captived,
Or to the unjust tribunals, under change of times,
And condemnation of the ungrateful multitude.
If these they scape, perhaps in poverty
With sickness and disease thou bow'st them down,
Painful diseases and deformed,
In crude old age ;   700
Though not disordinate, yet causeless suffering
The punishment of dissolute days.   In fine,
Just or unjust alike seem miserable,
For oft alike both come to evil end.
    So deal not with this once thy glorious champion,
The image of thy strength, and mighty minister.
What do I beg ? how hast thou dealt already !
Behold him in this state calamitous, and turn
His labours, for thou canst, to peaceful end.
    But who is this ? what thing of sea or land—   710

Female of sex it seems—
That, so bedecked, ornate, and gay,
Comes this way sailing,
Like a stately ship
Of Tarsus, bound for the isles
Of Javan or Gadire,
With all her bravery on, and tackle trim,
Sails filled, and streamers waving,
Courted by all the winds that hold them play ;
An amber scent of odorous perfume   720
Her harbinger, a damsel train behind ?
Some rich Philistian matron she may seem ;
And now, at nearer view, no other certain
Than Dalila thy wife.
   Sams. My wife ! my traitress ! let her not come near me.
   Chor. Yet on she moves ; now stands and eyes thee fixed,
About to have spoke ; but now, with head declined,
Like a fair flower surcharged with dew, she weeps,
And words addressed seem into tears dissolved,
Wetting the borders of her silken veil.   730
But now again she makes address to speak.
   Dal. With doubtful feet and wavering resolution   DALILA.
I came, still dreading thy displeasure, Samson ;
Which to have merited, without excuse,
I cannot but acknowledge.   Yet, if tears
May expiate (though the fact more evil drew
In the perverse event than I foresaw),
My penance hath not slackened, though my pardon
No way assured   But conjugal affection,
Prevailing over fear and timorous doubt,   740
Hath led me on, desirous to behold
Once more thy face, and know of thy estate,
If aught in my ability may serve
To lighten what thou suffer'st, and appease
Thy mind with what amends is in my power—
Though late, yet in some part to recompense

My rash but more unfortunate misdeed.

Sams. Out, out, hyæna ! These are thy wonted arts,
And arts of every woman false like thee—
To break all faith, all vows, deceive, betray ;   750
Then, as repentant, to submit, beseech,
And reconcilement move with feigned remorse,
Confess, and promise wonders in her change—
Not truly penitent, but chief to try
Her husband, how far urged his patience bears,
His virtue or weakness which way to assail :
Then, with more cautious and instructed skill,
Again transgresses, and again submits,
That wisest and best men, full oft beguiled,
With goodness principled not to reject   760
The penitent, but ever to forgive,
Are drawn to wear out miserable days,
Entangled with a poisonous bosom-snake,
If not by quick destruction soon cut off,
As I by thee, to ages an example.

Dal. Yet hear me, Samson ; not that I endeavour
To lessen or extenuate my offence,
But that, on the other side, if it be weighed
By itself, with aggravations not surcharged,
Or else with just allowance counterpoised,   770
I may, if possible, thy pardon find
The easier towards me, or thy hatred less.
First granting, as I do, it was a weakness
In me, but incident to all our sex,
Curiosity, inquisitive, importune
Of secrets, then with like infirmity
To publish them—both common female faults—
Was it not weakness also to make known
For importunity, that is for nought,
Wherein consisted all thy strength and safety ?   780
To what I did thou show'dst me first the way.
But I to enemies revealed, and should not !

ANIMAL IMAGERY

COMMON FEMALE
FAULTS !

Nor should'st thou have trusted that to woman's frailty :
Ere I to thee, thou to thyself wast cruel.
Let weakness, then, with weakness come to parle,
So near related, or the same of kind ;
Thine forgive mine, that men may censure thine
The gentler, if severely thou exact not
More strength from me than in thyself was found.
And what if love, which thou interpret'st hate,   790
The jealousy of love, powerful of sway
In human hearts, nor less in mine towards thee,
Caused what I did ?   I saw thee mutable
Of fancy ; feared lest one day thou would'st leave me
As her at Timna ; sought by all means, therefore,
How to endear, and hold thee to me firmest :
No better way I saw than by importuning
To learn thy secrets, get into my power
Thy key of strength and safety.   Thou wilt say,
' Why, then, revealed ?'   I was assured by those   800
Who tempted me that nothing was designed
Against thee but safe custody and hold.
That made for me ; I knew that liberty
Would draw thee forth to perilous enterprises,
While I at home sat full of cares and fears,
Wailing thy absence in my widowed bed ;
Here I should still enjoy thee, day and night,
Mine and love's prisoner, not the Philistines',
Whole to myself, unhazarded abroad,
Fearless at home of partners in my love.   810
These reasons in Love's law have passed for good,
Though fond and reasonless to some perhaps ;
And love hath oft, well meaning, wrought much woe,
Yet always pity or pardon hath obtained.
Be not unlike all others, not austere
As thou art strong, inflexible as steel.
If thou in strength all mortals dost exceed,
In uncompassionate anger do not so.

    Sams. How cunningly the sorceress displays
Her own transgressions, to upbraid me mine !   820
That malice, not repentance, brought thee hither
By this appears. I gave, thou say'st, the example,
I led the way—bitter reproach, but true ;
I to myself was false ere thou to me.
Such pardon, therefore, as I give my folly
Take to thy wicked deed ; which when thou seest
Impartial, self-severe, inexorable,
Thou wilt renounce thy seeking, and much rather
Confess it feigned.   Weakness is thy excuse,
And I believe it—weakness to resist   830
Philistian gold.   If weakness may excuse,
What murtherer, what traitor, parricide,
Incestuous, sacrilegious, but may plead it ?
All wickedness is weakness ; that plea, therefore,
With God or man will gain thee no remission.
But love constrained thee ! Call it furious rage
To satisfy thy lust. Love seeks to have love ;
My love how could'st thou hope, who took'st the way
To raise in me inexpiable hate,
Knowing, as needs I must, by thee betrayed ?   840
In vain thou striv'st to cover shame with shame,
For by evasions thy crime uncover'st more.
    Dal. Since thou determin'st weakness for no plea
In man or woman, though to thy own condemning,
Hear what assaults I had, what snares besides,
What sieges girt me round, ere I consented ;
Which might have awed the best-resolved of men,
The constantest, to have yielded without blame.
It was not gold, as to my charge thou lay'st,
That wrought with me. Thou know'st the magistrates 850
And princes of my country came in person,
Solicited, commanded, threatened, urged,
Adjured by all the bonds of civil duty
And of religion—pressed how just it was,

How honourable, how glorious, to entrap
A common enemy, who had destroyed
Such numbers of our nation : and the priest
Was not behind, but ever at my ear,
Preaching how meritorious with the gods
It would be to ensnare an irreligious   860
Dishonourer of Dagon.   What had I
To oppose against such powerful arguments ?
Only my love of thee held long debate,
And combated in silence all these reasons
With hard contest.   At length, that grounded maxim,
So rife and celebrated in the mouths
Of wisest men, that to the public good   *Duty before love.*
Private respects must yield, with grave authority
Took full possession of me, and prevailed ;
Virtue, as I thought, truth, duty, so enjoining.   870
   Sams. I thought where all thy circling wiles would end—
In feigned religion, smooth hypocrisy !
But, had thy love, still odiously pretended,
Been, as it ought, sincere, it would have taught thee
Far other reasonings, brought forth other deeds.
I, before all the daughters of my tribe
And of my nation, chose thee from among
My enemies, loved thee, as too well thou knew'st ;
Too well ; unbosomed all my secrets to thee,
Not out of levity, but overpowered   880
By thy request, who could deny thee nothing ;
Yet now am judged an enemy.   Why, then,
Didst thou at first receive me for thy husband—
Then, as since then, thy country's foe professed ?
Being once a wife, for me thou wast to leave
Parents and country ; nor was I their subject,
Nor under their protection, but my own ;
Thou mine, not theirs.   If aught against my life
Thy country sought of thee, it sought unjustly,
Against the law of nature, law of nations ;   890

No more thy country, but an impious crew
Of men conspiring to uphold their state
By worse than hostile deeds, violating the ends
For which our country is a name so dear ;
Not therefore to be obeyed.   But zeal moved thee ;
To please thy gods thou didst it !   Gods unable
To acquit themselves and prosecute their foes
But by ungodly deeds, the contradiction
Of their own deity, Gods cannot be—
Less therefore to be pleased, obeyed, or feared.   900
These false pretexts and varnished colours failing,
Bare in thy guilt, how foul must thou appear !

   Dal. In argument with men a woman ever
Goes by the worse, whatever be her cause.

   Sams. For want of words, no doubt, or lack of breath !
Witness when I was worried with thy peals.

   Dal. I was a fool, too rash, and quite mistaken
In what I thought would have succeeded best.
Let me obtain forgiveness of thee, Samson ;
Afford me place to show what recompense   910
Towards thee I intend for what I have misdone,
Misguided.   Only what remains past cure
Bear not too sensibly, nor still insist
To afflict thyself in vain.   Though sight be lost,
Life yet hath many solaces, enjoyed
Where other senses want not their delights—
At home, in leisure and domestic ease,
Exempt from many a care and chance to which
Eyesight exposes, daily, men abroad.
I to the lords will intercede, not doubting   920
Their favourable ear, that I may fetch thee
From forth this loathsome prison-house to abide
With me, where my redoubled love and care,
With nursing diligence, to me glad office,
May ever tend about thee to old age,
With all things grateful cheered, and so supplied

That what by me thou hast lost thou least shall miss.
   Sams. No, no ; of my condition take no care ;
It fits not ; thou and I long since are twain ;
Nor think me so unwary or accursed   930
To bring my feet again into the snare
Where once I have been caught.   I know thy trains,
Though dearly to my cost, thy gins, and toils.
Thy fair enchanted cup, and warbling charms,
No more on me have power ; their force is nulled ;
So much of adder's wisdom I have learned,
To fence my ear against thy sorceries.
If in my flower of youth and strength, when all men
Loved, honoured, feared me, thou alone could hate me,
Thy husband, slight me, sell me, and forgo me,   940
How would'st thou use me now, blind, and thereby
Deceivable, in most things as a child
Helpless, thence easily contemned and scorned,
And last neglected !   How would'st thou insult,
When I must live uxorious to thy will
In perfet thraldom ! how again betray me,
Bearing my words and doings to the lords
To gloss upon, and, censuring, frown or smile !
This jail I count the house of liberty
To thine, whose doors my feet shall never enter.   950
   Dal. Let me approach at least, and touch thy hand.
   Sams. Not for thy life, lest fierce remembrance wake
My sudden rage to tear thee joint by joint.
At distance I forgive thee ; go with that ;
Bewail thy falsehood, and the pious works
It hath brought forth to make thee memorable
Among illustrious women, faithful wives ;
Cherish thy hastened widowhood with the gold
Of matrimonial treason : so farewell.
   Dal. I see thou art implacable, more deaf   960
To prayers than winds and seas.   Yet winds to seas
Are reconciled at length, and sea to shore :

Thy anger, unappeasable, still rages,
Eternal tempest never to be calmed.
Why do I humble thus myself, and, suing
For peace, reap nothing but repulse and hate,
Bid go with evil omen, and the brand
Of infamy upon my name denounced?
To mix with thy concernments I desist
Henceforth, nor too much disapprove my own.   970
Fame, if not double-faced, is double-mouthed,
And with contrary blast proclaims most deeds;
On both his wings, one black, the other white,
Bears greatest names in his wild aery flight.
My name, perhaps, among the Circumcised
in Dan, in Judah, and the bordering tribes,
To all posterity may stand defamed,
With malediction mentioned, and the blot
Of falsehood most unconjugal traduced.
But in my country, where I most desire,   980
In Ecron, Gaza, Asdod, and in Gath,
I shall be named among the famousest
Of women, sung at solemn festivals,
Living and dead recorded, who, to save
Her country from a fierce destroyer, chose
Above the faith of wedlock bands; my tomb
With odours visited and annual flowers;
Not less renowned than in Mount Ephraim
Jael, who, with inhospitable guile,
Smote Sisera sleeping, through the temples nailed.   990
Nor shall I count it heinous to enjoy
The public marks of honour and reward
Conferred upon me for the piety
Which to my country I was judged to have shown.
At this whoever envies or repines,
I leave him to his lot, and like my own.

   Chor. She's gone—a manifest serpent by her sting
Discovered in the end, till now concealed.

Sams. So let her go. God sent her to debase me,
And aggravate my folly, who committed   1000
To such a viper his most sacred trust
Of secrecy, my safety, and my life.

Chor. Yet beauty, though injurious, hath strange power,
After offence returning, to regain
Love once possessed, nor can be easily
Repulsed, without much inward passion felt,
And secret sting of amorous remorse.

Sams. Love-quarrels oft in pleasing concord end ;
Not wedlock treachery endangering life.

Chor. It is not virtue, wisdom, valour, wit,   1010
Strength, comeliness of shape, or amplest merit,
That woman's love can win, or long inherit ;
But what it is, hard is to say,
Harder to hit,
Which way soever men refer it,
(Much like thy riddle, Samson) in one day
Or seven though one should musing sit.
   If any of these, or all, the Timnian bride
Had not so soon preferred
Thy paranymph, worthless to thee compared,   1020
Successor in thy bed,
Nor both so loosely disallied
Their nuptials, nor this last so treacherously
Had shorn the fatal harvest of thy head.
Is it for that such outward ornament
Was lavished on their sex, that inward gifts
Were left for haste unfinished, judgment scant,
Capacity not raised to apprehend
Or value what is best,
In choice, but oftest to affect the wrong ?   1030
Or was too much of self-love mixed,
Of constancy no root infixed,
That either they love nothing, or not long ?
   Whate'er it be, to wisest men and best,

Seeming at first all heavenly under virgin veil,
Soft, modest, meek, demure,
Once joined, the contrary she proves—a thorn
Intestine, far within defensive arms
A cleaving mischief, in his way to virtue
Adverse and turbulent ; or by her charms   1040
Draws him awry, enslaved
With dotage, and his sense depraved
To folly and shameful deeds, which ruin ends.
What pilot so expert but needs must wreck,
Embarked with such a steers-mate at the helm ?
    Favoured of Heaven who finds
One virtuous, rarely found,
That in domestic good combines !
Happy that house ! his way to peace is smooth :
But virtue which breaks through all opposition,   1050
And all temptation can remove,
Most shines and most is acceptable above.
    Therefore God's universal law
Gave to the man despotic power
Over his female in due awe,
Nor from that right to part an hour,
Smile she or lour :
So shall he least confusion draw
On his whole life, not swayed
By female usurpation, nor dismayed.   1060
    But had we best retire ? I see a storm.
    Sams. Fair days have oft contracted wind and rain.
    Chor. But this another kind of tempest brings.
    Sams. Be less abstruse ; my riddling days are past.
    Chor. Look now for no enchanting voice, nor fear
The bait of honeyed words ; a rougher tongue
Draws hitherward ; I know him by his stride,
The giant Harapha of Gath, his look
Haughty, as is his pile high-built and proud.
Comes he in peace ? What wind hath blown him hither 1070

HARAPHA of GATH .

I less conjecture than when first I saw
The sumptuous Dalila floating this way :
His habit carries peace, his brow defiance.

    Sams. Or peace or not, alike to me he comes.

    Chor. His fraught we soon shall know : he now arrives.

    Har. I come not, Samson, to condole thy chance,
As these perhaps, yet wish it had not been,
Though for no friendly intent. I am of Gath ;
Men call me Harapha, of stock renowned
As Og, or Anak, and the Emims old   1080
That Kiriathaim held. Thou know'st me now,
If thou at all art known. Much I have heard
Of thy prodigious might and feats performed,
Incredible to me, in this displeased,
That I was never present on the place
Of those encounters, where we might have tried
Each other's force in camp or listed field ;
And now am come to see of whom such noise
Hath walked about, and each limb to survey,
If thy appearance answer loud report.   1090

    Sams. The way to know were not to see, but taste.

    Har. Dost thou already single me ? I thought
Gyves and the mill had tamed thee. O that fortune
Had brought me to the field where thou art famed
To have wrought such wonders with an ass's jaw !
I should have forced thee soon wish other arms,
Or left thy carcass where the ass lay thrown ;
So had the glory of prowess been recovered
To Palestine, won by a Philistine
From the unforeskinned race, of whom thou bear'st   1100
The highest name for valiant acts. That honour,
Certain to have won by mortal duel from thee,
I lose, prevented by thy eyes put out.

    Sams. Boast not of what thou would'st have done, but do
What then thou would'st ; thou seest it in thy hand.

Har. To combat with a blind man I disdain,
And thou hast need much washing to be touched.

Sams. Such usage as your honourable lords
Afford me, assassinated and betrayed ;
Who durst not with their whole united powers   1110
In fight withstand me single and unarmed,
Nor in the house with chamber-ambushes
Close-banded durst attack me, no, not sleeping,
Till they had hired a woman with their gold,
Breaking her marriage-faith, to circumvent me.
Therefore, without feign'd shifts, let be assigned
Some narrow place enclosed, where sight may give thee,
Or rather flight, no great advantage on me ;
Then put on all thy gorgeous arms, thy helmet
And brigandine of brass, thy broad habergeon,   1120
Vant-brace and greaves and gauntlet ; add thy spear,
A weaver's beam, and seven-times-folded shield :
I only with an oaken staff will meet thee,
And raise such outcries on thy clattered iron,
Which long shall not withhold me from thy head,
That in a little time, while breath remains thee,
Thou oft shalt wish thyself at Gath, to boast
Again in safety what thou would'st have done
To Samson, but shalt never see Gath more.

Har. Thou durst not thus disparage glorious arms   1130
Which greatest heroes have in battle worn,
Their ornament and safety, had not spells
And black enchantments, some magician's art,
Armed thee or charmed thee strong, which thou from
          Heaven
Feign'dst at thy birth was given thee in thy hair,
Where strength can least abide, though all thy hairs
Were bristles ranged like those that ridge the back
Of chafed wild boars or ruffled porcupines.

Sams. I know no spells, use no forbidden arts ;
My trust is in the Living God, who gave me,   1140

AFFIRMATION of CHRISTIANITY.

At my nativity, this strength, diffused
No less through all my sinews, joints, and bones,
Than thine, while I preserved these locks unshorn,
The pledge of my unviolated vow.
For proof hereof, if Dagon be thy god,   *Samson v. Harapha.*
Go to his temple, invocate his aid   *= God v. Dagon.*
With solemnest devotion, spread before him
How highly it concerns his glory now
To frustrate and dissolve these magic spells,
Which I to be the power of Israel's God   **1150**
Avow, and challenge Dagon to the test,
Offering to combat thee, his champion bold,
With the utmost of his godhead seconded :
Then thou shalt see, or rather to thy sorrow
Soon feel, whose God is strongest, thine or mine.
   Har. Presume not on thy God.   Whate'er he be,
Thee he regards not, owns not, hath cut off
Quite from his people, and delivered up
Into thy enemies' hand ; permitted them
To put out both thine eyes, and fettered send thee **1160**
Into the common prison, there to grind
Among the slaves and asses, thy comrades,
As good for nothing else, no better service
With those thy boisterous locks ; no worthy match
For valour to assail, nor by the sword
Of noble warrior, so to stain his honour,
But by the barber's razor best subdued.
   Sams. All these indignities, for such they are
From thine, these evils I deserve and more,
Acknowledge them from God inflicted on me   **1170**
Justly, yet despair not of his final pardon,
Whose ear is ever open, and his eye
Gracious to re-admit the suppliant ;   *Remorse v. humble*
In confidence whereof I once again
Defy thee to the trial of mortal fight,
By combat to decide whose god is God,

Thine, or whom I with Israel's sons adore.

   Har. Fair honour that thou dost thy God, in trusting
He will accept thee to defend his cause,
A murtherer, a revolter, and a robber !   1180

    Sams. Tongue-doughty giant, how dost thou prove me
      these ?

   Har. Is not thy nation subject to our lords ?
Their magistrates confessed it when they took thee
As a league-breaker, and delivered bound
Into our hands ; for hadst thou not committed
Notorious murder on those thirty men
At Ascalon, who never did thee harm,
Then, like a robber, stripp'dst them of their robes ?
The Philistines, when thou hadst broke the league,
Went up with armed powers thee only seeking,   1190
To others did no violence nor spoil.

   Sams. Among the daughters of the Philistines
I chose a wife, which argued me no foe,
And in your city held my nuptial feast ;
But your ill-meaning politician lords,
Under pretence of bridal friends and guests,
Appointed to await me thirty spies,
Who, threatening cruel death, constrained the bride
To wring from me, and tell to them, my secret,
That solved the riddle which I had proposed.   1200
When I perceived all set on enmity,
As on my enemies, wherever chanced,
I used hostility, and took their spoil,
To pay my underminers in their coin.
My nation was subjected to your lords !
It was the force of conquest ; force with force
Is well ejected when the conquered can.
But I, a private person, whom my country
As a league-breaker gave up bound, presumed
Single rebellion, and did hostile acts !   1210
I was no private, but a person raised,

With strength sufficient, and command from Heaven,
To free my country.   If their servile minds
Me, their deliverer sent, would not receive,
But to their masters gave me up for nought,
The unworthier they ; whence to this day they serve.
I was to do my part from Heaven assigned,
And had performed it if my known offence
Had not disabled me, not all your force.
These shifts refuted, answer thy appellant,   1220
Though by his blindness maimed for high attempts,
Who now defies thee thrice to single fight,
As a petty enterprise of small enforce.

   Har. With thee, a man condemned, a slave enrolled,
Due by the law to capital punishment ?
To fight with thee no man of arms will deign.

   Sams. Cam'st thou for this, vain boaster, to survey me,
To descant on my strength, and give thy verdit ?
Come nearer ; part not hence so slight informed ;
But take good heed my hand survey not thee.   1230

   Har. O Baal-zebub ! can my ears unused
Hear these dishonours, and not render death ?

   Sams. No man withholds thee ; nothing from thy hand
Fear I incurable ; bring up thy van ;
My heels are fettered, but my fist is free.

   Har. This insolence other kind of answer fits.

   Sams. Go, baffled coward, lest I run upon thee,
Though in these chains, bulk without spirit vast,   COWARD.
And with one buffet lay thy structure low,
Or swing thee in the air, then dash thee down,   1240
To the hazard of thy brains and shattered sides.

   Har. By Astaroth, ere long thou shalt lament
These braveries, in irons loaden on thee.

   Chor. His giantship is gone somewhat crest-fallen,
Stalking with less unconscionable strides,
And lower looks, but in a sultry chafe.

   Sams. I dread him not, nor all his giant brood,

Though fame divulge him father of five sons,
All of gigantic size, Goliah chief.
 Chor. He will directly to the lords, I fear,   1250
And with malicious counsel stir them up
Some way or other yet further to afflict thee.
 Sams. He must allege some cause, and offered fight
Will not dare mention, lest a question rise
Whether he durst accept the offer or not ;
And that he durst not plain enough appeared.
Much more affliction than already felt
They cannot well impose, nor I sustain,
If they intend advantage of my labours,
The work of many hands, which earns my keeping, 1260
With no small profit daily to my owners.
But come what will ; my deadliest foe will prove
My speediest friend, by death to rid me hence ;
The worst that he can give to me the best.
Yet so it may fall out, because their end
Is hate, not help to me, it may with mine
Draw their own ruin who attempt the deed.
 Chor. O, how comely it is, and how reviving
To the spirits of just men long oppressed,
When God into the hands of their deliverer 1270
Puts invincible might,
To quell the mighty of the earth, the oppressor,
The brute and boisterous force of violent men,
Hardy and industrious to support
Tyrannic power, but raging to pursue
The righteous, and all such as honour truth !
He all their ammunition
And feats of war defeats,
With plain heroic magnitude of mind
And celestial vigour armed ;   1280
Their armouries and magazines contemns,
Renders them useless, while
With winged expedition

Swift as the lightning glance he executes
His errand on the wicked, who, surprised,
Lose their defence, distracted and amazed.
    But patience is more oft the exercise
Of saints, the trial of their fortitude,
Making them each his own deliverer,
And victor over all   1290
That tyranny or fortune can inflict.
Either of these is in thy lot,
Samson, with might endued
Above the sons of men ; but sight bereaved
May chance to number thee with those
Whom patience finally must crown.
    This Idol's day hath been to thee no day of rest,
Labouring thy mind
More than the working day thy hands.
And yet, perhaps, more trouble is behind ;   1300
For I descry this way
Some other tending ; in his hand
A sceptre or quaint staff he bears,
Comes on amain, speed in his look.
By his habit I discern him now
A public officer, and now at hand.   PUBLIC OFFICER .
His message will be short and voluble.
    Off. Ebrews, the prisoner Samson here I seek.
    Chor. His manacles remark him ; there he sits.
    Off. Samson, to thee our lords thus bid me say :   1310
This day to Dagon is a solemn feast,
With sacrifices, triumph, pomp, and games ;
Thy strength they know surpassing human rate,
And now some public proof thereof require
To honour this great feast, and great assembly.
Rise, therefore, with all speed, and come along,
Where I will see thee heartened and fresh clad,
To appear as fits before the illustrious lords.
    Sams. Thou know'st I am an Ebrew ; therefore tell them

Our law forbids at their religious rites   1320
My presence ; for that cause I cannot come.

   Off. This answer, be assured, will not content them.

   Sams. Have they not sword-players, and every sort
Of gymnic artists, wrestlers, riders, runners,
Jugglers and dancers, antics, mummers, mimics,
But they must pick me out, with shackles tired,
And over-laboured at their public mill,
To make them sport with blind activity ?
Do they not seek occasion of new quarrels,
On my refusal, to distress me more,   1330
Or make a game of my calamities ?
Return the way thou cam'st ; I will not come.

   Off. Regard thyself ; this will offend them highly.

   Sams. Myself ! my conscience, and internal peace.
Can they think me so broken, so debased
With corporal servitude, that my mind ever
Will condescend to such absurd commands ?
Although their drudge, to be their fool or jester,
And, in my midst of sorrow and heart-grief,
To show them feats, and play before their god—   1340
The worst of all indignities, yet on me
Joined with extreme contempt ! I will not come.

   Off. My message was imposed on me with speed,
Brooks no delay : is this thy resolution ?

   Sams. So take it with what speed thy message needs.

   Off. I am sorry what this stoutness will produce.

   Sams. Perhaps thou shalt have cause to sorrow indeed.

   Chor. Consider, Samson ; matters now are strained
Up to the highth, whether to hold or break.
He's gone, and who knows how he may report   1350
Thy words by adding fuel to the flame ?
Expect another message, more imperious,
More lordly thundering than thou well wilt **bear.**

   Sams. Shall I abuse this consecrated gift
Of strength, again returning with my hair

After my great transgression—so requite
Favour renewed, and add a greater sin
By prostituting holy things to idols,
A Nazarite, in place abominable,
Vaunting my strength in honour to their Dagon ?   1360
Besides how vile, contemptible, ridiculous,
What act more execrably unclean, profane ?

   Chor. Yet with this strength thou serv'st the Philistines
Idolatrous, uncircumcised, unclean.

   Sams. Not in their idol-worship, but by labour
Honest and lawful to deserve my food
Of those who have me in their civil power.

   Chor. Where the heart joins not, outward acts defile
     not.

   Sams. Where outward force constrains, the sentence
     holds :
But who constrains me to the temple of Dagon,   1370
Not dragging ? The Philistian lords command :
Commands are no constraints. If I obey them,
I do it freely, venturing to displease
God for the fear of man, and man prefer,
Set God behind ; which, in his jealousy,
Shall never, unrepented, find forgiveness.
Yet that he may dispense with me, or thee,
Present in temples at idolatrous rites
For some important cause, thou need'st not doubt.

   Chor. How thou wilt here come off surmounts my reach.

   Sams. Be of good courage ; I begin to feel   1381
Some rousing motions in me, which dispose
To something extraordinary my thoughts.
I with this messenger will go along—
Nothing to do, be sure, that may dishonour
Our Law, or stain my vow of Nazarite.
If there be aught of presage in the mind,
This day will be remarkable in my life
By some great act, or of my days the last.

Chor. In time thou hast resolved : the man returns.   **1390**

Off. Samson, this second message from our lords
To thee I am bid say : Art thou our slave,
Our captive, at the public mill our drudge,
And dar'st thou, at our sending and command,
Dispute thy coming? Come without delay ;
Or we shall find such engines to assail
And hamper thee, as thou shalt come of force,
Though thou wert firmlier fastened than a rock.

Sams. I could be well content to try their art,
Which to no few of them would prove pernicious ;   **1400**
Yet, knowing their advantages too many,
Because they shall not trail me through their streets
Like a wild beast, I am content to go.
Masters' commands come with a power resistless
To such as owe them absolute subjection ;
And for a life who will not change his purpose?
(So mutable are all the ways of men !)
Yet this be sure, in nothing to comply
Scandalous or forbidden in our Law.

Off. I praise thy resolution. Doff these links :   **1410**
By this compliance thou wilt win the lords
To favour, and perhaps to set thee free.

Sams. Brethren, farewell. Your company along
I will not wish, lest it perhaps offend them
To see me girt with friends ; and how the sight
Of me, as of a common enemy,
So dreaded once, may now exasperate them
I know not. Lords are lordliest in their wine ;
And the well-feasted priest then soonest fired
With zeal, if aught religion seemed concerned ,   **1420**
No less the people, on their holy-days,
Impetuous, insolent, unquenchable.
Happen what may, of me expect to hear
Nothing dishonourable, impure, unworthy
Our God, our Law, my nation, or myself ;

The last of me or no I cannot warrant.

  Chor. Go, and the Holy One
Of Israel be thy guide
To what may serve his glory best, and spread his name
Great among the Heathen round ;   1430
Send thee the Angel of thy birth, to stand
Fast by thy side, who from thy father's field
Rode up in flames after his message told
Of thy conception, and be now a shield
Of fire ; that Spirit that first rushed on thee
In the camp of Dan,
Be efficacious in thee now at need !
For never was from Heaven imparted
Measure of strength so great to mortal seed,
As in thy wondrous actions hath been seen.   1440
But wherefore comes old Manoa in such haste
With youthful steps ? Much livelier than erewhile
He seems : supposing here to find his son,
Or of him bringing to us some glad news ?

  Man. Peace with you, brethren ! My inducement hither
Was not at present here to find my son,
By order of the lords new parted hence
To come and play before them at their feast.
I heard all as I came ; the city rings,
And numbers thither flock : I had no will,   1450
Lest I should see him forced to things unseemly.
But that which moved my coming now was chiefly
To give ye part with me what hope I have
With good success to work his liberty.   *Dramatic Irony.*

  Chor. That hope would much rejoice us to partake
With thee. Say, reverend sire ; we thirst to hear.

  Man. I have attempted, one by one, the lords,
Either at home, or through the high street passing,
With supplication prone and father's tears,
To accept of ransom for my son, their prisoner.   1460
Some much averse I found, and wondrous harsh,

Contemptuous, proud, set on revenge and spite ;
That part most reverenced Dagon and his priests :
Others more moderate seeming, but their aim
Private reward, for which both God and State
They easily would set to sale : a third
More generous far and civil, who confessed
They had enough revenged, having reduced
Their foe to misery beneath their fears ;
The rest was magnanimity to remit,   1470
If some convenient ransom were proposed.
<u>What noise or shout was that ? It tore the sky.</u>

  Chor. Doubtless the people shouting to behold
Their once great dread, captive and blind before them,
Or at some proof of strength before them shown.

  Man. His ransom, if my whole inheritance
May compass it, shall willingly be paid
And numbered down.   Much rather I shall choose
To live the poorest in my tribe, than richest
And he in that calamitous prison left.   1480
No, I am fixed not to part hence without him.
For his redemption all my patrimony,
If need be, I am ready to forego
And quit.   Not wanting him, I shall want nothing.

  Chor. Fathers are wont to lay up for their sons ;
Thou for thy son are bent to lay out all :
Sons wont to nurse their parents in old age ;
Thou in old age car'st how to nurse thy son,
Made older than thy age through eye-sight lost.

  Man. It shall be my delight to tend his eyes,   1490
And view him sitting in his house, ennobled
With all those high exploits by him achieved,
And on his shoulders waving down those locks
That of a nation armed the strength contained
And I persuade me God had not permitted
His strength again to grow up with his hair
Garrisoned round about him like a camp

Of faithful soldiery, were not his purpose
To use him further yet in some great service—
Not to sit idle with so great a gift   1500
Useless, and thence ridiculous, about him.
And, since his strength with eye-sight was not lost,
God will restore him eye-sight to his strength.
   Chor. Thy hopes are not ill founded, nor seem vain,
Of his delivery, and thy joy thereon
Conceived, agreeable to a father's love ;
In both which we, as next, participate.
   Man. I know your friendly minds, and . . . O, what
      noise !
Mercy of Heaven ! what hideous noise was that ?
Horribly loud, unlike the former shout.   1510
   Chor. Noise call you it, or universal groan,
As if the whole inhabitation perished ?
Blood, death, and deathful deeds, are in that noise,
Ruin, destruction at the utmost point.
   Man. Of ruin indeed methought I heard the noise.
Oh ! it continues ; they have slain my son.
   Chor. Thy son is rather slaying them : that outcry
From slaughter of one foe could not ascend.
   Man. Some dismal accident it needs must be.
What shall we do—stay here, or run and see ?   1520
   Chor. Best keep together here, lest, running thither,
We unawares run into danger's mouth.
This evil on the Philistines is fallen :
From whom could else a general cry be heard ?
The sufferers, then, will scarce molest us here ;
From other hands we need not much to fear.
What if, his eye-sight (for to Israel's God
Nothing is hard) by miracle restored,
He now be dealing dole among his foes,
And over heaps of slaughtered walk his way ?   1530
   Man. That were a joy presumptuous to be thought.
   Chor. Yet God hath wrought things as incredible
D

For his people of old ; what hinders now ?

   Man. He can, I know, but doubt to think he will ;
Yet hope would fain subscribe, and tempts belief.
A little stay will bring some notice hither.

   Chor. Of good or bad so great, of bad the sooner ;
For evil news rides post, while good news baits.
And to our wish I see one hither speeding—
An Ebrew, as I guess, and of our tribe.   1540

   Messenger. O, whither shall I run, or which way fly
The sight of this so horrid spectacle,
Which erst my eyes beheld, and yet behold ?
For dire imagination still pursues me.
But providence or instinct of nature seems,
Or reason, though disturbed and scarce consulted,
To have guided me aright, I know not how,
To thee first, reverend Manoa, and to these
My countrymen, whom here I knew remaining,
As at some distance from the place of horror,   1550
So in the sad event too much concerned.

   Man. The accident was loud, and here before thee
With rueful cry ; yet what it was we hear not.
No preface needs ; thou seest we long to know.

   Mess. It would burst forth ; but I recover breath,
And sense distract, to know well what I utter.

   Man. Tell us the sum ; the circumstance defer.

   Mess. Gaza yet stands ; but all her sons are fallen,
All in a moment overwhelmed and fallen.

   Man. Sad ! but thou know'st to Israelites not saddest
The desolation of a hostile city.   1531

   Mess. Feed on that first ; there may in grief be surfeit.

   Man. Relate by whom.

   Mess.   By Samson.

   Man.   That still lessens
The sorrow, and converts it nigh to joy.

   Mess. Ah ! Manoa, I refrain too suddenly
To utter what will come at last too soon,

Lest evil tidings, with too rude irruption
Hitting thy aged ear, should pierce too deep.
 Man. Suspense in news is torture ; speak them out.
 Mess. Then take the worst in brief : Samson is dead. 1570
 Man. The worst indeed ! O, all my hope's defeated
To free him hence ! but Death, who sets all free,
Hath paid his ransom now and full discharge.
What windy joy this day had I conceived,
Hopeful of his delivery, which now proves
Abortive as the first-born bloom of spring
Nipt with the lagging rear of winter's frost !
Yet, ere I give the reins to grief, say first
How died he ; death to life is crown or shame.
All by him fell, thou say'st ; by whom fell he ?   1580
What glorious hand gave Samson his death's wound ?
 Mess. Unwounded of his enemies he fell.
 Man. Wearied with slaughter, then, or how ? explain.
 Mess. By his own hands.
 Man.   Self-violence ! What cause
Brought him so soon at variance with himself
Among his foes ?
 Mess.   Inevitable cause—
At once both to destroy and be destroyed.
The edifice, where all were met to see him,
Upon their heads and on his own he pulled.
 Man. O lastly over-strong against thyself !   1590
A dreadful way thou took'st to thy revenge.
More than enough we know ; but, while things yet
Are in confusion, give us, if thou canst,
Eye-witness of what first or last was done,
Relation more particular and distinct.
 Mess. Occasions drew me early to this city ;
And, as the gates I entered with sun-rise,
The morning trumpets festival proclaimed
Through each high street.   Little I had dispatched,
When all abroad was rumoured that this day   1600

Samson should be brought forth, to show the people
Proof of his mighty strength in feats and games.
I sorrowed at his captive state, but minded
Not to be absent at that spectacle.
The building was a spacious theatre,
Half round on two main pillars vaulted high,
With seats where all the lords, and each degree
Of sort, might sit in order to behold ;
The other side was open, where the throng
On banks and scaffolds under sky might stand :   1610
I among these aloof obscurely stood.
The feast and noon grew high, and sacrifice
Had filled their hearts with mirth, high cheer, and wine,
When to their sports they turned.   Immediately
Was Samson as a public servant brought,
In their state livery clad : before him pipes
And timbrels ; on each side went armed guards ;
Both horse and foot before him and behind,
Archers and slingers, cataphracts, and spears.
At sight of him the people with a shout   1620
Rifted the air, clamouring their god with praise,
Who had made their dreadful enemy their thrall.
He patient, but undaunted, where they led him,
Came to the place ; and what was set before him,
Which without help of eye might be assayed,
To heave, pull, draw, or break, he still performed
All with incredible, stupendious force,
None daring to appear antagonist.
At length, for intermission sake, they led him
Between the pillars ; he his guide requested   1630
(For so from such as nearer stood we heard),
As over-tired, to let him lean a while
With both his arms on those two massy pillars,
That to the arched roof gave main support.
He unsuspicious led him ; which when Samson
Felt in his arms, with head a while inclined,

And eyes fast fixed, he stood, as one who prayed,
Or some great matter in his mind revolved :
At last, with head erect, thus cried aloud :—
"Hitherto, Lords, what your commands imposed   1640
I have performed, as reason was, obeying,
Not without wonder or delight beheld ;
Now, of my own accord, such other trial
I mean to show you of my strength yet greater
As with amaze shall strike all who behold."
This uttered, straining all his nerves, he bowed ;
As with the force of winds and waters pent
When mountains tremble, those two massy pillars
With horrible convulsion to and fro
He tugged, he shook, till down they came, and drew   1650
The whole roof after them with burst of thunder
Upon the heads of all who sat beneath,
Lords, ladies, captains, counsellors, or priests,
Their choice nobility and flower, not only
Of this, but each Philistian city round,
Met from all parts to solemnize this feast.
Samson, with these immixed, inevitably
Pulled down the same destruction on himself ;
The vulgar only scaped, who stood without.
   Chor. O dearly bought revenge, yet glorious !   1660
Living or dying thou hast fulfilled
The work for which thou wast foretold
To Israel, and now liest victorious
Among thy slain self-killed ;
Not willingly, but tangled in the fold
Of dire Necessity, whose law in death conjoined
Thee with thy slaughtered foes, in number more
Than all thy life had slain before.
   Semichor. While their hearts were jocund and sublime,
Drunk with idolatry, drunk with wine   1670
And fat regorged of bulls and goats,
Chaunting their idol, and preferring

Before our living Dread, who dwells
In Silo, his bright sanctuary,
Among them he a spirit of phrenzy sent,
Who hurt their minds,
And urged them on with mad desire
To call in haste for their destroyer.
They, only set on sport and play,
Unweetingly importuned   1680
Their own destruction to come speedy upon them.
So fond are mortal men,
Fallen into wrath divine,
As their own ruin on themselves to invite,
Insensate left, or to sense reprobate,
And with blindness internal struck.
   Semichor. But he, though blind of sight,
Despised, and thought extinguished quite,
With inward eyes illuminated,
His fiery virtue roused   1690
From under ashes into sudden flame,
And as an evening dragon came,
Assailant on the perched roosts
And nests in order ranged
Of tame villatic fowl, but as an eagle
His cloudless thunder bolted on their heads,
So Virtue, given for lost,
Depressed and overthrown, as seemed,
Like that self-begotten bird
In the Arabian woods embost,   1700
That no second knows nor third,
And lay erewhile a holocaust,
From out her ashy womb now teemed,
Revives. reflourishes, then vigorous most
When most unactive deemed ;
And, though her body die, her fame survives,
A secular bird, ages of lives.
   Man. Come, come ; no time for lamentation now,

Nor much more cause.   Samson hath quit himself
Like Samson, and heroicly hath finished   1710
A life heroic, on his enemies
Fully revenged—hath left them years of mourning,
And lamentation to the sons of Caphtor
Through all Philistian bounds ; to Israel
Honour hath left and freedom, let but them
Find courage to lay hold on this occasion ;
To himself and father's house eternal fame ;
And, which is best and happiest yet, all this
With God not parted from him, as was feared,
But favouring and assisting to the end.   1720
Nothing is here for tears, nothing to wail
Or knock the breast ; no weakness, no contempt,
Dispraise, or blame ; nothing but well and fair,
And what may quiet us in a death so noble.
Let us go find the body where it lies
Soaked in his enemies' blood, and from the stream
With lavers pure, and cleansing herbs, wash off
The clotted gore.   I, with what speed the while
(Gaza is not in plight to say us nay),
Will send for all my kindred, all my friends,   1730
To fetch him hence, and solemnly attend,
With silent obsequy and funeral train,
Home to his father's house.   There will I build him
A monument, and plant it round with shade
Of laurel ever green and branching palm,
With all his trophies hung, and acts enrolled
In copious legend, or sweet lyric song.
Thither shall all the valiant youth resort,
And from his memory inflame their breasts
To matchless valour and adventures high ;   1740
The virgins also shall, on feastful days,
Visit his tomb with flowers, only bewailing
His lot unfortunate in nuptial choice,
From whence captivity and loss of eyes.   *Reason ?*

Chor. All is best, though we oft doubt
What the unsearchable dispose
Of Highest Wisdom brings about,
And ever best found in the close.
Oft He seems to hide his face,
But unexpectedly returns,   1750
And to his faithful champion hath in place
Bore witness gloriously ; whence Gaza mourns,
And all that band them to resist
His uncontrollable intent.
His servants He, with new acquist
Of true experience from this great event,
With peace and consolation hath dismissed,
And calm of mind, all passion spent.

NOTES.

PREFACE.

The Preface is mainly intended by Milton to be his Apology to the Puritans for writing a play. It is with this object that he appeals to the authority of Scripture, and to the example of a Father of the Church. Incidentally there follow Milton's expression of disesteem for the tragic compositions of his own time, and an explanation of his plan of reverting to the ancient Greek model.

said by Aristotle ... imitated. *Poetics*, vi. Twining's explanation of this difficult passage throws light on Milton's :—"The passions of savages or of men in the first rude stages of civilization, are ferocious and painful. They pity or they fear, either violently or not at all . In polished society where these passions are indulged in works of the imagination (tragedies, novels, etc.) the pain is converted into one strong and delightful feeling by the consciousness of fiction," *i.e.* of truth well imitated,..." and the habitual exercise of the passions in fiction has a tendency to soften and refine those passions, when excited by real objects in common life." See Ueberweg, *History of Philosophy*, i. 178 (Eng. transl.), for a different view.

for so, in physic ... humours. A reference to the doctrine, "similia similibus curantur," formulated by Paracelsus, long before Hahnemann made it the basis of Homœopathy. With Paracelsus this took the particular shape of the doctrine of Signatures, pointed out by Dunster. "which inferred the propriety of the use of any vegetable or mineral, in medicine from the similarity of colour, shape or appearance, which these remedies might bear to the part affected." Thus turmeric or saffron was given in liver complaints. Both doctrines were based upon Paracelsus's theory that Man, the microcosm, is only a miniature of Nature, the macrocosm.

a verse of Euripides. "Evil communications corrupt good manners." Newton quotes the verse, φθείρουσιν ἤθη χρήσθ' ὁμιλίαι κακαί. as from Menander of the New Comedy. Todd points out that it is also found in the fragments of the earlier writer, Euripides.

Paraeus. The latinized name of David Paré, a Calvinist theologian (1548-1622). In his *Reason of Church Government urged against Prelacy*, Milton in inquiring whether Tragedy is not "more doctrinal and exemplary to a nation" than the Epic, compares the *Song of Solomon* to a divine Pastoral Drama, and the *Apocalypse* of St. John (*i.e.* the book of Revelation) to a "high and stately Tragedy shutting up and intermingling her solemn scenes and acts with a sevenfold chorus of hallelujahs and harping symphonies": appealing, as here, to the authority of Paraeus. So, later, Ewald has looked upon the book of Job as a drama.

Dionysius the elder. Tyrant of Syracuse (421-367 B.C.). He carried off the first prize at the festival of the Lenaea with a play called *The Ransom of Hector*, besides contending repeatedly for the prize of tragedy at Athens.

Augustus Caesar (63 B.C.-14 A.D.) Suetonius (ii. 85) says that Augustus, being asked by his friends "how 'Ajax' was getting on," replied "My 'Ajax' has committed suicide with a—sponge" ("in spongiam incubuisse").

Seneca (d. 65 A.D.). Tutor to the Emperor Nero. There are ten Latin tragedies extant under his name, two being fragmentary. They are reproductions from the great Greek models, rhetorical in style, and false in depicting passion; but the Choruses set forth in strong epigrammatic language the doctrines of the Stoic philosophy.

Gregory Nazianzen (329-389), Bishop of Constantinople. When Julian the Apostate aimed at destroying culture and refinement among the Christians by prohibiting them from teaching grammar and rhetoric (362 A.D. Amm. Marcell. xxii. 10, quoted in Gibbon, xxiii.), Gregory attempted to counteract his insidious aim by creating a body of Christian literature on classical models for their use. A more general cause that contributed to the formation of this new literature was the aversion of the early Christians to heathen literature (cf. St. Augustin, *Confessiones*, i. 13). Gregory's *Christus Patiens* was a Greek adaptation, chiefly from the *Bacchae* of Euripides, this play being chosen, perhaps, because it had for its subject the rise of a new religion. It was the earliest example of the "Christian drama," which in Western Europe took the name of Mysteries and Miracle Plays. Later research ascribes the *Christus Patiens* to Apollinarius the elder, who, besides, wrote several dramas on the models of Euripides and Menander. He also turned Scripture History and the Psalms into Homeric hexameters, and the Gospels and Epistles into Socratic dialogues. (See Smith's *Dict. of Christian Biogr.* art. Apollinaris.)

interludes, used here contemptuously for 'Comedies.' An interlude properly was something acted in the intervals of a banquet or entertainment. It was the transition form between the old Moralities and Comedy properly so called, resembling the former in the absence of a plot, and the latter in containing real personages instead of the abstractions of the Moralities. Heywood's *Four P's* is an example.

intermixing comic stuff. This is a deliberate condemnation of a great part of Elizabethan tragedy, and an upholding of the classical drama, which, as a rule, avoids such intermixture. The *Alcestis* of Euripides is an exception.

no Prologue, in the sense of the author's Apology, meant to bespeak the goodwill of the audience, as used in English plays and Latin comedies. But a prologue in the Greek sense Milton himself uses in this drama. See Introd. p. xii.

Martial (43-104), Latin epigrammatist. These Epistles are addressed either to the Reader (books i. iii. x. xiii. xiv.) or to Friends (ii. ix. xii.) or to his patron Domitian (v. viii.).

Chorus ... Italians. The Chorus had been used in Italian literature since the revival of learning in the 15th century. It of course existed in the Melodrama or the Opera, which rose into importance in Italy in the 17th century, while dramatic literature proper fell into decay. This age of decadence in Italy, contemporary with Milton's age in England, is called the era of the *Seicentisti*. Sismondi does not name any of the seicentisti dramatists, and among those named by Hallam, Andreini (d. 1652), who wrote the drama of *Adamo*, is alone of any interest to us. This work has choruses of Angels, Spirits and Phantoms. Chiabrera (d. 1637), better known as a lyric poet, was also the father of the Melodrama in Italy, and Rinuccini (d. 1621) employed in his choruses the 'apolelymenon' measure of Milton.

Apolelymenon ... Alloeostropha, 'freed from the restraints' of division into *Strophé* (the song sung by the chorus in moving rhythmically from right to left on the orchestra), *Antistrophé* (sung similarly in moving from left to right), and *Epode* (an 'after-song' sung while standing still). The Strophé and Antistrophé were stanzas of exactly the same rhythmic construction. *Monostrophic* (ode) is a choral ode of a single stanza, and an *Alloeostropha* is a choral ode of several irregular stanzas, neither of which is capable of division into strophés and antistrophés.

stanzas ... music. Such was the origin of the Greek chorus from the Dithyramb (lyrical songs in honour of Bacchus), to which was afterwards added a new element, the Dialogue.

stage ... intended. The objection of the Puritans to acting had been deepened since the appearance of actresses on the stage after the Restoration.

fifth act. The omission of the Chorus in the new Comedy of Greece (judging from its Roman imitators) gave rise to the division into Acts. Such an omission in the Greek classic drama (or in *Samson Agonistes*) would not always give the number of acts as five. This number was laid down for tragedy by Horace (*Ars Poet.* 189).

intricate or explicit. This is Aristotle's classification of Plots (μῦθοι) into *simple* (ἁπλοῖ) and *complex* (πεπλεγμένοι) (*Poet.* x.). A plot is simple when ' the catastrophe is brought about without either revolution or discovery ; complex, when with one or both.' See Introd. p. xvi. *Explicit* is used in the literal Latin sense of ' unfolded,' *i.e.* simple.

twenty-four hours. This is the Unity of Time. See Introd. p. xvi.

THE PLAY.

Title.—**Samson.** This is the Greek spelling in the Septuagint (Σαμψών) ; the Hebrew is *Shimshon*, which becomes in German *Simson*. The word means ' sun-like '; but Josephus (*Antiq.* v. 8. 4) says it means "one that is strong." **Agonistes**, Greek 'an athlete, a contender in public games, a champion.' The epithet draws attention to the particular act of Samson constituting the catastrophe. Cf. 'antagonist' l. 1628. Such distinguishing epithets were used in the titles of Greek dramas forming parts of a trilogy.

1-11. *These lines are addressed to the guide, perhaps the same 'lad that held him by the hand' (Judges, xvi. 26) in the last scene. The touching sight and words serve to open the play with what is technically called 'pathos' (Arist. Poet. xi.). Compare the similar entry of the blind Œdipus led by his daughter Antigone, in the opening of the Œdipus Coloneus of Sophocles.*

2. these, a Graecism for ' my.' In Attic dialogue the demonstrative ὅδε often refers to the speaker. **dark,** 'of one that cannot see.' Richardson compares Eur. *Phoen.* 848, ἡγοῦ πάροιθε, θύγατερ, ὡς τυφλῷ ποδὶ | ὀφθαλμὸς εἶ σύ, "A little onward lead me, be an eye | To these dark steps, my daughter." In the same play Œdipus says (1555), τί μ', ὦ παρθένε, βακτρεύμασι | τυφλοῦ ποδὸς ἐξάγαγες εἰς φῶς ; " Why, virgin, ... why hast thou brought my blind, staff-guided steps ... to light ? " Cf. ' dark orbs,' l. 591.

3. hath, 'affords.' Samson knows this, we may suppose, from habit.

4. There ... sit. Prof. Masson aptly quotes the painter Richardson's description of the blind Milton's own habits in his last years :—" ... He used also to sit, in a grey coarse cloth coat, at the door of his house, near Bunhill Fields, in warm weather, to enjoy the fresh air ; and so, as well as in his room, received ... visits ...." **wont.** This word, as well as the growth of the 're- dundant locks' (l. 568), implies that Samson has been some time in prison. See l. 938 and note.

5. **servile toil,** viz. the task of grinding corn (l. 35), which among the ancients was a degrading labour. Thus among the Jews " the maid-servant behind the mill " was the antithesis of "Pharaoh upon his throne " (*Exod.* xi. 5), and captives of war were condemned to grind at the mill (*Lam.* v. 13). Among the Greeks, female slaves were not permitted to retire for sleep before they had ground their daily portion of corn (Homer, *Od.* xx. 105 *sq.*) ; and among the Romans the corn-mill or pounding-house (*pistrinum*) was a place of punishment for refractory slaves (Terence, *Andr.* i. 2. 28).

6. **common prison,** where he has to endure the society of con- victs (l. 1224 and note), or, as l. 1162 has it, of slaves and drudging beasts. **else,** 'at other times,' 'elsewhile,' when not relieved by chance. This use of ' else ' to refer to *time* is rare. Cf. Beau. and Fl. *Wit at Several Weapons,* ii. 2, " Birds that build nests | Have care to keep 'em. | *Cunn.* That's granted ; | But not continually to sit upon 'em, | 'Less in the youngling season ; *else* they desire | To fly abroad, and recreate their labours."

8. **air, imprisoned also** ; double sense, (1) stuffy, ill-ventilated, (2) put into prison, like me (' pathetic fallacy.') Landor needlessly censures this as a ' prettiness.' Milton here only imitates the practice of the Greek dramatists.

9. **Unwholesome draught,** ' unhealthy to breathe.' *Draught* (what is ' drawn in ' with the breath) in apposition with ' air.'

11. **day-spring,** 'dawn.' Cf. *P. L.* v. 139, vi. 521. The ex- pression occurs in *Luke,* i. 78, " The day-spring from on high hath visited us"; in a slightly different form in Gower, *Conf. Am.* ii. " For till I se the *daies spring* | I sette sleepe nought at a risshe " (quoted by Wright, *Bible Word-Book*), and in the *Plumpton Papers,* " The *spring of the day.*"

12-22. *These lines set forth the occasion—namely a feast in hon- our of Dagon—upon which the entire action of the drama hinges. The opening of the drama with the mention of that very incident which leads to the catastrophe that closes it, well indicates how care- fully Milton had planned the unity of action. Johnson did not note the significance of these lines.*

13. **Dagon.** A god who had his principal sanctuaries at Gaza and Ashdod, but was worshipped in every Philistine town. His shape, described as half human and half fish (*P. L.* i. 463), is in- ferred from the Hebrew *Dag,* ' fish,' and from 1 *Sam.* v. 4, which

in the original was 'only Dagon was left to him,' the marginal
reading supplying 'the fishy part of.' This shape is referred to
in the expression *sea-idol*.

16. **popular noise**, 'noise made by a large concourse of people.'
Cf. l. 434, and *P. L.* vii. 487, "Popular tribes of commonalty"
(of the ant).

20. **armed**, *sc.* 'with stings.' Cf. l. 623. Todd quotes from
Sidney's *Arcadia*, "A new swarm of thoughts stinging her mind."
Found agrees with 'me' (next line). The construction is not
strictly grammatical, since 'found' being a participle, the two
sentences introduced by the conjunctions 'no sooner' and 'but,'
are not co-ordinate, as they should be. The ordinary construction would be, 'that rush thronging upon me, *as soon as found*
alone,' (participle) or 'that no sooner *am I found* (indicative)
alone, but rush upon me thronging.' Milton has blended the
two constructions together.

23-64. *Samson's thoughts go back from the present to the past:—
The comparison of the angel's prediction at his birth with its miserable falsification in his captivity, and of the secret of his glorious
strength with the weakness of mind that made him betray it, drives
him almost to question God's providence; but he checks himself and
acknowledges that it was his own frailty (the ἁμαρτία of Aristotle)
that was to blame.*

24. **Twice by an Angel**. Viz. once to his mother whose name
is not mentioned (*Judges*, xiii. 3), and again to both his parents
(*ib.* 11). **at last**, *i.e.* on the *second* of these occasions.

26. **From off**, 'off from.' Cf. l. 922, 'from forth'; and see
Abbott, § 157.

27. **As in a fiery column charioting**. 'Seeming to carry away
in a fiery column as in a chariot.' Milton here follows Josephus
v. 8. 3, "And the angel ascended openly, in their sight, up to
heaven, by means of the smoke, as by a vehicle." In the corresponding passage in *Judges* no chariot is mentioned, but in ii
Kings, ii. 11, the prophet Elijah is described as rapt up to heaven
in a "chariot of fire."

28. **god like**, used here in the sense of 'divine'; but Milton
frequently uses 'gods' and 'god-like' to mean 'angels' and
'angelic.' Cf. *P. L.* i. 358, ix. 708-718. **presence**. This use of
the abstract for the concrete to invest a personage with awe is
frequent in Milton. Cf. *P. L.* viii. 312, "Had not he … appeared, presence divine," x. 144, "To whom the sovran Presence
thus replied." Compare honorific titles like 'your Majesty,'
'your Grace.' **and from some great act revealed**. A Latinism
for 'and from the revelation of some great act.' The construction is 'ascended … as charioting … and *as* from some great act.'

30. **breeding**, 'course of education,' cf. Shak. *All's Well*, ii. 3.

121, "She had her breeding at my father's charge." **prescribed,** 'appointed, laid down beforehand' (literal Latin use).

31. **separate,** 'set apart.' Milton uses 'secret' in the same sense (*P. L.* i. 6, "Secret top of Sinai," *Nativity Ode,* 27, "Secret altar"). 'Separate' has the allied sense of 'apart by oneself in *P. L.* ix. 422 and 424. For the omission of the participial termination *-d* v. Introd. p. xliv). **separate to God.** The expression is biblical; cf. *Numb.* vi. 2, "Separate themselves unto the Lord"; *Rom.* i. 1, "Paul separated unto the Gospel of God."

33. **captived.** Latin accent, so Spenser frequently : *F. Q.* ii. 4, 16 ; 5. 27 ; 7. 15. **both,** *i.e.* 'with both'; 'and' prevents this **from** being a nominative absolute.

35. **brazen,** literal, cf. *Judges,* xvi. 21, "And bound him with fetters of brass"; used metaphorically in *P. L.* x. 697, "Brazen dungeon." **under task,** 'bound to perform a certain amount of work daily,' like the Israelites during their bondage in Egypt.

37. **labour of a beast.** Samson was condemned to work with asses in turning mills. The employment of asses for this work is indicated in the Greek version of Matt. xviii. 6, where μύλος ὀνι-κός is rendered by Wyclif "the mylnstoon of asses," where the *A.V.* has merely "millstone"; cf. Ovid, *Fasti,* vi. 318, "Et quae pumiceas versat asella molas," "And the ass that turns the mills of soft stone."

38. **Promise was.** For the omission of 'there' see Abbott, § 404, cf. expressions like 'time was (when),' 'reason is (that).'

39. *Judges,* xiii. 5, "And he shall begin to deliver Israel out of the hand of the Philistines."

40. **Ask ... and find.** 'If you ask ... you shall find.' This use of 'and' to indicate a contingent consequence is old. It occurs in Wyclif, *Matt.* vii. 7, and resembles the *incressive* use of καί in Greek. (*Jelf,* § 759.)

41. Landor punctuates this line thus :—" Eyeless, in Gaza, at the mill, with slaves," each clause setting forth a distinct cause of Samson's misery. **in Gaza,** *i.e.* at the seat of Dagon's idolatrous worship, and the scene of Samson's former triumph over his enemies (*Judges,* xvi. 3).

44. **What if.** Schmidt (*Shak. Lex.*) explains this to be "what should you say if," in which case "what if" is analogous in constr. to "what then." It is better taken as a contraction of "what wonder if," in some contexts (as here). The full expression is old ; it occurs in Hampole's *Pricke of Conscience* ("what wonder es yf"), see l. 790.

45. **but,** 'were it not.' **mine own,** cf. l. 459, "mine eyes," and see Abbott, § 237. This euphonic use of 'mine' for 'my,' and 'thine' for 'thy' occurs in Wyclif (*Luke,* ii. 30, "For *myn* eyen

han seyn *thin* helthe;" *A.V.* "For *mine* eyes have seen thy salvation"). Still earlier in M.E. *min, thin,* are the common adj. possessive pronouns used alike before vowels and consonants, as in A.S., *e.g. min heorte, mine mihte* (*The Orison of our Lady,* 1210) : *mine song, thine neste* (*Owl and Nightingale,* 1250).

47-49. 'In what part lodged,' and 'how easily bereft me,' are noun clauses objectives to 'keep,' and co-ordinate with 'gift.' **bereft me,** taken away from me ; for this use of 'bereft' with the object of the person cf. Shak. *Othello,* i. 3. 258, "The rites for which I love him are bereft me." See l. 85, n.

50. **must reveal,** 'could not help revealing,' 'could not resist the temptation to reveal.' In Germ. *müssen* is similarly used. In English 'needs' is often added ironically.

53-56. Samson's character in this respect resembles that of *Ajax,* cf l. 206, v. Introd. p. xxiii. Cf. Soph. *Ajax,* 1250 *sq.,* οὐ γὰρ οἱ πλατεῖς οὐδ' εὐρύνωτοι φῶτες ἀσφαλέστατοι, ἀλλ' οἱ φρονοῦντες εὖ κρατοῦσι πανταχοῦ, "The high-built frame, | The massy structured limb, | Yield not protection ; but the prudent mind | The conquest everywhere obtains." Ovid, *Met.* xiii. 363, "Tu vires sine mente geris ; mihi cura futuri est," "Thou possessest bodily strength without a mind ; in me is prudence," *ib.* 365, "Tu tantum corpore prodes, nos animo," "Thou excellest in body alone, we in mind" (addressed by Ulysses to Ajax), (quoted by Jortin). Hor. *Od.* iii. 4. 65, "Vis consili expers mole sua ruit," "Strength without counsel is crushed by its own weight" (quoted by Richardson). **double share,** *i.e.* 'wisdom in proportion to a double share of strength.'

55. **Proudly secure,** 'careless through excessive self-confidence'; cf. Shak. *Merry Wives,* ii. 1. 241, "Though Page be a secure fool"; Quarles, *Emblems* ii. 14, "He never yet stood safe, that stands secure."

56. **By weakest subtleties.** 'Through subtleties contrived by the weakest,' *i.e.* by a woman. Todd quotes Soph. *Ajax* 1077 *sq.,* ἀλλ' ἄνδρα χρή, κἂν σῶμα γεννήσῃ μέγα, δοκεῖν πεσεῖν ἂν κἂν ἀπὸ σμικροῦ κακοῦ, "And it behoves a man, though large his limbs | And vast his strength, to think that he may fall | E'en by a petty ill."

57. **subserve,** 'to serve under another.' The word is not used again by Milton. It is a Latin use occurring in Plautus, *Men.* v. 2.

58. **withal,** 'at the same time,' as in *P.L.* xii. 82, "Yet know withal, true liberty is lost." For the various shades of meaning this word has, see Abbott, § 196, and Schmidt *Shak. Lex.*

59. *Judges,* xvi. 17, "If I be shaven, then my strength will go from me, and I shall become weak, and be like any other man." **slight,** 'of which I could be easily deprived.' The same idea of in-

stability is implied in 'hung.' So on a single golden hair growing on the head of Nisus, king of Megara, depended his life (Ovid, *Met.* viii.), and on a single hair of his head depended the life of Orillo, the magician of Egypt (Ariosto, *Or. Fur.* xv. 85 *sq.*).

60. **quarrel with**, 'find fault with,' 'upbraid.'

61. **highest dispensation**, 'the dispensation of the Highest.' **dispensation** is here used generally for 'providence'; literally it means 'a weighing out,' and in Scripture (*Eph.* iii. 2, *Col.* i. 25) has the particular meaning of 'the task of preaching.'

62. **above my reach**, 'beyond my comprehension'; cf. l. 1380. The constr. is elliptical : 'ends *which it is* above, etc.'

63. **Suffices**, elliptical, '*it* suffices *for me to know*.'

65-109. *In Samson's lamentation over his blindness we are reminded of Milton's own calamity, and ll. 75-78 are a painful reference to the neglect and ingratitude shown by his daughters. In his will Milton calls them 'undutiful.'* (See Masson, *Introd.* to *P. L. pp.* 67-69.) *With Samson's lament compare Milton's lines on his own blindness in P. L.* iii. 40 *sq.*

66. **ask a life**, 'require a life-time,' cf. *P. L.* iv. 632, "Ask riddance." Shak. *M. N. D.* i. 2. 27, "Ask some tears."

69. **decrepit**, 'broken down with age,' Lat. *decrepitus* (*crepo*, Eng. 'crack,' 'creak'), that makes no noise ; hence, of an old man, creeping about noiselessly, like a shadow.

70. **the prime work**. *Gen.* i. 3, and l. 84. Light was the first creation of God on earth.

71. **her**. 'Light' in Latin is '*lux*,' which is feminine. Milton avails himself of the Latin gender when it suits the idea ; so in *P. L.* i. 592, 'form,' and in ii. 984, 'region' are fem. See ll. 613-4, n.

73. **Inferior** agrees with 'me' inferred from 'my' (l. 72) ; a Latinism.

74. **here**, 'herein,' viz. in the following circumstance that they 'yet see.'

75. **dark in light**, 'blind in the midst of light.' A similar oxymoron occurs in Soph. *Ajax* 394, ἰὼ σκότος, ἐμὸν φάος, ἔρεβος ὦ φαεννότατον, ὡς ἐμοί, "O darkness now my light ! Ye dreary shades | Of Erebus, to me sole brightness now."

77. **still**, 'always,' 'ever,' cf. *Comus*, 560. The meaning of this word in Anglo-Saxon was 'quiet' (from the root STA- to stand). In Middle English it retains this meaning, but also acquires a new one of 'silent' in the *Owl and the Nightingale* (1250) ; it is used as an adverb meaning 'secretly' in Layamon's *Brut* (1205), and 'silently' in the *Lay of Havelock the Dane* (1290). Long before, however, in the *Blickling Homilies* (971) (Northern

dialect) ' still ' is used to mean ' always '; it is so used in the
Legend of King Horn of the same date as *Havelock*. The word
in this meaning passed into general use with Chaucer, and continued to be so used in prose till at least the beginning of the
18th century. In poetry it occurs quite recently (as in Long-
fellow, " still achieving still pursuing "). The present meaning
' yet ' occurred as a northern dialectic peculiarity as early as
1330, in the *Romance of the Seven Sages*, and passed into the
Standard English (*i.e.* English as spoken in London) of the time
at about the date of the *Paston Letters* (1433).

80. So too Œdipus laments his blindness, Soph. *Oed. Tyr.*
1313 *sq.* From this line to the end of the lament the metre is
irregular, like that of the chorus. Milton uses this irregular
metre where deep emotion has to be expressed, cf. ll. 606-651.
noon. Originally this was the ninth hour (Lat. *nona*) of the day,
or 3 P.M., at which a service called the *nones* was celebrated at
church. ' Noon ' acquired its present meaning when the time of
this service was shifted towards mid-day. The older meaning is
evident in the following :—" At myd-day ant at non, he sende
hem thither fol son " (M.E. *Lyrics circ.* 1300). The original form
' nones ' occurs in *Piers Plowman*.

81. **Irrecoverably,** ' from which there is no recovery or deliverance,' ' for ever.'

82. **all,** ' any '; cf. *Heb.* vii. 7, " Without all contradiction,"
which in Wyclif is " With outen ony ayenseiying."

83. **great Word.** Milton follows, partly, the Targum on *Gen.*
i. 3 (" The word of God said ' let there be light ' ") and partly
St. John, i. 1, 3 (" In the beginning was the Word ... and the
Word was God ... all things were made by him.")

85. **bereaved,** see l. 47. This use of the passive in a transitive
sense may follow from a similar use of the active ; cf. *P. L.* x.
809, " But say | That Death be not one stroke, as I supposed, |
Bereaving sense " ; *ib.* 918, " Bereave me not, | Whereon I live,
thy gentle looks."

87. **silent as the Moon.** The expression ' *luna silens* ' occurs
in Pliny (*Hist. Nat.* xvi. 74, " Quem diem alii interlunii, alii
silentis lunae appellant," " Which some call the interlunar day,
others the day of the silent moon " ; xviii. 74, " Hoc silente luna
seri jubent," " They direct that this should be sown during the
silent moon ";) and Cato (*Re Rust.* 29, " Luna silenti "); and, as the
first passage indicates, means ' new moon.' Todd quotes from
Dante, *Inf.* i. 60, " Mi ripingeva là, dove 'l sol tace," " Impelled
me where the sun in silence rests"; and v. 26, " I' venni in luogo
d' ogni luce muto," " Into a place I came | Where light was silent
all " ; where silence is attributed to the sun and to dark places.
In such epithets there is a transfer of the language used to

express the impressions of one sense to those of another; thus painters speak of 'warm' or 'loud' colours.

88. **deserts.** The expression 'nocte deserta' Todd points out occurs in Seneca, *Hippol.* 308. Cicero humorously speaks of his *lamp* deserting him (*Att.* vii. 7, " Nisi me lucerna desereret ").

89. **vacant,** 'when she ceases from her work of giving light to the world'; cf. Pliny, *Hist. Nat.* ii. 6, "(Luna) quae mensis exitu latet, quum laborare non creditur," " The moon that hides herself at the end of the month, when she is believed to cease from her task." **Interlunar.** Milton coins the adj. from the Lat. subst. *interlunium* used frequently by Pliny (in books ii. and xviii.) to mean the time intervening between the last waning and the first waxing, crescent; *i.e.* as equivalent to 'luna silens' above, and the opposite of 'plenilunium'—full moon. **cave.** In the Homeric Hymn to Demeter (22-26, οὐδέ τις ἀθανάτων, οὐδὲ θνητῶν ἀνθρώπων | ἤκουσεν φωνῆς, οὐδ' ἀγλαόκαρποι ἑταῖραι, | εἰ μὴ Περσαίου θυγάτηρ ἀταλὰ φρονέουσα | ἄιεν ἐξ ἄντρου, Ἑκάτη λιπαρο-κρήδεμνος | Ἥέλιός τε ἄναξ, Ὑπερίονος ἀγλαὸς υἱός, " Nor god nor mortal heard her cry, nor her companions, bestowers of the fruits of earth; but only bright-filleted Hecate, Perseus' daughter, ever watchful over youth from within her cave, and lordly Helios, bright son of Hyperion ") Hecate, who is there identified with Artemis, the goddess of the moon (ἀταλὰ φρονέουσα is κουροτρόφος, an attribute of Artemis), is represented as abiding in a cave whence she witnesses the abduction of Persephone by Pluto. Shelley, in one of his lyrics (*To a Lady with a Guitar*) has borrowed from Milton—" The silent moon in her interlunar swoon."

92. **light is in the soul.** This philosophic notion occurs in the *Nosce Teipsum* of Sir John Davies, where the nature of the union of the soul with the body is explained to be not that of a spider to its web, or of an impression with the wax, or of a voice with the air : " But as the fair and cheerful morning light | Doth here and there her silver beams impart, | And in an instant doth herself unite | To the transparent air in all and every part. | So doth the piercing soul the body fill | Being all in all, and all in part diffused." Milton uses the same idea in *P. L.* iii. 51. *sq.*, " So much the rather thou, Celestial Light, | Shine inward, and the mind through all her powers | Irradiate." Spenser has a similar idea in the *Hymn of Beautie*—"For of the soule the bodie forme doth take, | For soule is forme, and doth the bodie make."

93. **She all in every part.** Cf. ll. 4 and 6 in the quotation from Sir J. Davies, who derived the notion from the mystic doctrine of Plotinus and the Neo-Platonists, that the soul is present in all parts and in every part of the body ; μεριστή (ἡ ψυχή), ὅτι ἐν πᾶσι μέρεσι τοῦ ἐν ᾧ ἐστιν, ἀμέριστος δέ, ὅτι ὅλη ἐν πᾶσι καὶ ἐν ὁτῳοῦν αὐτοῦ ὅλη, " The soul is divisible, inasmuch as

it is found in every part of the body in which it is, but undivisible,
inasmuch as it is entire in all and every part of the body."
Ennead, iv. 2. **all,** *i.e.* ' is all,' ' is diffused.'

94. **confined,** instead of being diffused like ' light,' or the
sense of touch, throughout the surface of the body.

95. **obvious,** in the Latin sense of ' exposed to injury ' ; cf.
P. L. xi. 374, " Obvious breast." The word is also used by
Milton in its literal Latin sense of ' lying in the way ' ; in *P. L.*
vi. 69, " Obvious hill " ; x. 105, " Obvious duty " (duty of
coming to meet God) ; *Doctr. and Disc. of Divorce,* i. 6, " Love ...
consorts him with these obvious and suborned striplings."

96. **feeling,** ' the sensation of touch.'

98. **exiled.** Latin accent.

99. **As,** ' so as,' co-ordinate with ' thus ' (l. 98). It would be
omitted in modern prose.

100. **a living death.** The same oxymoron occurs in *P. L.* x.
788, " Who knows but I shall die a living death ? " Todd
quotes from several English poets, and from Petrarch, *Sonetto*
102, " O viva morte, o dilettoso male," " O living death, O
delightful ill ! " Cf. also Soph. *Antig.* 1167, οὐ τίθημ' ἐγὼ ζῆν
τοῦτον, ἀλλ' ἔμψυχον ἡγοῦμαι νεκρόν, " For upon such a man I look
not as having life, but consider him as the living dead " ;
Lucretius, iii. 1046, " Mortua cui vita est prope jam vivo atque
videnti," " Whose life is dead, even while he lives and sees " ;
Shak. *Rich. III.* i. 2. 153, " They kill me with a living death."

101. **yet more miserable,** *i.e.* ' a circumstance yet,' etc.

102. **a moving grave.** It would not be surprising if Milton
meant one of his perfectly serious puns here, the secondary
meaning being, ' a grave the sight of which (whom) is harrow-
ing ' ; see l. 1529. The idea of the body being the grave of the
soul occurs in Plato, *Crat.* 17 (400 B), καὶ γὰρ σῆμά τινές φασιν
αὐτὸ (τὸ σῶμα) εἶναι τῆς ψυχῆς, ὡς τεθαμμένης ἐν τῷ νῦν παρόντι,
" For some say that the body is the grave of the soul, as being
buried in this present life " ; and *Gorgias* 47 (493 A), καὶ τὸ μὲν
σῶμά ἐστιν ἡμῖν σῆμα, " For the body is a grave to us " ; to which
Stallbaum adds in a note that the idea was propounded by the
Pythagorean Philolaus.

103. **exempt** ; this is the true past pt. form Lat. exempt (-us) ;
see note l. 1556.

105. **pains and wrongs** ; hendiadys for ' wrongful pains ' ;
in apposition with ' worst.' **pains,** ' punishments.' Though the
Lat. *poena* had this meaning in both sing. and pl., in technical
legal language the plural was so used, and is still so used in the
expression ' pains and penalties.' Samson looks upon his
wrongful imprisonment as the next worse evil after his blindness.

106. obnoxious, in the Latin sense of 'exposed,' 'liable': cf.
P. L. ix. 170, "Obnoxious first or last to basest things"; Bacon,
Essays, 36, "Obnoxious to ruin." The word literally means 'liable
to punishment for (*ob*) injury (*noxa*) committed': see Trench,
Sel. Gloss.

108, 109. Each thought occupies a line by itself. This slowness
of rhythm is meant to express the intensity of grief that each
thought by itself causes.

110-114. *These lines introduce the Chorus, according to the practice in Greek dramas of heralding every fresh entrance on the stage
by words that draw the attention of the audience to the new comer.
See ll.* 326, 710, *etc.*

110. joint pace. The Greek chorus moved rhythmically to and
from the orchestra.

111. steering, intrans. 'moving,' 'directing their course': cf.
P. L. x. 328, "Satan, betwixt the Centaur and the Scorpion
|Steering his zenith" (*i.e.* for or towards his zenith); Spencer, *F.
Q.* ii. 1. 7, "A comely palmer ... that with a staffe his feeble
steps did stere." Hurd quotes from Chaucer, *The Flower and the
Leaf,* "Stering so fast, that all the earth trembled."

112. Cf. Soph. *Ajax,* 367, οἴμοι γέλωτος, οἷον ὑβρίσθην ἄρα, "O!
How to derision and insults exposed!"

114. Their daily practice, *sc.* 'it being.' **more,** *i.e.* 'more and
more.'

115-175. *Through this ode there runs a parallelism with Samson's
last speech. The Chorus supplements Samson's account of himself
by dwelling on his glorious deeds, as Samson had dwelt on his frailty.
Here again Milton skilfully blends the present with the past, through
the exclamation of surprise and pity with which the narration begins
(l. 124), and the sympathetic lament over his blindness and captivity with which it ends (l. 150 sq.). The entire ode is spoken as an
'aside.'*

115. softly, *i.e.* 'let us move or tread softly.' Dunster quotes
Eur. *Orest.* 136, ὦ φίλταται γυναῖκες, ἡσύχῳ ποδὶ χωρεῖτε, "Dearest
of women, softly set your feet."

116. break in upon him, 'rudely disturb his solitude.'

117. beyond report, 'worse than rumour had represented it to
be.'

118. at random, 'with limbs not orderly disposed,' in familiar
Eng. 'he lies *anyhow.*' **random** (Germ. *rande,* edge, brim) was
originally a subst. meaning 'force' (as of a brimming river, Cotgr.)
as in the *Romance of Alexander* (*circ.* 1300), "Priked the stedes
with gret randoun," and in Mandeville's *Travels* (1356), "They
runnen togidre a grate randoun": it is used as a verb in *Ferrex and
Porrex* (1571) i. 2, "Leave them free to randon of their will"; **it**

appears as part of the adverbial phrase 'in a randoun' in Barbour's
Bruce (1375), *i.e.* 'in a furious course'; the present adv. expr.
"at random" has been traced to Bp. Jewel (1560) (Oliphant), and
is soon after used by Spenser, *F. Q.* ii. 4. 7, "But as a blindfold
bull at random fares," so in iii. 10. 36.   The final 'n' afterwards
passed into 'm.'   **diffused**, 'stretched out as through languor.'
This Latin use of the word is rendered into Saxon Eng. by Spenser, *F. Q.* i. 7. 7, "Pour'd out in looseness on the grassy grownd."
Thyer quotes from Ovid, *Ex Ponto*, iii. 3. 8, "Fusaque erant toto
languida membra toro," "Poured were my languid limbs all on
the couch"; and Todd from Eur. *Heracl.* 75, ἐπὶ πέδῳ χύμενον,
"Poured on the ground." Cf. also Virg. *Aen.* ix. 317, "Per
herbam Corpora fusa vident," "They see their bodies poured upon
the grass."   (In Elizabethan literature the word implies 'negli-
gence in dress,' Shak. *Hen. V.* v. 2. 61, "Diffused attire"; Beau.
and Fl. *The Nice Valour*, iii. 3, "Go not so diffusedly.")

119. **languished**, 'languishing'; cf. 'festered,' l. 186, 'blandished,' l. 403, 'clattered,' l. 1124, 'flourished' (flowering), *P. L.*
iv. 699, for this use of '-ed' for '-ing.'

120. **abandoned**, viz. 'by his friends,' balancing the thought in
the next line 'abandoned by himself.'

122. **habit**, 'dress.' The word now has only a particular application—a lady's riding dress; it is so first used in Miss Burney's
Cecilia; in Foxe's *Book of Martyrs* it is used of a priest's
garments.   **ill-fitted**, 'ill-fitting,' 'hanging loose upon him.'
weeds, like 'habit,' has now only a particular application—
'a widow's weeds.'   The word is used in the pl. in Anglo-Saxon
for a magnificent dress, robe (Cynewulf, *Dream of the Rood*,
"Geseah ic wuldres tréow wàedum geweorthod wynnum scínan,"
"I saw the tree of glory, adorned with robes, shining beautifully";)
in M. E. *Homilies* (*circ.* 1200) occurs the sing. "bicumliche ('becoming') wede"; and immediately afterwards the pl. "unbicum-
liche weden."   In Shakspere, in both sing. and pl., it means simply
'dress.' Milton uses the pl. (as here) and the sing. (*Comus*, 189,
"palmer's weed").

123. **O'er-worn**, 'threadbare,' 'tattered.'   This is a touch of
Euripides, who is fond of dwelling upon the rags and squalor of
misery, for which he is ridiculed by Aristophanes. This aspect
of Samson's misery is insultingly alluded to in the scene with
Harapha (ll. 1107, 1138, 1167).

126. **unarmed.** *Judges*, xiv. 6, "And he nad nothing in his
hand." Cf. Chaucer, *Monkes Tale*, 3214, "Sampson, the noble
mighty champioun, withouten wepen save his hondes tweye."

127. *Judges*, xiv. 6, "And he rent him (the young lion) as he
would have rent a kid."

129. embattled, 'drawn up in battle array'; cf. *P. L.* vi. 16, "Embattled squadrons"; i. 129, "The imbattled seraphim."

131. arms, *sc.* 'of his enemies,' as on the occasions referred to in ll. 138, 142. **forgery,** 'forging,' 'fabrication,' in the literal sense.

132. hammered cuirass; so in *P. R.* iii. 328, "Cuirassiers all in steel"; in both places 'cuirass' has lost its original meaning of a breastplate made of *leather* (Fr. *cuir*, Lat. *corium*).

133. Chalybean. The accentuation is doubtful: it may be either 'Chalýbean' on the analogy of 'Aégean' (*P. L.* i. 746), and 'Thyéstean' (x. 688), or 'Chalybéan,' following the Latin accent, and on the analogy of 'adamantéan' (l. 134), and 'empyréan,' which is used six times by Milton, with the accent always so. The Chalybes were a people of Pontus in Asia Minor, famous among the ancients for their work in iron. Æschylus calls them 'iron workers' (σιδηροτέκτονες, *Prom. Vinct.* 733) and uses 'Chalybs' for hardened iron, steel (*ib.* 134). This mention of the Chalybes by Hebrews is an anachronism; for the fame of this people was entirely confined to Greek literature. **tempered,** 'hardened' to the proper degree by being suddenly cooled after being heated. Cf. *P. L.* ii. 813, "Those bright arms though temper'd heavenly." **frock of mail,** 'coat of mail.' The Germ. '*rock*,' from the same root as 'frock,' is the common word for a 'coat.'

134. Adamantean proof, 'impenetrable armour.' 'Proof' is here a noun; in compounds like 'shot and shell proof' and 'ague-proof,' 'shame-proof' (Shak.) it is an adj. 'Proof' for 'proof armour' also occurs in Shak. *Macb.* i. 2. 54, "Lapp'd in proof," *Rich. III.* v. 3. 219, "Arm'd in proof"; so Beau. and Fl. *The Chances,* i. 11, "You clap on proof on me." *Adamantine* is from Gr. *adamas,* 'steel,' literally 'the unbreakable,' ά- privative, and *δαμάω, tame, conquer. ('Adamant' once had the meaning of magnet; cf. Shak. *Tr. and Cr.* iii. 2. 186, "As iron to adamant"; Webster, *Vittoria Corrombona,* ii. 1, "You are the adamant shall draw her to you.") The word is a doublet of 'diamond.'

136. insupportably, 'irresistibly.' Thyer quotes Spenser, *F. Q.* i. 7. 11, "That when the knight he spide, he gan advance | With huge force and insupportable mayne."

137. proud arms, 'arms on whose strength they prided themselves.' **tools.** In Stanyhurst's *Aeneid* the word is so used for 'arms'; cf. Spenser, *F. Q.* ii. 3. 37, "Those deadly tools, which in her hand she held"; Shak. *Rom. and Jul.* 1. 1. 37, "Draw thy tool."

138. Ascalonite. *Judges,* xiv. 19 (quoted in l. 1186 n.); also see l. 981, n.

139. lion ramp, 'his onset fierce as a lion's.' The word is more common as a verb (*P. L.* iv. 343), and as an adj. 'rampant' (*P. L.* vii. 466). The original meaning of the verb in French (*ramper*) was 'to climb,' 'rise on the hind legs'; this still survives in the heraldic term 'lion rampant,' and is well shown in Spenser, *F. Q.* i. 5. 28, "Her twyfold teme ...*trampling the fine element*, would fiercely ramp." In Chaucer and Spenser the meaning of the verb is 'to rage with anger': this still survives in the slang 'rampageous' and 'rampage.' In *Ralph Roister Doister* the meaning changes to 'frisking about, playing wanton tricks' (a girl "ramps abroad like a Tomboy": Oliphant). Hence the 'rampallian' of Shak. and Beau. and Fl., and the modern 'romp.'

140. **plated,** 'protected with plates of armour.' **under his heel.** A bold *zeugma* or *verbum praegnans* must be understood in 'turned' here : 'old warriors turned their backs and fled, and, overtaken in their flight, were trampled under his heel.' Without this we get the meaning of 'old warriors turned turtle under his heel.'— which is neither poetic nor dignified.

141. **grovelling,** 'fallen flat on the ground.' For the termination, *-ling*, cf. 'flatling,' 'headlong.' Chaucer uses the word without the termination, *Prioress Tale*, "And *groff* he fell al platte upon the ground."

142. **with.** The construction requires this word to be joined with 'fell,' l. 144. We should now say either 'with .. *he felled* a thousand' or '*before* (or *to*) him ... a thousand fell.' **trivial,** lit. 'what can be found at the meeting of three ways' (*tres, viae*); hence 'picked up in the road.' In older English the word meant 'well-worn,' 'often-used.' Thus H. More speaks of Charity, Humility, and Purity, as 'trivial names.' Both here and in l. 263 the word has a subsidiary meaning of 'seemingly inadequate for the great havoc it produced' in Samson's hand among the Philistines.

144. **foreskins,** 'uncircumcised Philistines,' 1 *Sam.* xviii. 25. The Philistines are so called frequently in the books of *Judges* and *Samuel.* Some of the Canaanitish nations seem, like the Israelites, to have been circumcised : *Jer.* ix. 25. **Palestine,** 'Philistia'; the land of the Philistines is called 'Palestina' in *Exod.* xv. 14. The incident is related in *Judges,* xv. 17, "And he found a new jaw-bone of an ass, and put forth his hand, and took it, and slew a thousand men therewith." This contact with the dead would have defiled an ordinary Nazarite (see l. 318 n.), but Samson, according to the Mishna, belonged to a class of perpetual Nazarites called after him Samson-Nazarites, who were considered free from defilement in such cases.

145. **Ramath-lechi,** *Judges,* xv. 17, marginal reading, "The lifting up or casting away of the jaw-bone." **famous to this day.** Landor objects to this as a feeble truism on the ground that such a wonderful exploit was not likely to be forgotten in the course

of a few years (twenty, according to Usher's *Chronology*). But the allusion evidently is to the perpetuation of the memory of the victory through the renaming of the place by Samson, which name (and not the old one) says the Chorus, is still used.

146. The Alexandrine is meant to be an echo of the sound to the sense.

147. **Azza,** used for 'Gaza' in *Deut.* ii. 23, and *Jer.* xxv. 20. For the exploit see *Judges*, xvi. 3. **massy.** Milton seems always to have used this form (see ll. 1633, 1648). His contemporary, Sir T. Browne, uses it too. So do Shakspere and Spenser. The French form 'massive,' now common, occurs in Cotgrave's *Dict.*

148 **Hebron ... giants old.** Hebron was the city of Arba, father of Anak . *Joshua*, xv. 13. Anak and his descendants the Anakim were giants : *Numb.* xiii. 33.

149. An Alexandrine. From *Acts*, i. 12 ("Then returned they unto Jerusalem, from the mount called Olivet, which is from Jerusalem a *Sabbath day's journey*") the distance indicated would be seven-eighths of a mile, which tradition allowed a Jew to travel without violating the law forbidding Sabbath travelling (*Exod.* xvi. 29). This distance was pitched upon as being that of the Tabernacle from the farthest parts of the camp. The journey from Gaza to Hebron would be along a distance of about forty miles. **and loaded so.** The use of 'and,' which here has the force of 'while,' prevents this from being a nom. abs., and brings it near a common Irish provincialism ; see l. 1480 n.

150. **Like whom,** 'like *him* whom' ; a Latinism, see Introd. p. xlii. The allusion is to Atlas, son of Iapetus and brother of Prometheus, condemned by Zeus to bear up the heavens on his head and shoulders as a punishment for having joined in the war of the Titans. Milton here follows Hesiod (*Theog.* 517, Ἄτλας δ' οὐρανὸν εὐρὺν ἔχει κρατερῆς ὑπ' ἀνάγκης, "Atlas holds up the broad heavens compelled by powerful necessity "). Homer's account (*Od.* i. 52) is somewhat different. **Gentiles.** (Heb. *Goyîm*.) All nations idolatrous, uncircumcised and unclean were so called by the Israelites ; the distinction points to deeper national hatred than that between Greek and Barbarian. **feign.** Milton uses this word again in *P. L.* iv. 706, v. 381, contemptuously of the fictions of Greek mythology. For the anachronism see Introd. p. xxvi.

151. The Chorus solves its own doubt almost immediately by bewailing Samson's blindness first, as the greater calamity of the two.

153. **Prison within prison,** like a dungeon in a castle ; the inner and more horrible prison being Samson's blindness.

154. **Inseparably dark?** Samson could issue out of the darkness of the prison at Gaza, but he could not separate himself from the ' ever during dark ' of the prison of his blindness. *P. L.* iii. 45.

156. **The dungeon of thyself**: a less impassioned echo of Samson's words, "myself my dungeon" (l. 102), cf. *Comus*, 384, "Himself is his own dungeon."

157. An Alexandrine. **Which**; the antecedent is 'the fact that the soul of man is imprisoned in the body,' to be inferred from ll. 156, 158. **oft without cause**; for often the 'ills of life' that men complain of are more fancied than real. **complain**, transitive as in Shak. *Rich. II*. iii. 4. 18, "What I want it boots not to complain."

158. **Imprisoned now indeed.** A reference to Plato's doctrine that the body is the soul's prison (*Phaedo*, vi. 62 B), ὁ μὲν οὖν ἐν ἀπορρήτοις λεγόμενος περὶ αὐτῶν λόγος, ὡς ἔν τινι φρουρᾷ ἐσμεν οἱ ἄνθρωποι, "The analogy set forth in the secret or esoteric doctrines (of the Pythagoreans), that we human beings are in a sort of prison" in which we are confined like an oyster in its shell; (*Phaedr.* xxx. 250 c), καθαροὶ ὄντες καὶ ἀσήμαντοι τούτου, ὃ νῦν σῶμα περιφέροντες ὀνομάζομεν, ὀστρέου τρόπον δεδεσμευμένοι, "Being free and having thrown off the mask of that which we carry about with us now and call the body, tied to it like an oyster." Virg. *Aen.* vi. 734, speaks of the lives of living beings as confined in a dark prison, "Clausae tenebris et carcere caeco," "(Souls) confined in darkness and a blind prison."

159. **real**, not a fancied evil. **darkness of the body**; hendiadys for 'dark body,' *i.e.* a body deprived of its eyesight.

160. **outward light**, 'physical light,'. as opposed to the light of the soul, l. 92, 'inward light,' l. 162.

161. **To incorporate with**, reflexive in sense, '*so as* to join itself to,' 'to dwell in,' 'to be wedded to,' used transitively in this sense in Shak. *Rom. and Jul.* ii. 6. 37, "Incorporate two in one."

163. **visual beam**; see note, l. 92. The Chorus here speaks of two distinct 'lights': one the 'outward' or physical light which his blindness prevents from *entering into* him through his eyes, laden with the impressions of external nature; the other the 'inward' light of the soul which his blindness as effectually prevents from *issuing forth*, as it were, from his eyes, bearing his soul's response to the messages that external nature sends to it.

164. When Œdipus withdraws after bidding a last farewell to light, the chorus in similar strains laments over his fate, and over the transitoriness of human happiness. Soph. *Œd. Tyr.* 1186 *sq.*

165. **Since man on earth**, *sc.* 'was.' The constr. may also be taken as a modified form of the Latinism occurring in *P. L.* i. 673, "Since created man," in which case 'since' becomes a preposition and no 'was' is understood.

166. **The rarer.** There is a slight discrepancy here if 'unparalleled' above is interpreted in its strict sense.

167. By how much; a Latinism (*exemplum tanto rarius quanto...*); the English constr. is 'inasmuch as.' For the sentiment, cf. Soph. *Antig.* 1158, τύχη γὰρ ὀρθοῖ καὶ τύχη καταρρέπει τὸν εὐτυχοῦντα τόν τε δυστυχοῦντ᾽ ἀεί, "For fortune ever raises or casts down | The happy and th' unhappy at her will." Ariosto, *Or. Fur.* xlv. 1, "Quanto più sull' instabil ruota vedi | Di Fortuna ire in alto il miser uomo, | Tanto più tosto hai da vedergli i piedi | Ove ora ha il capo, e far cadendo il tomo," "By how much higher we see poor mortal go | On Fortune's wheel, which runs a restless round | We so much sooner see his head below | His heels ; and he is prostrate on the ground."

169. pitch, 'depth.' Elsewhere Milton always uses this word for 'height.' In music, however, 'pitch' is both high and low, and in M. E. 'picche' (past tense 'pighte') means 'to throw down headlong' (Chaucer, *Knightes Tale*, 1831, "He pighte him on the pomel of his heed.")

170-176. For the rhymes in these lines, see Introd. p. xlvii.

170. him ... estate, 'he does not hold a high rank in my estimation.' **estate,** 'condition of life,' cf. *P. L.* xii. 351, "In mean estate." Cf. Ovid, *Ex Ponto*, i. 9. 39, "Nec census nec clarum nomen avorum | Sed probitas magnos ingeniumque facit," "It is not wealth, nor the fame of ancestors, but uprightness and talent that make men great."

172. sphere of fortune. The goddess Fortune (Gr. Τύχη) was represented with a sphere or ball *in her hand*, Plutarch *de Fort. Rom.*), which although it represents instability of fortune cannot 'raise' a man. Milton seems to have been thinking of the *wheel* of Fortune (Tibullus, *El.* i. 5. 70, "Versatur celeri Fors levis orbe rotae," "Unstable Fortune turns upon the swift-revolving circle of her wheel"; Ovid, *Trist.* v. 8. 8, "Nec metuis dubio Fortunae stantis in orbi numen?" "Fearest not thou the divine power of Fortune, as she stands upon her unstable wheel?"). It is also likely that by 'sphere' Milton meant 'circle' or 'wheel,' as elsewhere he so confuses three dimensions with two ; cf. *P. L.* v. 593, where 'orb' means 'circle,' vi. 552, 399, where 'cube' and 'cubic' stand for 'square.' (These passages, however, may be interpreted in the ordinary meaning of these words.) The same confusion occurs in Elizabethan poetry ; cf. Shak. *M. N. D.* ii. 1, 7, "Swifter than the moon's sphere"; so ii. 1. 153; Marlowe, *Faustus*, i. 3, "Be it to make the moon drop from her sphere." (These passages, again, may be interpreted after the Ptolemaic system, according to which the moon is fixed immovably in a sphere which has a motion of its own.)

173. But thee, *sc.* 'I reckoned'; the past tense is necessary. **her,** the Lat. *fortitudo* is fem.

176. In a Greek tragedy, here would commence the first

episode when the Chorus ceases to be lyric, and begins to take a part in the dialogue. The word 'episode' shows how, in the oldest form of Greek tragedy, the lyric was the chief, and the dramatic the subordinate, element.

177. **unjointed,** 'rendered inarticulate.'

178-186. *The Chorus state the object of their visit, which, in accordance with the functions of the Greek Chorus, consist in bringing counsel and sympathy.*

178. **Matchless in might.** The Chorus end their 'aside,' and address Samson.

180. **not unknown.** *Litotes* or *Meiosis.* Contrast this modest self-introduction with the bluster of Harapha's self-announcement (l. 1076 *sq.*).

181. **Eshtaol and Zora.** These were two of the towns included in the lot of land that fell to the tribe of Dan (*Joshua,* xix. 41). **Eshtaol** was one of the places in which Samson's youth was spent, and where he first felt the inspiration of heaven (see l. 1435, n.) **Zora** was his birthplace, and the residence of Manoah (*Judges,* xiii. 2). **fruitful** : both these places were situated in the valley (*Joshua,* xv. 33).

182, 183. Milton may have, as Calton says, dictated 'visit *and* bewail.' **or, if better ... bring.** The constr. is 'or we come *to see* if better we may bring, etc.' **if better,** 'if more appropriately,' 'if more befittingly.' Probably by the use of 'or' and 'if' in these lines, Milton intends to indicate the delicacy and hesitation the Chorus feel in addressing Samson. The same feeling is implied in ll. 116 and 180.

184. **Salve,** 'as a salve'; cf. Shak. 3 *Henry VI.* iv. 6. 88, "But let us hence, my sovereign, to provide a salve for any sore that may betide." Todd quotes Spenser, *F. Q.* vi. 6. 5, "Give salves to every sore, but counsell to the mind." **swage,** assuage, allay. The form occurs in Wyclif, *Acts,* xiv. 17, "And thei seiynge these thingis unnethis ('with difficulty') *swaqiden* the puple." Nares quotes Gascoigne, "As by no meanes their malice could be swaged." Palsgrave's *Dict.* also gives the form. For the sentiment, cf. Aesch. *Prom. Vinct.* 386 (quoted by Thyer) ; ὀργῆς ζεούσης (var. νοσούσης) εἰσὶν ἰατροὶ λόγοι, "Soft speech is to distempered wrath medicinal," and Dante, *Purg.* xi. 119, "Lo tuo ver dir m'incuora | Buona umiltà. e gran tumor m'appiani," "Thy true words plant in my heart healing humility, and allay the great tumour rankling there."

186. **festered,** 'festering'; see l. 119, 'languished.' Skeat quotes, for the form, *Piers Plowm.* C. xx. "So festered aren hus wondes." Derivation doubtful.

187-209. *The Chorus's sympathy gives a new turn to Samson's grief, in which the sense of shame for the moral stain upon his*

*character overpowers the sense of physical bereavement. When
alone he bewailed to himself the loss of eyesight: in the presence of
others he is almost reconciled to this loss, since it conceals his shame
to some extent (l. 196). This sensitiveness of the fallen hero is one
of Milton's finest touches to his character.*

188. **of**, 'from.' **by**, 'from,' 'through.'

189. **friends**, 'the title of 'friends'.' The same metaphor
occurs in Theognis, *El.* 119, κιβδήλου δ' ἀνδρὸς γνῶναι χαλεπώτερον
οὐδὲν, Κύρνε, "Nothing is harder than to detect a counterfeit
friend, O Kyrnus."

190. **superscription**, used in *Matt.* xxii. 20 ("Whose is this
image and superscription?"), for the writing over or around the
image stamped on the obverse of a coin; see l. 1737, n. **the
most .. understood**, 'I wish to be understood to speak of the
majority of those professing friendship.' Samson, by using
'most,' implies that he does not include the Chorus in this class
of friends.

192. Keightley quotes Ovid, *Trist.* i. 9, 5, "Donec eris felix,
multos numerabis amicos; | Tempora si fuerint nubila, solus
eris," "As long as thou prosperest, thou wilt number many
friends; if the times become cloudy, thou wilt be left alone."

195. This line indicates a rise in the scale of Samson's grief;
see ll. 187-209, n.

197. **heave**, 'raise.' The word had a more extended meaning
formerly; cf. *Will. of Palerne* (1350), "Heve up that hende (cour-
teous) childe bihinde him on his stede"; Chaucer, *Prol.* 550,
"Heve a dore of harre" (off its hinge); Spenser, *F. Q.* i. 2. 39,
"His raging blade he heft."

198. The same simile is used of a foolish man in Soph. *Antig.*
715 *sq.*; Dunster points out that in the epistle of *James*, iii. 4, the
tongue is compared to the "very small helm" that turns the
great ship. **shipwracked**, 'wrack' is an older verb and subst. for
'wreck,' and the vowel '*a*' occurs in the Dutch cognate '*wraken*';
the older form occurs in Chaucer, *Man of Lawes Tale*, 513. Cf. Ben
Jonson, *The Case is Altered*, iii. 1, "O in what tempests do my
fortunes sail | Still wracked with winds"; Dryden, *The Tempest*,
i. 1, "Supposing that they saw the duke's ship wracked."

200. **a word, a tear**; the importunities of Delilah, *Judges*,
xvi. 16.

201-202. Cf. Tasso. *Ger. Lib.* xix. 84, "Femmina è cosa garrula
e fallace, | Vuole e disvuole; è folle uom che sen fida," "Woman's
a false and chattering thing, she wills and wills not; foolish is the
man that trusts her."

203. **sung**, 'ridiculed in songs.' **proverbed for**, 'named in
proverbs as'; the use of this word as a verb is rare. It occurs

in a different sense in Shak. *Rom. and Jul.* i. 4. 36, "For I am
proverb'd with a grandsire phrase." Cf. *Job*, xxx. 9, "And now
I am their song, yea, I am their byword."

205. Yet why? in prose we should say either '*and* why?' or
'yet why *not?*'

207. of wisdom ... mean, 'but of wisdom they beheld in me
nothing more than the average of it that ordinary men possess':
cf. l. 53, n.

208. paired, 'corresponded,' 'been proportioned to.'

209. transvérse (Latin accent), 'out of my due course'; cf. *P.
L.* iii. 487, "A violent cross-wind from either coast | Blows them
transverse ten thousand leagues awry."

210-276. *The Chorus informing Samson of the general feeling of
surprise at his two Philistine marriages, give him an opportunity
of vindicating his action on this point. He shows that in both his
marriages he was acting under divine impulse working for Israel's
deliverance ; that it was not his fault but that of the rulers of
Israel that deliverance had not come ; and that it was their
apathy, envy and suspicion that led them to desert him when
deliverance was almost within grasp at the rock of Etam.*

210. Tax, 'blame'; cf. Shak. *Much Ado*, i. 1. 46, "Faith, niece,
you tax Signior Benedick too much"; the word in this sense has
an indirect object governed by 'with' as in *Lear*, iii. 2. 16.
Wisest men ; Solomon, for instance, was betrayed into idolatry by
his wives. The sentiment occurs again in ll. 759, 1034. Todd
quotes from *Tetrachordon*, "The best and wisest men, amidst
the sincere and most cordial designs of their hearts, do daily err
in choosing" (speaking of marriage-choices).

212. shall again, *sc.* 'err and be deceived.' **pretend** ! ... **wise**,
'though they pretend to be ever so wise,' *i.e.* 'though they may
desire to act with all wisdom and circumspection in the matter.'
pretend, in the older sense of 'intend,' 'aim at,' cf. Shak. *Two
Gen. of Ver.* ii. 6. 37, "Their pretended flight." Bacon, *Adv. of L.*
i. 4. 11, "Alchemy pretendeth to make separation, etc." Cowley
Adv. of Exper. Phil. "If he pretend to the place." Milton uses
the subst. in *P. L.* vi. 421, "Too mean pretence" (aim), and in
ii. 822, "Just pretences" (claims). **Ne'er**, is often used in Elizabethan literature where now 'ever' would be used ; see Abbott,
§ 52 ; so *Ps.* lviii. 5, "Charm he never so wisely." For the omission of 'to be' cf. *P. L.* iv. 947, "Pretending first wise to fly pain."

213. deject not thyself, 'be not dejected.' The transitive form
occurs in Shak. *Tr. and Cr.* ii. 2. 121, "Deject the courage of
our minds," and in Sir T. Browne, *Rel. Med.* ii. 9, "Deject his
cool'd imagination."

215. truth to say, the definite article is more frequently omitted in the corresponding phrase 'sooth to say' (Shak. *Com. of Err.* iv. 4. 72).

217. **thy tribe,** that of Dan, one of the twelve tribes of Israel.

218. **as noble.** Milton in this, perhaps the only instance, seems to have written without authority. There is nothing in Scripture to indicate that either of his wives was noble ; Josephus expressly denies it in the case of Delilah.

219. **The first ... Timna.** *Judges,* xiv. 1. Warton pointed out that there was an allusion here to Milton's own first marriage. This is especially true in one particular—the circumstance of Mary Powell leaving Milton only a few weeks after marriage, partly at the instigation of her relatives, finds a parallel in that of Samson's first wife being withheld from him by her father on the pretext that "he utterly hated her" ; this taking place apparently shortly after the marriage festivities. **and she pleased Me.** The meaning of the corresponding passage in Scripture (*Judges,* xiv. 3, "Get her for me, for she pleaseth me well") is 'she is right in my eyes,' *i.e.* 'she is suitable for a purpose I have in view,' (Kitto) ; see l. 224.

220. The constr. is "but it *pleased* not my parents that, etc."

221. **infidel,** 'a gentile'; see l. 150, n.

222. **motioned,** 'proposed'; cf. *P. L.* ix. 229, "Well hast thou motion'd ... how we might best fulfil the work," Shak. 1 *Henry VI.* i. 3. 63, "One that still motions war." **of,** from. Cf. Josephus, *Antiq.* v. 8. 5, "Yet because this marriage was of God."

223. **intimate,** 'inward,' 'internal.' This word, formed from the Lat. superl. *intimus* (inmost), was properly spelt in older English (as it is in modern French) '*intime*'; it was subsequently confounded with the verb 'intimate' formed from the past pt. of the Lat. verb *intimo,* 'to inform.'

224. **by occasion hence,** 'by the opportunity thus afforded.' **occasion,** 'opportunity,' like Lat. *occasio,* Gr. εὐκαιρία, frequently used in this sense, see ll. 237, 423, 1329, 1716. So used also in Chaucer (*Doctoures Tale,* "That ben occasiouns of daliances"), Wyclif (2 *Cor.* xi. 12, "Y kitte awei (cut off) the occasioun of hem that wolen (desire) occasioun" (ἀφορμήν in Gr. text), and in *Judges,* xiv. 4 (to which the present passage refers), "But his father and his mother knew not that it was of the Lord that he sought an occasion against the Philistines."

226. **divinely called,** 'summoned by divine providence': the announcement was made by an angel (*Judges,* xiii. 5). **she proving false,** *Judges,* xiv. 12-20. She had enticed Samson to tell her the answer to the riddle he had proposed to the 'thirty companions' for a wager, and had then disclosed it to them.

227. **to wife.** This use of 'to' for 'as' or 'for' perhaps survives

only in the expression 'with God to friend.' It is common in Elizabethan English ; see Abbott, § 189.

228. fond, 'foolish,' very common in Milton and in Elizabethan literature in this sense. In Wyclif the word occurs as *'fonned'* (1 *Cor.* i. 27, "But God chees tho (chose those) thingis that ben fonned of the world") ; in Chaucer the adj. *'fonne,'* a subst. *'fonne,'* and a verb *'fonnen'* are used (*Rom. of Rose,* " The rich man ful fonde is ywis | That weneth that he loved is " ; *Reeves Tale,* " Ili haile Alein, by God thou is a fonne " ; *Court of Love,* " As freshly than thou shalt begin to fonne and aote in love.") Of these forms the subst. 'fon' is the oldest, occurring in the M. E. dialects *circ.* 1290. The word is of Scandinavian origin. The present meaning of 'fond' ('loving') appears as early as 1530 in Palsgrave's *Dict.* " I waxe fonde upon a woman—je m'enamoure."

229. vale of Sorec. *Judges,* xvi. 4. A vale here is what eastern travellers call a 'Wady.' The place was in the Philistine country : its site cannot now be identified. 'Sorec' means 'choice wine,' *Is.* v. 2. *Dálila,* accented on the first syllable throughout the piece, so in *P. L.* ix. 1061. The spelling in the *A. V.* is ' *Delilah.*'

230. specious, 'fair,' 'handsome,' like Latin *speciosa.* Wherever Milton uses this word (*P. R.* ii. 391, *P. L.* ix. 361, ii. 484) it means, as here, 'a fair exterior hiding inward foulness.' The simple meaning of 'beautiful' occurs in Fuller (*Pishgah Sight,* " Almug trees ... as sweet to the smell, as specious to the sight." See Trench, *Sel. Gloss.* **accomplished snare.** Warburton saw a quibble here. Perhaps Milton meant one, though the sense of the words have to be strained to bring it out—(1) 'my accomplished (which also ironically means 'artful') ensnarer ' ; (2) 'she who accomplished my ensnaring.'

231. lawful, *i.e.* not offensive to God, who had sanctioned the first marriage.

232. end, governed by 'from' understood, which by *zeugma* may be here used for '*with.*'

234. prime, chief ; see ll. 70, 85, 388 for other shades of meaning.

235. peal. There is an anachronism here in the reference to artillery. The word was used for the sound of bells and trumpets as early as in the *York Mysteries* (1362) ; but Shak. had used it for a 'discharge of ordnance' (in 1 *Henry VI.* ii. 3. 60, stage direction) before Milton ; and the use of 'fort' in the context, and 'tongue-batteries,' l. 404, makes it clear that the older meaning cannot be understood here, in order to avoid the anachronism. The word is a contraction of 'appeal.'

236. fort of silence. There is a double meaning in 'fort' : **(1)**

'fortress,' which is the metaphor ; (2) 'strength,' which lay in silence regarding its secret source.

237. provoke, in the Latin sense of 'challenge' (*provoco*, Cic. *Tusc.* iv. 22), lit. 'call forth (to fight)' ; so in l. 466 ; cf. Beau. and Fl., *The Island Princess,* iii. 3, "Daily provok'd thee, and still found thee coward."

240. serves, 'are subject to the Philistines.' **Israel .. with all his sons,** 'the whole of Israel,' 'the entire nation.' This servitude refers to the Restoration. Jortin pointed out that Milton intended to reproach his countrymen with the Restoration of Charles II., which he accounted the restoration of slavery.

241. me, reflex. 'myself.'

243. seeing ... acknowledged not, cf. *Matt.* xiii. 14, "And seeing ye shall see, and shall not perceive" ; Æsch. *Prom. Vinct.* 455, βλέποντες ἔβλεπον μάτην, "Seeing they yet saw in vain."

245. considered, 'valued,' 'cared for.' Cf. Shak. *Meas. for Meas.* i. 2. 114, "You that have worn your eyes almost out in the service, you will be consider'd." The word is a remnant of old belief in astrology, and lit. means 'to inspect the stars' (*sidera*).

247. ambition, 'a going about (Lat. *ombitio, ambi,* and *eo*) seeking for popular favour' ; the original Lat. meaning was 'a going about seeking votes,' 'canvassing.'

248. spoke the doer, 'proclaimed his worth.'

249. persisted deaf, 'persisted *in being* deaf.' **deaf** is predicative.

250. count, 'account,' 'consider,' see l. 949.

251. the Philistines. These people dwelt along the sea-coast in the plain known as the Shephelah, extending from Gaza to Ekron northwards. *Gen.* x. 14, makes them to be of Egyptian origin ; *Amos,* ix. 7, states that they migrated from Caphtor or Crete, whence in *Deut.* ii. 23, they are called Caphtorim. When the Israelites took possession of Canaan under Joshua, the Philistines formed a powerful confederation of the five states of Gaza, Ashdod, Askalon, Gath, and Ekron, ruled by 'Princes.' Soon after Joshua's death they are found, in alliance with the Ammonites, holding the Israelites in bondage, and henceforth a protracted guerila war was waged by the Israelites against their oppressors, under the successive leaderships of Shamgar, "who slew of the Philistines 600 men with an ox goad," of Jephthah, whose sacrifice of his daughter took place on the return from one of these successful raids, and of Samson. In the battle of Aphek the Philistines carried off the Ark of the Covenant from the Tabernacle, but they suffered a signal defeat at the hands of Samuel at the battle of Mizpeh. The struggle was renewed under Saul and David. when occurred the

episode of the duel between David and the giant Goliath. From
oppressors the Philistines next pass into a conquered people, successively under the sway of Sennacherib of Assyria, and of Psam-
metichus of Egypt, and the last trace of Philistine nationality
disappeared with the capture of Gaza by Alexander the Great.
Their lords, *Judges,* xv. 11, "Knowest thou not that the
Philistines are rulers over us ? "

252. **Judea,** here used in the restricted sense of the tract of land
allotted to the tribe of Judah. *Judges,* xv. 9, "Then the Philistines went up and pitched in Judah." The name of 'Judea'
was applied to the whole of the country inhabited by the Jews
only after the return from the Captivity.

253. **Safe,** proleptic, 'in order to be safe from sudden attack.'
the rock of Etham, *Judges,* xv. 8. Josephus calls it a "strong
rock," *i.e.* a stronghold. **was retired,** 'had retired'; modern
usage still fluctuates between the forms 'I am come' and 'I have
come.' Both the pass. and reflex. forms occur in Shak. *Tim. of
Ath.* v. 1. 62, "Hearing you were retir'd, your friends fallen off";
ii. 2. 171, "I have retir'd me to a wasteful cock, | And set mine eyes
at flow." For a similar use of the pass. cf. *P. L.* ix. 401, "She to
him as oft engaged to be returned by noon." Shak. *M. N. D.* ii.
1. 191, "They were stolen unto this wood."

254. **forecasting,** 'planning,' 'casting about in my mind'; so
'cast' is used in *P. L.* iii. 634.

255. **advantaged,** potential, 'might be of advantage'; cf. *P. R.*
iv. 208, "Me nought advantaged missing what I aimed."

257. **harass.** This seems to be the only instance in Milton (or
any other author as far as I can ascertain) where this word is
used as a subst. Littré leaves the origin as uncertain ; Prof.
Skeat proposes O. Fr. *harer,* to urge on (*sc.* of dogs, *harer un
chien*). The suggestion is obvious that Milton meant to use ' harass' for 'harrying' or 'harry,' *i.e.* 'overrunning with an army'
(A.S. *here*-army), 'ravaging'; but I can find no parallel passage
to support it.

258. **on some conditions.** *Judges,* xv. 12, 13, " ... And Samson
aid unto them, Swear unto me, that ye will not fall upon me
yourselves. And they spake unto him, saying, No ; but we will
bind thee fast, and deliver thee into their hand : but surely we
will not kill thee. And they bound him with two new cords ..."

259. **yield,** past tense, *-ed* omitted ; see l. 31, n.

262. **Touched with the flame.** *Judges,* xv. 14, "And the cords
that were upon his arms became as flax that was burnt with fire,
and his bands loosed from off his hands."

263. **trivial weapon,** 'a weapon picked up in the road'; cf.
Holland's Pliny xxv. 39, " ... Notwithstanding it (the hearbe

waibread or plantains) be a triviall and common hearbe, trodden under every man's foot," *i.e.* a herb growing along the road, see ll. 142, 143, nn.

265. **Judah**, the tribe of that name. **one whole tribe.** Keightley takes this to mean a subdivision of the tribe of Judah, and refers to *Numb.* xiv. 18, *Judges*, xx. 12, 1 *Sam.* ix. 21, where the Hebrew '*shebet*' ('tribe') is so used for a 'subdivision.'

266. **by this**, 'by this time,' see l. 483; cf. Spenser, *F. Q.* i. 2. 1, "By this the Northerne Wagoner had set His sevenfold teme." **Gath**, see l. 251, n. This was one of the cities which the Philistines had taken away from the Jews (1 *Sam.* vii. 14), and the lost chance of its recovery is here referred to. So Josephus places Gath in the territory of Dan.

267. **lorded.** The use of this verb has been traced by Mr. Oliphant to Chaucer's *Legend of Good Women;* cf. Shak. *Temp.* i. 2. 97, "Being thus lorded." The word is now used in the form 'to lord it,' which has been traced back to Foxe's *Book of Martyrs.*

268-276. An allusion to the England of the Restoration, with, Dunster suggested, a particular reference to General Lambert, see Introd. p. xxxii. Prof. Masson, however, sees in these lines a reference to Milton's own deserted condition at the Restoration.

268. **what more oft**, 'what is more frequent.' **oft** is an adj.: see l. 382, n.

271. **Bondage with ease**, cf. Virg. *Georg.* iv. 564, "Studiis florentem ignobilis oti," "Lapped in the enjoyment of inglorious ease." **with**, 'coupled with.' **strenuous liberty**, 'liberty purchased and maintained with toil.' For the opposite sentiment cf. *P. L.* ii. 255, quoted in the note to l. 464.

273. **of**, 'through.' Cf. the modern expression 'of his own accord.'

274. **aught**, 'anything,' contraction of 'a whit' ('wight' is 'a creature,' lit. 'something moving' from the same root as 'weigh,' 'wag').

275 **How frequent**, *sc.* 'is it for them.'

277-289. *The Chorus corroborate Samson by citing other examples of the ingratitude of the Hebrews towards God's chosen.*

278-281. **Succoth ... kings.** *Judges*, viii. 8 *sq.* **Gideon** (the Breaker or Destroyer), fifth judge of Israel, was raised from poverty by special tokens from heaven to be the deliverer of his people from the Midianites, a nomadic race, descended from Abraham, dwelling around the eastern head of the Red Sea, who made annual raids into the Hebrew country. During one of these raids Gideon attacked and defeated their **kings**, Zebah and Zalmunna, and pursued them to the Jordan. Here however the name of Midian was still a terror, and the people of **Succoth** and **Penuel** with mingled cowardice and ingratitude refused to supply bread

to Gideon's followers, faint with hunger. **the fort of Penuel,**
since in *Judges*, viii. 17, the '*tower* of Penuel' is mentioned.
Madian ; this is the spelling in the *Septuagint*, the *A. V.* has
' Midian.'

282-287. **ingrateful Ephraim ... died. Jephtha,** ninth judge of
Israel. An outcast from his own tribe and family, he lived for
some years the life of an eastern Robin Hood, and was chosen
captain of the Gileadites against their enemies the Ammonites.
Finding negotiations fruitless he made his "rash vow" (*Judges*,
xi. 30), marched across the country of the **Ephraimites**, and, without seeking their aid, defeated the king of Ammon. This gave
offence to the Ephraimites, who had crossed over in large bodies
to share in the glory and spoil of victory. A battle was fought
in which Jephthah and the Gileadites defeated the Ephraimites,
and slew the fugitives in large numbers at the fords of the Jordan.

282. **ingrateful,** because in their narrow-minded tribal jealousies
they had forgotten the national deliverance wrought by Jephthah.
They had displayed similar feelings towards Gideon. In *P. L.*
iii. 97, Milton uses '**ingrate**.' The prefix **un-** makes the word, as
now spelt, a hybrid.

283. **Had dealt,** 'would have dealt.' They had threatened to
burn down his house upon him, *Judges*, xii. 1. **by argument**.
Before giving battle, Jephthah opened negotiations with the King
of Ammon, in which, against the grievance alleged by the latter
that "Israel took away his land," he maintained that the Israelites held their land by right of conquest and actual possession.
We are reminded here of Milton himself defending, 'by argument' with his pen, the rights of Puritanism.

286. **prowess.** The word originally meant virtue, excellence,
a sense found in Chaucer's subst. 'prow'—'advantage' ("Men han
ful ofte more harm than prow," *Pardoners Tale*); but as early as
in *King Horn* (*circ.* 1300) the word acquired its present meaning
of 'valour' ("Ich wulle do pruesse for thi luve"). The word
degenerated into meaning 'the affectation of virtue,' and supplied
the noun 'prude,' and Congreve with his character of *Miss Prue*.
The old etym. from Lat. *probus*, fails to account for the 'd' in
'prude,' and for the French form *prud'homme*, and is discarded
in favour of a derivation from the Lat. prep. *pro*, 'for the advantage of,' which acquires a 'd' in the compound *prodesse*, 'to be
advantageous.'

289. **Shibboleth.** *Judges*, xii. 4-6. The retreat of the Ephraimites after their defeat was cut off by Jephthah who stationed his
men at fords of the Jordan, with instructions to ask every man
that wished to cross to pronounce the word '*Shibboleth*' ('a
stream' or 'flood'), and to kill every man that pronounced it
'*Sibboleth*,' this being evidently a dialectic variety of pronuncia-

tion prevailing among the Ephraimites. Forty-two thousand men were detected by this test and slain.

288. Without reprieve, ' on the spot,' ' no mercy being shown.' The word is another form of ' reprove,' ' set aside a sentence.' So Spenser, *F. Q.* i. 9. 29, spells ' repriefe ' for ' reproof.'

291. easily; for they had done so more than once before (in the cases of Gideon and Jephthah). Ingratitude, Samson implies, seems to come naturally to the Israelites. **mine,** 'my countrymen.'

292. not so, 'not easily,' 'not with impunity.' Samson devoutly ascribes the terrible retribution that had befallen the Israelites on former occasions to God's anger against their ingratitude towards Himself.

293-325. *The dialogue ends, and the second choral ode commences. The Chorus solves its own doubt (raised in ll. 215-218) by asserting that the ways of God are just in the eyes of all except of the atheist and the sceptic. God being above His own Laws, if He chooses to employ a particular method and a particular agent for the fulfilment of His ends, though He might have dispensed with both, human reason has no right to question the wisdom of His procedure. Therefore, if God willed to deliver Israel through Samson's marriage with a Philistine woman, that marriage must have been right and proper. In this and similar arguments of Milton there is, no doubt, a touch of the spirit of controversial theology prevalent in his times.*

293. Just ... God. It was to prove this that Milton wrote *Paradise Lost.* (*P. L.* i. 26, "To justify the ways of God to man.")

295. think not God at all, 'think that God does not at all exist.' ' To be' as a subst. verb is understood; cf. for the constr. *P. L.* xi. 292, "Where he abides think there thy native soil." It is a Graecism like the use of $\nu o\mu i\zeta\epsilon\iota\nu$ (Æsch. *Pers.* 500, $\theta\epsilon o\grave{v}s$ $\nu o\mu i\zeta\omega\nu$), and $\dot{\eta}\gamma\epsilon\hat{\iota}\sigma\theta a\iota$ (Eur. *Bacc.* 1327, $\dot{\eta}\gamma\epsilon\hat{\iota}\sigma\theta\omega$ $\theta\epsilon o\acute{v}s$) to mean ' believe in the existence of.' **there be who;** a Latinism, *sunt qui*; antecedent omitted. This and the following lines refer to the Atheist.

297. ' Such a doctrine never commanded a body of adherents.' The use of ' school ' implies that Milton has in view ' philosophic atheism.'

298. The anapaestic measure suddenly tripping in after the grave iambics, together with the rhyme, is meant to express contempt for the light-hearted atheism of the fool. Cf. *Ps.* xiv. 1, liii. 1, "The fool hath said in his heart, There is no God." ' Fool ' in such passages means ' wicked,' ' having a perverted rather than a weak, intellect' (cf. *Ps.* x. 4, "The wicked ... all his thoughts are, There is no God ").

299. doctor, " one ' learned ' in this ' school '." Thyer thought this "quaint conceit" out of place in the serious speech of the Chorus.

300. **his ways,** sc. 'to be.' **doubt,** 'suspect'; for this meaning and constr. cf. Shak. *Merry Wives*, i. 4. 42, "I doubt he be not well." In modern prose the 'not' would not be used after 'doubt.' This and the following lines refer to the Sceptic.

301. **to ... contradicting.** The preposition 'to' is here used on the analogy of the Lat. *contradico* which governs the *dative;* so the Fr. *contredire* takes the prep. *à* before the object of the person.

302. **wandering,** 'wild,' 'having no stay and support in faith.'

303-306. A rhymed stanza: cf. ll. 688-91, 1053-1060.

303. **diminution;** a Latinism: *majestatem minuere* and *crimen laesae majestatis* were Roman law terms for 'high treason.' The halting hendecasyllabic measure in this and l. 306 are meant to be an echo of the perplexed and lame conclusions of this class of thinkers.

305-306. **ravel,** is to *unweave* a woven texture, and in so doing to *entangle* the loose threads; cf. Shak. *Two Gen. of Ver.* iii. 2. 52, "Therefore as you unwind her love from him, lest it should ravel and be good to none, you must provide to bottom it on me"; *Rich. II.* iv. 1. 288, "And must I ravel out my weav'd up folly?" **resolv'd,** 'having one's doubts removed,' 'convinced'; cf. Shak. 3 *Henry VI.* iv. 1 35, "Resolve my doubt"; *Jul. Caes.* iii. 2. 183, "To be resolved if Brutus so unkindly knock'd or no." Middleton and Dekker, *The Roaring Girl,* i. 1, "Now you're resolv'd, sir, it was never she." A play upon the double meaning of the word ('convinced,' and 'determined') occurs in Ben Jonson, *The Devil is an Ass,* ed. Gifford, v. 68, "*Wit.* Go, you are an ass. *Fitz.* I am resolv'd on it, sir. *Wit.* I think you are." The expressions 'resolve me,' 'resolve you' are frequent in Beau. and Fl., and Shakspere uses 'resolution' and 'resolvedly' in corresponding senses.

307. **the Interminable,** 'The Infinite,' 'The Eternal.' Latin use; cf. Boethius, *Consol.* v. 6, "Interminabilis vitae plenitudinem," "The fulness of the life everlasting"; which Chaucer renders "All the plentie of the life interminable." Tertullian has "Interminabilis aetas."

308. **prescript,** 'edict,' 'ordinance.'

309. **our laws;** 'the Mosaic Law.'

310. **To exempt,** sc. 'him': omission of antecedent; a Latinism.

311. **Whom so,** sc. 'to exempt'; in modern prose in the case of the omission of a transitive verb 'to' would be used : "whom it pleases him *to.*" **by choice,** 'in preference to others,' 'chosen out from among others.'

312. **From,** to be joined with 'exempt,' l. 310. **national obstriction.** 'obligations binding upon the nation to which he

belongs.' The reference is to the Mosaic law forbidding marriage with Gentiles (*Deut.* vii. 3), and Idolaters (*Exod.* xxxiv. 16). **obstriction.** This word seems to be Milton's own coinage from the Lat. *obstringo*, ' to bind.'

313. **legal debt,** 'a penalty for having broken the law.' For this meaning of ' debt' cf. the Lord's Prayer in the *A. V.* " Forgive us our debts " (which in the Prayer Book stands as " Forgive us our trespasses "); Wyclif, " And forgyve to us oure dettis " ; *Ancren Riwle,* " Forgif us ure dettes."

314. **with...dispense,** 'suspend'; lit. ' to weigh out,' 'distribute,' as in *P. L.* v. 330. See l. 1377, n.

315. **wanted,** 'was without' : see l. 916.

316. **in respect of,** 'with regard to' ; cf. *Ps.* xxxix. 6, " Mine age is even as nothing in respect of thee."

318. **Nazarite.** Two derivations of this word are given. (1) A Hebrew word meaning 'separation' (so that a Nazarite is one separated or consecrated to the service of God by certain vows) ; (2) a particular use of this word to mean ' a distinctive badge,' 'a crown' (so that a Nazarite is one crowned with unshorn flowing locks). The vows consisted in abstinence from wine and strong drink, in not allowing a razor to come upon his head, and in avoiding contact with the dead. These vows might be taken for a limited period, or, as in the cases of Samson, Samuel, and John the Baptist, for life. Violation of any of them required expiation and sacrifice. The life of a Nazarite was thus an example of self-denial and holy living (*Numb.* vi. 1-21). **heroic,** to the ordinary peaceful functions of the Nazarite as a devotee, Samson added that of a warrior.

319. **strictest purity;** as the vows make no reference to celibacy, this must be taken to mean abstinence from marriage with one ' unclean and unchaste.'

322. **Unclean;** the application of the word to a Gentile is derived from *Leviticus.* **unchaste,** Josephus, v. 8, 11, and *P. L.* ix. 1060.

324. **moral verdit.** The law of nature, looking only to our common humanity, did not pronounce a Gentile unclean as the Mosaic law did. The form ' verdit' is coined by Milton on the analogy of 'perfet' (l. 946), though in this case there is no corresponding French form, both the English and the French word being ' verdict.' **quits.** 'acquits, 'frees from the charge' ; see l. 509, n. ; cf. Marlowe, *Massacre at Paris,* " And so to quite your grace of all suspect." **unclean,** adj. for subst. like ' suspect' in Marlowe.

327. **careful step,** 'slow steps indicating a mind full of anxiety.' **white as down ;** an unusual simile, the usual attribute of ' down' in similes being its 'softness.'

328. **advise,** ' consider' ; cf. *P. L.* ii. 376, " Advise if this be

worth attempting," v. 729, "Let us advise, and to this hazard
draw.' In Spenser (as in Fr. *s'aviser*), the word in this sense is
reflexive. (*F. Q.* ii. 7. 38, "Avise thee well"; ii. 6. 27, "Gan
him avise.")

330. **Ay me**, 'woe's me.' This form occurs frequently in
Shakspere, and in Gascoigne's *Steele Glas*, O. Fr. *aimy*, It.
ahime, Gr. οἴμοι. 'Ay' here is a different word from 'ay,' 'aye,'
still used in Lowland Scotch for 'yea,' and from 'aye,' 'ever.'
another inward grief, namely, the thought that Samson had
brought disgrace upon his father's name. Manoah's death is not
mentioned in Scripture ; *Judges*, xvi. 31, does not necessarily
imply that he died before Samson.

333. **uncouth place**, 'strange land.' The Danites, like pious
Hebrews, were not likely to show themselves in the land of
idolaters. The successive stages in the meaning of this word
are :—(1) 'unknown' (A.S. *uncúth*, *un*, not, *cunnan*, to know),
e.g. "Uncúth gelád" (unknown path) Beowulf ; (2) 'strange,'
'foreign,' *e.g.* "Uncúthe londe" (foreign land) Layamon ; (3)
'unusual,' 'unaccustomed'; "Uncouth smart," Spenser, *F. Q.* i.
1. 15 ; "Uncouth light," i. 12. 20 ; (4) 'awkward,' its modern
meaning. **old**, 'felt in days past.'

334. **once gloried**, 'once gloried *in*,' 'of whom you once were
proud.'

335. **informed**, in the Lat. sense of 'shaped,' 'directed' (*forma*,
'shape'); cf. *Comus*, 180, "Where else shall I inform my unacquainted feet ?"

336. Newton pointed out that this line is introduced to
account for Manoah's coming later than the Chorus. Manoah
had evidently set out at once on hearing that Samson would be
allowed out of prison that day.

337. **say if he be here.** It is strange that the father cannot
recognize his son. Perhaps this is purposely introduced to show
the great change in Samson's appearance. The Chorus recognized him.

339. **erst**, 'erewhile,' 'once'; the word is the superlative of 'ere'
whence 'early,' orig. an adv. ('ere-ly'). 'Ere,' orig. positive,
acquired a comparative meaning as in Ger. *eher*, 'rather,' and
passed into a prep. meaning 'before.'

340-372. *Manoah, too, bewails his son's condition, and once again
the contrast between the present and the past is brought into play,
but in a different manner ; for the Chorus, like outsiders, found the
contrast in the change from the hero to the blind captive ; the
father feels it more deeply in the cruel justice by which the blessing
of God, granted in answer to his earnest prayer, has been turned
into a curse ; and in his grief Manoah almost inveighs against
Providence.*

340. Cf. Virg. *Aen.* ii. 274, " Ei mihi ! qualis erat, quantum mutatus ab illo."

341. Scan thus :—" Thát ìn | vìncì | blè Sám | sòn fár | rè-nównʼd | . The sharp ring of the two trochees opening the verse is another instance of Milton's consummate skill in adapting sound to sense. What Prof. Masson truly calls the "horror" of accentuating the word as 'invincíble' (which Landor very strangely preferred) is not warranted either by the ear, or by the Latin accent, which is *invincĭbilis*.

342. strength of Angels, which surpasses that of man, 2 *Pet.* ii. 11.

343. walked their streets ; this may be inferred from *Judges*, xvi. 3.

345. Duelled, 'fought single-handed' ; 'duel' is derived, through the Ital. *duello*, from the Lat. *duellum*, the older form of *bellum*, 'war,' contention of *two* parties (Lat. *duo*, 'two'). The reference is to the incident mentioned in l. 144.

348. one spear's length. This evidently implies that Samson's remaining strength was still a match for any *unarmed* Philistine ; the coward, armed, would venture near enough to wound Samson, *but not near enough* to get within reach of his bare arms ; cf. l. 1235.

349. what not, 'what *is there* not.' In prose the negative would be used in the relative sentence—'what is there in man that is not deceivable ?'

351. but, 'that … not.' **proves,** *sc.* ' to be.'

352. prayed. Milton here follows Josephus (*Antiq.* v. 8. 2). **barrenness.** This was the hardest lot that could befall a Hebrew woman ; cf. *Gen.* xxx. 23, " God hath taken away my reproach " ; *Luke*, i. 25, " The Lord looked on me … to take away my reproach among men."

353. gained, 'obtained through prayer,' Lat. 'impetravi filium.'

354. such … as, ' such … that ' ; see Abbott, § 109, so Bacon, *Adv. of L.* ii. 2. 4, " *Such* being the workmanship of God, *as* he doth hang the greatest weight upon the smallest wires." Newton refers to the words of the happy father in Terence, *Andr.* i. 1. 69 *sq.*

355. now, emphatic, ' when he sees the condition my son has come to.'

358, 359. tempt … our prayers, 'tempt us to offer prayers.'

359, 360. The constr. is 'then, being given, … why do his gifts draw, etc.' **graces.** This seems to be the only instance in which Milton uses the pl. of this word to mean 'favour.' It is so used in the *Ayenbite of Inwyt* (1340), and still survives in the expr. 'to be in one's good graces' (Oliphant). The pl. is used by Wyclif (*Luke*, xxii. 17, " And whanne he hadde take the cuppe, he *dide gracis* ("gratias egit" Vulg.), in the Latin sense of 'thanks.' The meaning of 'favour' is more common in the sing. (*e.g.* Chaucer, *Chanouns Yemannes Tale*, "To stonde in gracè of his lady dere"; Spenser, *F. Q.* ii. 7. 59, "Of grace, I pray thee" (Fr. *de grace*). Elsewhere Milton uses the pl. 'graces' always in the sense of 'beauty.' **scorpion**. Cf. *Luke*, xi. 12, " If he (the son) shall ask an egg (from his father), will he offer him a scorpion?"

362. **plant**, cf. *Is.* v. 7, " For the vineyard of the Lord of Hosts is the house of Israel, and the men of Judah his pleasant plant"; and the beautiful allegory of the vine in *Ps.* lxxx., beginning with "Thou hast brought a vine out of Egypt." Dunster refers to *Il.* xviii. 57, ὁ δ' ἀνέδραμεν ἔρνεϊ ἶσος, τὸν μὲν ἐγὼ θρέψασα, φυτὸν ὡς γουνῷ ἀλωῆς, "Like a young tree he throve : I tended him, | In a rich vineyard as the choicest plant"; and Theocr. *Idyll.* xxiv. 102, Ἡρακλέης δ' ὑπὸ ματρὶ νέον φυτὸν ὡς ἐν ἀλωᾷ, ἐτρέφετ', "Hercules was nursed by his mother like a young plant in an orchard."

364. **miracle**, 'an object of wonder or admiration'; the expr. occurs in Shak. 2 *Henry IV.* ii. 3. 33, "O miracle of men."

365-366. The suddenness of the calamity is depicted by the *asyndeta* (omissions of the conjunction) and accumulation of epithets; so in the third day's battle, *P. L.* vi. 851, the rebel angels are left " Exhausted, spiritless, afflicted, fallen." For the asyndeta, cf. Aesch. *Prom. Vinct.* 679-80; Soph. *Od. Tyr.* 1314-15.

368-372. Landor pointed out the allusion here. The remains of Cromwell were disinterred and hanged at Tyburn, then decapitated, and the head fixed on Westminster Hall, 1661, see l. 694.

368. **methinks**, 'it seems to me.' The confusion in spelling between the two distinct A.S. verbs *thyncan* (to seem) and *thencan* (to think) took place as early as the B-text of *Piers Plowman* (Skeat). In Ger. the corresponding forms *dünken* and *denken* are kept apart. For the omission of the impersonal 'it' compare Ger. *mich dünkt*, and Fr. *me semble*.

369. **frailty**, 'a momentary weakness' as opposed to deliberate sin and vice.

370. **thrall**, 'a slave.' Trench's derivation of this word from the A.S. *thyrlian*, 'to pierce,' because Jewish slaves had their ears bored (*Exod.* xxi. 6), is disproved by the fact that while the A.S. *thral*, 'a slave,' is derived from the Norse word '*thraell*,' the A.S. *thyrlian*, 'to drill,' does not occur in Norse. Besides there is no phonetic law by which the Norse '*ae*' can be changed

into the A. S. '*y*.' The Norse '*thraell*' is from a root THRAG
akin to Gr. τρέχω, 'to run'; hence a 'thrall' is lit. ' one who
runs on errands,' 'a servant.'

373-419. *Samson gravely reproves Manoah for arraigning God's
providence, and takes all the blame upon himself. The skilful balance of sentiment that runs throughout the work is again observable
here. To the Chorus Samson had defended his Philistine marriages in refutation of the public condemnation of them, but to his
father he lays bare that fatal weakness that led him, in spite of
experience, to betray the forbidden secret. The Hebrews had
selfishly condemned Samson's marriage, because they thought it had
hindered their own deliverance :—his reply to their selfish fault-
finding was full of indignation—it was their fault, not his, that
they were not free. But Manoah complains against God's justice
that His hand should lie heavy on one whom He had chosen for his
servant :—Samson's reply to one who errs through love for him, is
full of self-condemnation—it was his own fault that God's hand so
lies on him. The conclusion of Samson's speech again illustrates
that rise in the scale of his grief (noted before in ll. 187-209 n.) by
which it becomes sublimer in measure as it passes from lament over
physical sufferings to remorse at past moral frailties.*

373. **Appoint.** A difficult word. Warburton took it to mean
'arraign, summon to answer.' This meaning is supported by the
French use of the word as a law-term, meaning 'to refer a cause,'
Brachet; ('*appointer*, régler un appointement en justice; *appointement*, réglement en justice par lequel, avant de faire droit aux
parties, le juge ordonnait de produire par écrit ... ou encore de
prouver par témoins les faits articulés.' Littré). Todd understood it to mean ' blame, lay the fault on.' For this meaning cf.
Harington's *Nugae Antiquae* (in Halliwell), "If any of these
wants be in me, I beseech your lordships *appoint* them to my extreme state"; where 'appoint' means 'impute.' Keightley goes
back to the ord·nary sense of 'arrange or direct.' Richardson
explains it as 'point not at (providence)' *sc.* 'as the cause.' A
modification of the literal meaning gives good sense :—'do not
point out to Providence what it should do'; 'do not take upon
yourself the arrangement of matters that are at the disposal of
Providence alone'; cf. for this use of the word Surrey's Virgil,
Aen. ii. "A blazing sterne (star) ... by long tract appointing us
the way." For the sentiment (according to Todd's interpreta-
tion), cf. Pindar, *Olymp.* ix. 56, λοιδορῆσθαι θεοὺς ἐχθρὰ σοφία,
"To blame the gods is a hateful wisdom."

375. Cf. Aristoph. *Nub.* 1454, αὐτὸς μὲν οὖν σαυτῷ σὺ τούτων
αἴτιος, στρέψας σεαυτὸν ἐς πονηρὰ πράγματα, "Thyself rather art the
cause of these evils to thyself, having turned thyself to wicked
courses."

377. **my ... who**, antecedent 'me' contained in the poss. 'my.'

380. Canaanite, here in the general sense of Gentile. Canaan ('the low or depressed country') was the land between the Jordan valley and the Mediterranean, originally peopled by the descendants of Canaan, grandson of Noah. At the time of the Exodus there were 'seven nations' dwelling in Canaan, among whom the Philistines are not named (*Gen.* xv. 18-21), but Philistia and Phoenicia are included in Canaan by the prophet Zephaniah (ii. 5), and in the settlement of Canaan after the Jewish conquest Philistia is again included in the division. The country is now called Palestine.

382. oft, adj. 'frequent.' For this archaic use of the word cf. Barbour, *Bruce,* "Bot I haf herd *oftsiss* say" ('oft sithe,' 'oft times'); Chaucer, *Clerkes Tales,* "She wolde bringe wortes or othere herbes *tymes ofte.*" Later 'often' was similarly used, *e.g.* Tyndale, *N. T.* "Thyne often diseases," *A. V.* "Thine often infirmities" (1 *Tim.* v. 23).

383. she Of Timna. Her name too is never mentioned in the Bible.

384. The secret. See l. 1016.   **highth**; this spelling, which gives the termination in full (-th), is always preferred by Milton; cf. *P. L.* i. 24, 552, etc. The common spelling 'height' occurs as early at least as Chaucer ('hyghte').

385. nuptial love professed, *Judges,* xiv. 16, 17, "And Samson's wife wept before him, and said, Thou dost but hate me, and lovest me not ... and she wept before him the seven days while their feast lasted." (This was the marriage feast.)

386. my spies, see l. 1197. Milton here again follows Josephus. In *Judges,* xiv. 11, merely "thirty companions" are mentioned, corresponding to what are now called 'groomsmen,' or as they are styled in *Matt.* ix. 15, "children of the bride-chamber." But Josephus, *Antiq.* v. 8. 6, mentions "thirty of the most stout of their youth, in pretence to be his companions, but in reality to be a guard upon him." Quarles in his *History of Samson* adopts this notion.   **corrupted,** 'obtained information by a breach of confidence,' or to use Samson's own metaphor "ploughed with his heifer," *Judges,* xiv. 18. (Ben Jonson, *New Inn,* Gifford, v. 336, refers to this.)

387. rivals. From *Judges,* xiv. 20, and l. 1020, it is evident that there was *one* rival in the ordinary sense of the word. The sense here is rather of 'rivals in the confidence of his wife,' cf. 'underminers,' l. 1204.

388. prime of love, 'first bloom of love,' 'nuptial love.' The word is used of the morning in *P. L.* v. 170, "While day arises that sweet hour of prime," of the new creation, *ib.* 295, "Nature here wantoned as in her prime."

389. Spousal embraces, governed by 'in' understood.   **vitiated,**

'corrupted,' qualifies 'who' above. *Judges*, xvi. 5, "And the lords of the Philistines came up to her, and said unto her, Entice him ... and we will give thee every one of us eleven hundred pieces of silver."

390. **offered**, qualifies 'gold.' **scent**, spelt 'sent' in the original, and always so spelt by Milton (Masson). This is also the spelling in Spenser (where it either means 'sense' as in *F. Q.* i. 1, 43, "A fit false dreame that can delude the sleeper's sent" : or ' power of smell ' as in *F. Q.* iii. 4. 46, " And sent of houndës trew ") ; and in Holland's *Pliny*. **by the scent**, 'before she had touched the gold,' 'by the mere promise of it,' the expression is a metaphor for what precedes—"though offer'd only,"—with perhaps a sarcastic allusion to the keenness of avarice that can smell what to the ordinary sense is inodorous. Keightley's allusion to Juno's conception of Mars by means of a flower, Ovid, *Fasti* v. 229 *sq.*, would have been apposite, were it not that it is the *touch* (not the *smell*) that effects it (cf. l. 254, "Flos dabit ... tetigi, nec mora, mater erat"). More probably the allusion is to the story of Danaë who conceived Perseus through the medium of a shower of gold (Ovid, *Met.* iv. 610, "Neque enim Jovis esse putabat Persea, quem pluvio Danaë conceperat auro"). **conceived**, verb to the nom. 'who,' l. 388.

391. **Treason.** The comma after 'conceived' indicates that the object of this verb is 'treason,' and that 'first-born' is in apposition with this object. **spurious ;** so too is Perseus called in Ovid, quoted above.

392. **thrice she assayed**, *Judges*, xvi. 6-14.

394. **capital secret**, in a double sense ; (1) 'secret that lay in (the hair of) my head' ; (2) 'great secret, one whose divulgence would endanger my life.' For the first sense, cf. *P. L.* xii. 383, "Needs must the serpent now his capital bruise | Expect with pain " (in allusion to *Gen.* iii. 15) : for the second cf. the expr. "capital treason," "capital crime" (Shak.). The constr. is 'that she might know in what part, etc.'

395. **Summed**, 'concentrated,' ' summed up,' as in *P. L.* viii. 473, ix. 113. 'Summed' is used in *P. L.* vii. 421 in a different and very peculiar sense (see Nares).

400. **contempt**, *sc.* 'for Samson,' who, she thought, could not see through the pretence of her love.

401. **traitor to myself**, 'betrayer of my own secret ' cf. Shak. *Com. of Err.* iii. 2. 167, "But her fair sister ... hath almost made me traitor to myself."

403. **blandished**, 'flattering,' 'full of blandishments' ; cf. 'languished,' l. 119. Propertius similarly uses this word in the pass. with an active meaning : *El.* iv. 6. 72, "*Blanditaeque* fluant per mea colla rosae," " And charming rose-wreaths flow

around my neck." **Parleys,** 'conversation,' like the ordinary French use of *parler*. The metaphor occurs in Shak. *Macb.* ii. 3. 87, "calls to parley the sleepers of the house." Doublet "parable," l. 500.

404. **Tongue-batteries.** Cf. "peal of words," l. 235. Todd quotes Shak. 1 *Henry VI.* iii. 3. 79, "I am vanquish'd; these haughty words of hers have batter'd me like roaring cannon-shot." **surceased,** 'ceased.' Cf. Shak. *Rom. and Jul.* iv. 1. 97, "For no pulse shall keep his native progress, but surcease." The word is derived from Fr. *sursis,* subst. from verb *surseoir,* Lat. *supersedeo,* 'to desist from.' The proper spelling is 'sursease,' as in Fabian's *Chronicle,* but from confusion with 'cease' (Lat. *cedo,* 'to give way'), the '*s*' was changed into '*c.*'

405. **over-watched,** 'tired out'; lit. 'kept awake too long.' *Judges,* xvi. 16, "His soul was vexed unto death." The metaphor is from a sentinel.

406. **At times,** 'at the time.' The phrase in modern prose would mean 'now and then.' **most,** adv. to 'seek.'

407. **unlocked.** *Judges,* xvi. 17, "He told her all his heart." **my heart,** *i.e.* 'the citadel of my heart,' as the metaphor requires.

408. **resolved,** 'resolute.' The word has a different meaning in l. 305. **well,** 'fully,' 'firmly.' The line may be paraphrased 'who, if I had a grain of firm, manly resolution,' inverting the noun into an adjective and the adjective into a noun, as is frequently Milton's practice.

410. **effeminacy** has here the sense of 'uxoriousness.' Cf. 'effeminately,' l. 562.

412. **To.** We should say 'upon' in modern prose.

414. **degree,** 'condition,' 'stage.' Cf. Shak. *Twelfth Night,* i. 5. 143, "He's in the third degree of drink."

416. **servitude,** like "servile mind" (l. 412), refers to his "foul effeminacy" (l. 410).

418. **True slavery.** Because by it the mind is enslaved to another's will. **blindness,** *sc.* 'was.'

420-447. *What in the language of musicians would be called the first 'motive' of the piece, ends at l. 433. Up to that place the dominant thought has been Samson's Philistine marriage, and its consequences to himself and to his nation. From reflections upon these past calamities, we come in l. 434 sq. face to face with a present evil—the latest consequence of Samson's error—namely, the public celebration of the triumph of idolatry over the Hebrew religion: for a feast is about to be held in honour of Dagon, who had delivered Samson into the hands of his enemies, and in dishonour of the God of Israel who had failed to effect His people's deliverance.*

The announcement of this celebration is appropriately made through one who, next to Samson, feels most keenly the dishonour it brings.

421. **approved not**, *sc.* 'I,' *Judges*, xiv. 3.

423. **occasion**, see l. 224 *n*. **infest**. 'attack,' 'molest,' like Lat. *infesto* (from an adj. *infestus*, 'hostile'). Cf. Spenser, *F. Q.* ii. 1. 48, "The bitter pangs that doth your heart infest." In modern prose the word is commonly used in the sense of 'to render unsafe,' *e.g.* 'a sea infested with pirates,' which is also a Latin use (*mare infestum*, Cic. *Att.* 16. 1).

424. **I state not that**, 'I do not pretend to establish or settle that point,' namely, 'whether you were right or I was.' Cf. Sir T. Browne, *Christian Morals*, iii. 7, "Not celestial figures but virtuous schemes must dominate and state our actions." The Fr. *constater* is similarly used. The word occurs in the sense of 'establish,' 'station in a place,' in Marlowe, *Jew of Malta*, ii. 2, "My lord, remember that to Europe's shame | the Christian isle of Rhodes from whence you came | was lately lost, and you were *stated* here | to be at deadly enmity with Turks." **this**, 'of this.' Here, by a kind of *synesis*, 'be sure' is taken to be a transitive verb in sense equivalent to 'know surely,' 'know for certain.' See l. 1408.

426. **triumph**, *i.e.* 'an object of triumph.' **the sooner**, *sc.* 'than thou would'st have found had thy choice of a wife been otherwise.'

429. **within thee**, 'within thy breast.'

430. **Tacit**, in the pass. sense of 'secret,' so used in Latin, *e.g. Tacitum aliquid tenere*, Cic. *de Or.* iii. 17, 64. **True** is emphatic (not concessive) here, ''Tis very true,' ''Tis too true.'

431. **burden**, 'heavy consequences.' **more**, 'more than enough,' the punishment has been heavier than the fault deserved.

433. **rigid**, 'from which no abatement will be made.' **score**, 'reckoning.' From A.S. *sceran*, 'to cut,' two M.E. forms were derived—'shear' and 'score'—both preserving the original sense, *e.g.* in Nigel Wireker's *Poems*, 1180. Soon after, from the custom of cutting notches in a stick for counting, 'score' came to mean 'twenty,' *e.g. Genesis* and *Exodus*, 1230, "you woren seven score yere"; and by an easy transition the 'account' itself, whether scored on a stick or written, was called a 'score,' *e.g.* in *Midland Poems*, *circ.* 1280. The same custom of notching up accounts is seen in the word 'tally,' Fr. *tailler*, 'to cut.' **remains**, *sc.* 'to be told.' Samson already knows the *fact* that the feast is going to be held (l. 12), but, we may suppose, not its *object*, which Manoah at the same time announces (l. 437 *sq.*).

434. **popular**, 'public'; see l. 16 n.

436. **pomp**, 'solemn procession,' in the lit. Greek sense πομπή, from πέμπειν, 'to send.' Cf. *L'All.* 127, "And pomp and feast

and revelry." *P. L.* vii. 563, "While the bright pomp ascended jubilant"; viii. 61, "A pomp of winning graces waited still."

437. *Judges*, xvi. 23, "Then the lords of the Philistines gathered together for to offer a great sacrifice unto Dagon their god, and to rejoice : for they said, Our god hath delivered Samson our enemy into our hand."

439. **Them out of thine.** The constr. is, 'and who hath delivered them out of thy hands.' An antithesis is meant between 'thee *into* their hands' and 'them *out of* thine.' **who slew'st ... slain**, proleptic constr. with the cognate accusative, 'who slewest to their loss many a man who was thus slain.' The tautology (which Landor needlessly found fault with) can be paralleled from the classics. Cf. Hom. *Il.* xiv. 6, θερμὰ λοετρὰ θερμήνῃ, lit. 'heat the hot baths.' Soph. *Œd. Col.* 1200, τῶν σῶν ἀδέρκτων ὀμμάτων τητώμενος, lit. 'blinded of your blind eyes,' and from modern usage, *e.g.* the expression 'shot him dead.' **them**, the so-called *ethical dative*, which sometimes means 'at the cost of,' as here and in l. 537 ; and sometimes (more commonly) 'for the benefit of,' *e.g. Numbers*, xxiii. 7, "Come, curse me, Jacob." See Abbott, § 220. **slew'st**, 'slay,' in A.S. meant 'to smite' (Germ. *schlagen*), and the expression 'slain to death,' akin to that in the text, occurs in *Judith*, x. "Oferdrencte his duguthe ealle, swilce hie waéron deáthe geslægene," "Plied all his retainers excessively (with wine, so that they lay) as if they were smitten with death."

440. **magnified**, 'exalted.' Cf. *P. L.* vii. 606, "Thee that day thy thunders magnified" ; *Luke*, i. 46, "My soul doth magnify the Lord" ; *i.e.* praise ; lit. make much of ; opp. belittle.

441. **Besides**, 'beside,' 'except.' This use of the word as a prep. is incorrect, but occurs in M.E. The prep. originally was 'byside,' meaning 'near,' *e.g. Robert of Gl.* 1298, "Biside Hastings to Engelond hi come " ; frequently in Chaucer, as "Stonden hem bisyde " (*Tale of Gamelyn*), "Stonden her bisyde " (*Clerkes Tale*). In *Old English Homilies* (*circ.* 1200) the form ' bi-sides ' (properly an adv. formed by the addition of the genitive ' *s* ') occurs as a prep., " Bi-sides Jerusalem on the fot of the dune the men clepen Munt Olivete " ; so later in Wyclif, *Matt.* xiii. 1, " Jhesus ... sat bisidis the see " ; and, later still, in Shak. *M. N. D.* iv. 1. 120, "Besides the groves " (' near ') ; *Temp.* iii. 1. 57, "Nor can imagination form a shape, besides yourself, to like of " (by the side of, compared with).

442. **Disglorified**, 'divested, shorn of his glory.' For the prefix cf. ' disallied,' l. 1022 ; ' disenthrone,' *P. L.* ii. 229, ' disrelish,' v. 305, ' displode,' vi. 605, ' disespouse,' ix. 17. Milton shares with Spenser his frequent use of this prefix ; cf. ' discounsell,' ' dis-likeful,' ' dispart,' ' disthronize,' ' distroubled,' occurring, among others, in *F. Q.* **had**, *i.e.* ' held.'

443. rout, 'disorderly crowd'; see l. 674, used in a similarly contemptuous sense in *Comus*, 533. In Foote's plays and in the days of the Regency this very word significantly came to mean 'a *fashionable* assembly.' The word is the same as 'rout' ' defeat,' and 'route' 'way' (lit. a road *cut* through a 'forest'), all from Lat. *rupta* (*rumpo*, to break).

444. Which ... come, a Latinism for 'and that this has come.'

446. the most with shame, *i.e.* 'the most shameful.'

448-478. *Manoah's information draws forth from Samson a fresh outburst of accusations against himself as the instrument of dishonour to Israel's God ; but with this is coupled the noble utterance of his hope that the contest now being between God and Dagon, Dagon never can triumph, as he had triumphed over Samson. The lines containing this hope* (ll. 460-471) *furnish the* Middle *of the Action of the piece* (see Introd. p. xvi). *They are emphasized by Manoah's solemn reply, " These words I as a prophecy receive."*

450. advanced, 'promoted,' cf. *P. L.* 359, "Into our room of bliss thus high advanced | Creatures of other mould."

452. opened the mouths, a frequent expression in Scripture both in a good and a bad sense : for the latter see *Ps.* cix. 2.

453. scandal, 'disgrace.' Another form of the word is 'slander'; from Gr. σκάνδαλον, 'offence,' 'stumbling block'; the idea is from disturbing the stick or spring in a trap and thereby causing it to shut.

455. propense, 'inclined': cf. Sir T. Browne, *Religio Medici*, i. 8, "Heads that are disposed unto schism, and complexionally propense to innovation."

456. with idols, *i.e.* 'in idol-worship.'

459. harbour, 'receive,' 'entertain.' The word was orig. a subst. 'herbergh,' meaning lit. a shelter for an army (A.S. *here*, 'army,' *beorgan*, 'to shelter'): it is used by Chaucer for an inn ; both subst. and verb occur in Wyclif, *Matt.* xxv. 36, "Y was herborles and ye herboriden me."

461. With me, 'as far as I am concerned '; the issue of the strife no longer depends on Samson. **contést,** Latin accent.

463. Me overthrown ; an imitation of the Latin ablative absolute constr. : the English case absolute is the nominative—'I (being) overthrown.' **enter lists with,** 'match himself against'; 'lists' is from Lat. *licium*—a border, an enclosure for a tournay. For the omission of the article cf. Chaucer, *Squieres Tale*, "That faught in listes with the bretheren two of Canace ": Spenser *F. Q.* ii. 1. 6, "Well could he tournay and in listes debate."

464. deity, an abstract noun, as in l. 899; cf. 'Godhead,' l. 1153 ; cf. *P. L.* vi. 157, "A third part of the gods in synod met | Their deities to assert." **preferring before,** 'placing or ranking above,' see l. 1672; cf. *P. L.* ii. 255, "Preferring | Hard liberty before the easy yoke | Of servile pomp."

466. connive, 'tolerate,' 'endure,' lit. 'to shut the eyes (to an offence),' used again of God in *P. L.* x. 624. **provok'd**, see l. 237, n.

467. will arise, a frequent biblical expression, cf. *Ps.* vii. 6, "Arise, O Lord, in thine anger"; xii. 5, "Now will I arise, saith the Lord." **assert**, 'vindicate,' 'establish,' cf. *P. L.* vi. 157, quoted above (l. 464).

468. Dagon must stoop. Although these lines certainly refer to the catastrophe, it is probable that Milton had also in his mind an incident outside the action of the piece, narrated in 1 *Sam.* v. 2, 3, "When the Philistines took the Ark of God, they brought it into the house of Dagon, and set it by Dagon. And when they of Ashdod arose early on the morrow, behold Dagon was fallen upon his face to the earth before the ark of the Lord."

469. discomfit, 'discomfiture,' 'defeat'; cf. Shak. 2 *Henry VI.* v. 2. 86, "Incurable discomfit reigns."

470. trophies, 'moral causes of triumph rather than any material tokens of victory (such as Samson's hair).' The "*ph*" is a misspelling that passed into English from the Fr. *trophée*, derived from the Gr. τροπαῖον, a memorial of victory (τροπή 'a putting to flight,' τρέπω 'to turn').

471. confusion, 'destruction': the word had formerly a stronger meaning than now. Cf. *P. L.* ii. 996, "With ruin upon ruin, rout on rout, | Confusion worse confounded"; *Is.* xxiv. 10, "The city of confusion" (doomed to destruction'); Hall's *Chronicle* (quoted by Wright), "Kyng Rycharde perceivyng them armed, knewe well that they came to his confusion." **blank**, 'to make pale,' frequently used as an adj., *e.g.*, *Comus*, 452, "Blank awe"; *P. L.* ix. 890, "Adam ... astonied stood and blank." *P. R.* ii. 120, "Solicitous and blank he thus began." The verb occurs in Shak. *Hamlet*, iii. 2, "Each opposite that blanks the face of joy." The word is derived from O.H.G. *blinchen*, 'to shine,' and is cognate with 'bleak,' 'blink,' 'blench,' but different from 'black,' although in A.S. the two are distinguished only by the accent.

473. prophecy. Josephus (*Antiq.* v. 8. 4) says of Samson, "it appeared evidently that he would be a prophet." Samson here fulfils that function more literally than the passage has been interpreted to mean Examples are numerous in classical literature of the belief in omens drawn as here from spoken words. Æneas accepts the omen of words spoken in jest by his son Iulus (Virg. *Aen.* vii.); the seer Teiresias prophesies in angry words the impending blindness of Œdipus (Soph. *Œd. Tyr.*); and muttering voices presage his end (*Œd. Col.*); Clytaemnestra's dream is interpreted by the Chorus in prophetic words as a presage of coming retribution (*Elect.*). The taking of omens from spoken words was not unknown to the Jews ; see 1 *Sam.* xiv. 1-14.

477. doubtful, predicative—' to be or to remain doubtful.' **God,** *i.e.* ' Our God,' ' Jehovah,' as he announced his name to be to Moses (*Exod.* vi. 3). **Lord,** 'supreme.'

478-540. *The Chorus could only offer counsel. The father brings something more substantial—namely, a proposal of ransom for his son. (This incident not only serves to bring out the loving, active, practical character of Manoah, but is a skilful contrivance for heightening the pathos of the tragic end ; for Samson dies just when his father has all but succeeded in carrying his purpose through). But Samson's spirit that had flashed forth in prophesying the triumph of God over Dagon, droops and sinks when his own interests are concerned, and he despairingly tells his father that he is unworthy of ransom. Manoah reproves him and points out that the sin of pride and ' over-justice' underlies his self-abandonment. Samson replies that life has ceased to have any attraction for him, and again recurs to the constant theme of his past folly.*

479. forgot, ' forgotten ' ; this use of the past tense for the past participle is common in Elizabethan English ; see Abbott, § 343. It arose as follows :—The A.S. past pt. was formed by prefixing *ge-* to all verbs (weak or strong) and affixing *-en* to strong, and *-ed* to weak verbs, with or without a vowel change. In M.E. the prefix *ge-* was weakened into *i-* or *y-*, and altogether dropped in the northern dialect ; while the suffix *-en* was weakened to *-ë* and then to *-e* (silent) in the southern and midland dialects. The past pt. thus mutilated sometimes corresponded with the form of the past tense as in ' forgot' here, and sometimes with that of the infinitive as in 'forsake,' l. 629, or ' take.' In both cases the form of the past tense was used for the past pt. For 'take'; cf. *Comus*, 558, "Silence was took ere she was ware."

481. made way, ' made my way,' ' obtained access to'; in modern prose ' made way' would mean 'progressed ' (as a ship).

482. with whom : a Latinism for ' with them ' ; see l. 444.

483. by this, see l. 266, n.

484. utmost of revenge, ' utmost feelings of revenge'; for this use of the adj. for the subst. cf. l. 1153 ; *P. R.* iv. 535, "To the utmost of mere man."

485. pains, ' punishments,' see l. 105, n. **slaveries,** ' tasks performed by slaves.' The common distinction is that the abstract singular means the condition or state, the plural, the various actions incident to it.

487. Spare, ' waste not,' ' forbear from '; cf. Shak. *Wint. Tale,* iii. 2. 92, "Spare your threats " ; *M. N. D.* ii. 1. 142, "I will spare your haunts."

489. pay on, 'continue to suffer'; a Latinism like '*pendere poenas*,' '*solvere poenas*.'

492. Secrets of *men*. A contrast is here meant with God's "holy secret," l. 497 ; similarly **the secrets of a friend**, of one equal in rank, are contrasted with "God's counsel" entrusted to his humble servant.

493. had, potential, 'would have.' **fact**, 'act,' lit. 'what is done' (Lat. *factum*), see l. 736 ; cf. *P. L.* ii. 457, "Bloody fact," ii. 124, "Fact of arms." 'Fact' here is a superfluous nominative.

494. The grammar here is defective, as it often is in Milton when the sense is clear. Grammatically 'deserving contempt and scorn' refers to '**fact**,' but the sense requires 'excluded' and 'avoided' to refer to the *person*, although both adjs. are co-ordinate with 'deserving.' By *attraction* this last adj. may also be made to refer to the person. Milton had, no doubt, the Latin construction in mind, where the transition from the act to the actor would have been indicated by a corresponding transition from the *neut.* gerundive pt. (-*dum*) to the *masc.* (-*dus*). A similar transition occurs in ll. 500, 501. **excluded** ; the modern constr. 'excluded *from*' is, strictly, a *pleonasm*, (for *ex-*=from).

495. avoided. Perhaps Milton alludes to *Prov.* xvii. 12, "Let a bear robbed of her whelps meet a man, rather than a fool in his folly."

496, 497. The lines are printed as in the text of the first two editions ; giving an iambic tetrameter in the first, and an Alexandrine hypermetric in the second line. Warton transferred **But I** from the second to the first line, thus making l. 496 an iambic pentameter, and l. 497 an iambic pentameter hypermetric. Both readings stand on good grounds :—That in the text by lengthening the line makes the mind dwell upon Samson's anguish at the thought : Warton's, by bringing in the terminal pause after "But I," brings out strongly the contrast between Samson and the less guilty betrayer of mere human secrets. The constr. in l. 496 is "how deserving the mark of fool (to be) set, etc." The nom. absol. constr. would be very feeble here. There are two references to Scripture combined in this passage : for the 'fool' as a 'blab' cf. *Prov.* x. 8, "A prating fool shall fall" ; xxix. 11, "A fool uttereth all his mind." In **mark** Milton was perhaps thinking of those that had received the "mark of the beast" "on their forehead" (*Rev.* xiv. 11, xx. 4), and who were visited with the first "vial of the wrath of God" (*Rev.* xvi. 2). "The mark of Cain" (*Gen.* iv. 15), and "The mark upon the foreheads of the men that sigh" (*Ezek.* ix. 4) have a different signification. **front**, 'forehead,' like Lat. *frons*, cf. *P. L.* iv. 300, "His fair large front."

497. kept, 'kept secret' ; cf. the expression "to keep one's own counsel."

500. A covert anachronism. The allusion is to the story of Tantalus (Ovid, *Ars. Am.* ii. 603), who for his garrulity in revealing the secrets of Zeus was punished with a raging thirst while immersed in water, which receded from his lips whenever he attempted to drink ("Garrulus in media Tantalus aret aqua," "Tantalus for his blabbing is parched with thirst while in the midst of water"), while a rock suspended overhead ever threatened to fall and crush him (Eur. *Orest.* 6). **parable,** 'fable,' 'allegory,' lit. 'narration,' 'comparison' (Gr. παρά, 'by the side of,' βάλλω, 'to throw'). The word is a doublet of 'parley,' l. 403.

501. Abyss, Hades, or the lowest part of it, Tartarus. **pains,** see l. 485, n. **confined,** grammatically agrees with 'sin,' but in sense with 'sinner' inferred from it. The constr. is a *synesis;* see l. 494, n.

502. contrite, Latin accent; lit. 'crushed in spirit': Lat. *tero,* 'to bruise.'

503. 'Be not an agent in afflicting thyself.'

505. bids, *sc.* 'thee do so,' *i.e.* 'to avoid it.'

508. penal forfeit, lit. 'the fine imposed as a punishment,' hence 'the punishment itself'; cf. 'debt,' l. 313, from Low Lat. *forisfactum,* 'trespass,' lit. 'an acting beyond limits' (*foris,* 'out of doors,' *facio,* 'to do').

509. quit ... debt, 'release thee from the debt due to him.' **thee,** dat. 'to thee.' **quit,** 'remit,' cf. Shak. *Com. of Err.* i. 1. 23, "Quit the penalty"; *Mer. of Ven.* iv. 1. 381, "Quit the fine." 'Quit' has the sense of 'pay,' 'be released from,' in *P. L.* iv. 51, "Quit | The debt immense of endless gratitude." The word is derived from the same root as 'quiet' and 'quite,' and was originally an adj. meaning 'at rest.' 'free,' occurring in the *Ancren Riwle* (1210), and *Rob. of Gl.* (1298) (Skeat), and Chaucer (*Seconde Nonnes Tale,* "Goon al quit"); it occurs as a verb in M.E. poems of 1240 in the expression "quyten hire ale"; so in Chaucer (*Monkes Tale* "Hir cost for to quyte," *Tale of Gamelym* "Quitte hem his dette"); cf. the expr. 'quit rent,' 'we are quits.' Hence, in l. 1709, the derived meaning of 'discharging one's duty.'

512. The contrast between the characters of Samson and David is strongly brought out here. David *did* implore mercy (2 *Sam.* xii.).

513. self rigorous, 'judging himself rigorously.'

514. Which, *i.e.* 'which course of conduct.' **argues,** 'proves'; for this meaning and the omission of 'to be' cf. l. 1193; *P. L.* iv. 830, "Not to know me argues yourself unknown"; *ib.* 949, "To say and straight unsay ... argues no leader, but a liar traced." The lit. meaning is 'to make clear,' Lat. *arguo* (root ARG, whence *argentum,* 'silver,' 'the shining metal').

515. *i.e.* 'For having offended his own sense of pride (through his failure) than for having offended God (by his disobedience).'

516, 517. The constr. is 'reject not then those offered means which, who knows but God, etc.' This peculiar use of 'what' as a compound relative, where we should expect it to be used as the indefinite 'whatever,' points to a confusion with another constr.—'reject not then *whatever* offered means God hath (*for all that we know*) set, etc.' **set before us**, 'placed within our reach.' **return**, lit. 'turn back,' hence 'render back,' 'restore'; cf. *P. R.* iv. 374, "I found thee there, | And thither will return thee"; Spenser *F. Q.* ii. 3, 19, "Ne ever backe retourned eie"; Lydgate, *Storie of Thebes*, "Whilys that I retourne ageyn my style unto the king." The modern intransitive meaning 'to come or go back' is derived from the intermediate reflexive use, as in *P. L.* iv. 906, "Satan ... | And now returns him from his prison scaped."

518. **sacred house**, 'the Tabernacle.' The Temple was not yet built. Samson at Gaza was of course precluded from exercising the public rites of his religion.

520. **renewed**, *sc.* 'in place of those that he had violated.'

525. **exploits**, accent on the stem (not on the prefix as now); so accented also in l. 32.

526. **instinct**, 'impulse,' Latin accent and meaning ; cf. Shak. *Rich. III.* ii. 3, "By a divine instinct men's minds mistrust | Ensuing dangers." Used as an adj. 'animated' in *P. L.* ii. 937, xi. 562.

528. **sons of Anak**, 'the Anakim,' see l. 148, n. The Hebrew spies sent to 'search the land,' reported that they felt themselves to be 'grasshoppers' before these giants (*Numb.* xiii. 33); "Who can stand before the children of Anak?" was the common saying (*Deut.* ix. 2). **blazed**, 'proclaimed aloud'; cf. Spenser, *F. Q.* i. 11. 7, "That I this man of God his godly armes may blaze"; ii. 9. 25, "Bablers of folly and blazers of crime." The derivation from the same root as 'blare,' 'blast,' 'blow,' is shown in Chaucer, *House of Fame*, iii. "With his blake clarion | He gan to blasen out a soun as lowde | As bloweth wynde in helle;" (Skeat). Hence is derived 'blazon.'

529. **petty god**, 'demi-god,' 'hero.' The notion is more Greek than Jewish.

530. **of**, 'by'; cf. *P. L.* v. 878, "Forsaken of all good."

531. **hostile ground**, 'the country of my enemies,' cf. l. 343. **my affront**, 'to face me'; the subst. occurs in Shak. *Cymb.* v. 3. 87, "There was a fourth man, in a silly habit, that gave the affront with them"; Ben Jonson, *Alchemist* (Gifford, iv. 51), "This day thou shalt have ingots ; and to-morrow give lords th' affront"; used of a friendly meeting in Greene's *Tu Quoque* (Dodsley, vii. 78), "Sir, this I must caution you of, in your

affront or salute, never to move your hat." For the use of the word as a verb, see *P. L.* i. 391 ; Shak. *Haml.* iii. 1. 31.

533. **venereal trains**, 'artifices of love'; cf. l. 932 ; *P. L.* xi. 624, "To the trains and to the smiles of these fair atheists"; Shak. *Macb.* iv. 3. 118, "Devilish Macbeth | By many of these trains hath sought to win me"; Spenser, *F. Q.* ii. 1. 4, "With cunning traynes him to untrap unwares." From Lat. *traho*, 'to draw,' through Fr. *trainer.* From Cotgrave the meaning seems to be, originally, 'something drawn or spread out,' 'a snare.'

534. **Softened**, 'rendered effeminate.'

535. The constr. is 'I fell ... *so as* at length to lay,' the inf. 'to lay' depending on 'I fell,' l. 532. The modern constr. would be 'I fell ... *so that* at length *I laid.*' **head and hallow'd pledge**; *hendiadys* for 'the hallowed pledge of my head.' So Cymochles lays his head on the lap of Phaedria (Spenser, *F. Q.* ii. 6), and Rinaldo on that of Armida (Tasso, *Ger. Lib.* xvi.).

536. **lascivious** by *hypallage*, qualifying 'concubine.'

537. **shore me**; see l. 439, n.

538. The scathing self-contempt conveyed by this simile will be remarked by the reader.

541–605. *The Chorus observing that Manoah's efforts are fruitless, try to draw Samson out of his despondency by recalling his virtues as a set-off against his one failing, upon which he has so repeatedly dwelt; but in vain:—Samson replies that it is better for him to work for his bread in captivity, than to live the life of a drone in inglorious freedom ; and that, captive or free, life, now that it has ceased to be useful to his nation and religion, has no charms for him. Hereupon Manoah, who had in the case of his wife seen the power of God turn her barrenness into fertility, reminds his son that the same power can restore his eyesight, if it pleases,— for why else has God permitted his miraculous strength to return to him ? To this Samson in the most deeply affecting words, replies— he has no hope—he feels death to be near. Manoah seeing that words are of no avail, departs to see what action can do (namely in the matter of the ransom). He commends Samson, meanwhile, to the care of the Chorus.*

543. **dancing ruby**, 'red sparkling wine'; cf. *Comus,* 673, "Behold this cordial julep here | That flames and dances in his crystal bounds"; *P. L.* v. 633, "And rubied nectar flows in pearl." The allusion, perhaps, is to *Prov.* xxiii. 31, "Look not upon the wine when it is red, when it giveth its colour in the cup." **ruby** lit. means 'red,' which is one of Homer's epithets for wine, οἶνος ἐρυθρὸς, *Od.* ix. 163.

545. *Judges,* ix. 13, "Wine which cheereth god and man." Milton changes 'god' into 'gods' to make the allusion to the demi-

gods or heroes clearer. Keightley says that *Elohim*, 'gods,' often means 'great men' in Hebrew, so that 'gods and men' would mean 'high and low.'

546. crystalline, 'clear as glass'; accent on the second syllable; cf. *P. L.* vii. 271, "Crystalline ocean."

547. fresh current, 'current of fresh water' as opposed to a 'stagnant pool.'

548. eastern ray, 'rising sun.' **Against**, 'towards,' so as to meet and flash back the rays of the morning sun. The reference here is to the 'holy waters' that Ezekiel saw in vision, and to his Guide's description of their virtue. *Ezek.* xlvii. 1, "Behold waters issued out from under the threshold of the house *eastward*"; ib. 8, "These waters issue out towards the east country and go down into the desert, and go into the sea: which being brought forth into the sea, *the waters shall be healed*"; ib. 9, "And everything shall live whither the river cometh." I owe to Mr. Tawney the following apposite references: Burton, *Anat. of Mel. II.* ii. 1. 1, "Rain water is purest ... next to it fountain water that riseth in the east, and runneth eastward, from a quick running spring"; Wirt Sikes (*British Goblins*, iv. 2), speaking of mystic wells, says, "Formerly and indeed until within a few years past no water would do for baptizing but that fetched from the Ffynon Mair, though it were a mile or more from the church. That the water flowed southward was in some cases held to be a secret of its virtue. In other instances wells which opened and flowed *eastward* were thought to afford the purest water." This beautiful picture of Samson's attention being first attracted by the flashing of the water in the rays of the *morning* sun is meant to contrast with the 'dancing ruby sparkling outpour'd' that cheers the *night* revels of wassailers. The fine imagery of this and the next line forms, in the mouth of the Nazarite, what may be called the glorification of water-drinking, before which the Chorus's praise of wine sounds faint and common-place. For the sake of effect Milton has made a slight sacrifice of truth in associating thirst with the morning. Todd quotes from Tasso, *Del Mondo Creato*, iii. 8.

549. ethereal, 'celestial,' 'pure'; cf. *P. L.* i. 285, "Ethereal temper," v. 418, "Ethereal fires," Sir T. Browne, *Christian Morals*, ii. 7, "Ethereal particles and diviner portion of man." From Greek αἰθήρ, 'the upper air' (αἴθω 'I burn'). **fiery rod**, 'the rays of the sun.' Dunster quotes Eur. *Suppl.* 652, λαμπρὰ μὲν ἀκτὶς ἡλίου κανὼν σαφὴς ἔβαλλε γαῖαν, "The sun's bright beam, like to a glowing rod, shot o'er the earth"; cf. also *Comus*, 340, "Long-levell'd rule of streaming light." **touch**, Milton perhaps has in mind the rod of Moses with which he struck the rock at Rephidim, causing water to flow (*Exod.* xvii.). Samson implies that even the humble needs of his daily life were the special care of Providence, as on one occasion particularly narrated ; see l. 581, n.

550. milky juice, 'clear fluid,' so in *P. L.* v. 306, "Milky stream" means 'water.' The expression 'juice' keeps up comparison closer between water and wine.

551. refreshed. The construction is either (1) 'refreshed myself' (co-ordinate with 'drank') or (2) 'being refreshed' (co-ordinate with 'allaying thirst'). **nor ... grape.** Cf. Ovid, *Met.* xv. 322, "(Clitorio) quicunque sitim de fonte levâret | Vina fugit, gaudetque meris abstemius undis." *Grape* used here for 'wine,' as 'liquor' indicates; so in Ovid, *Fasti* v., *racemus* is used for 'wine.'

552. turbulent liquor, *hypallage* for 'liquor causing turbulence in those that drink of it,' as opposed to water which 'refreshes.'

553. use of ... drinks, *sc.* 'to be.'

555. with these forbidden, 'the use of these being forbidden.'

556. compare, 'comparison.' Cf. *P. L.* vi. 705, "Power above compare"; i. 588, "Beyond compare of mortal prowess."

558. temperance, 'restraint of the appetites.' **this,** 'in this particular respect,' 'with regard to this one appetite.' This older and wider meaning of 'temperance' is illustrated in the second book of the *Faery Queene*, where Sir Guyon, who represents this virtue, resists the temptations of the World (in the cave of Mammon), the Flesh (in Acrasia's bower), and the Devil (in the siege of the castle of the Soul).

560. boots, 'profits,' 'avails,' from the same root as 'bet' (older form of 'better'). The word was originally a subst. 'bote,' 'help,' 'remedy,' frequent in A.S., whence the M.E. verb 'bêtan' 'to amend,' 'make better'; the subst. reappears in the modern expression 'to boot,'—'for the advantage,' 'to the good.'

562. Effeminately, 'through effeminacy,' in the sense it has in l. 410.

563. For this heaping up of epithets cf. ll. 366, 417. **quelled,** 'crushed,' 'destroyed'; used, as here, of an individual in Shak. *M. N. D.* v. 1. 292. "Quail, crush, conclude and quell!"; Spenser, *F. Q.* ii. 2. 20, "The scorned life to quell."

564. To what, 'to what purpose,' 'for what.'

565. work, governed by 'serve' understood, which by *zeugma* means 'perform.'

566. But to sit idle, grammatically depending upon 'serve' or 'be useful,' understood in an ironical sense.

567. burdenous. Cf. Shak. *Rich. II.* ii. 1. 260, "Burdenous taxation." **A drone,** 'an idler.' Cf. for the metaphor *P. L.* vii. 490, "The female bee that feeds the husband drone"; and

Plato, *Rep.* viii. 7, ὡς ἐν κηρίῳ κηφὴν ἐγγίγνεται σμήνους νόσημα, οὕτω καὶ τὸν τοιοῦτον (τὸν ἀναλωτὴν) ἐν οἰκίᾳ κηφῆνα ἐγγίγνεσθαι, νόσημα πολέως, "As the drone grows up in the hive to be the plague of the bees, so also does such a man [one who is only a consumer of the resources of the state] grow up as a drone in his house, to be the plague of the state." The word is the same as 'drone,' 'a humming sound' ("the drone of a Lincolnshire bag-pipe"). **visitants**, 'visitors.' Cf. *P. L.* xi. 225, "While the great visitant approached."

568. **redundant,** 'flowing.' This adj. with the Fr. term. '*ant*' occurs again in *P. L.* ix. 503, "Floated redundant" (of the folds of the serpent's body), and with the Saxon term. '*ing*' in *P. L.* ii. 889, "Cast forth redounding smoke." Cf. Spenser, *F. Q.* i. 3. 8, "Redounding teares," from Lat. *red* (*re*), 'back,' *undo*, 'to flow.' This is the first indication in the drama that Samson's hair has grown again to something like its former luxuriant growth (*Judges*, xvi. 22). The next two lines imply that his miraculous strength has returned with his locks. The two circumstances prepare us for Manoah's utterance in ll. 588, 589.

569. **Robustious,** 'strong.' The allied meaning of 'sturdy,' 'violent,' occurs in Shak. *Hamlet*, iii. 2. 10, "A robustious peri-wig-pated fellow"; *Henry V.* iii. 7. 159, "Robustious and rough coming on." Samson's locks are 'robustious' in the sense that they are a sign of (recovered) strength. Cf. 'boisterous,' l. 1164, and see l. 1354, n.

570. **Vain monument,** 'vain,' because Samson never hopes to exercise this strength again; 'monument,' because they are merely a memorial of past exploits, and not a pledge of future achievements. Samson gives expression to sentiments bearing the strongest possible contrast to Manoah's hopeful utterances, ll. 588, 589.

571. **craze,** 'break down.' Cp. *P. L.* xii. 210, "And craze their chariot-wheels"; Shak. *Rich. III.* iv. 4. 17, "So many miseries have crazed my voice"; Spenser, *F. Q.* iii. 9. 26, "Her crased helth"; Chaucer, *Chanouns Yemannes Tale*, "I am ryght siker that the pot was crased." This word and 'crush,' and Fr. *écraser* are from a Norse root.

572. The placing of an adjective on each side of the noun qualified is in imitation of classical usage.

574. **draff,** 'refuse.' Cf. *P. L.* x. 630, "To lick up the draff and filth"; Shak. 1 *Henry IV.* iv. 2. 38, "From eating draff and husks"; Chaucer, *Persones Tale*, "Why should I sowen draf out of my fist?" The word is as old as Layamon's *Brut* (1205). **servile food,** 'food such as is given to slaves.'

578. **annoy,** 'hurt,' 'injure,' used in a much stronger sense than it is now. Cf. *P. R.* iii. 365, "By invasion to annoy their

country "; Wyclif, *Judith*, xvi. 7, "The Lord Almyghti anoyede hym"; *Mark*, xvi. 18, "And if thei drynke ony venym, it schal not noye hem"; Chaucer, *Man of Lawes Tale*, "Anoyeth neither see, ne land, ne tree." Prof. Skeat discards the old derivation from Lat. *noceo*, 'to hurt,' and substitutes Lat. *in odio* (habere), 'to hold in hatred,' whence Fr. *ennui*.

579. **bed-rid**, 'confined to one's bed.' This is the correct form of the word, from M.E. 'bed-rida' (*bed*, and *ridda* 'a rider'). Cf. *Piers Plowman*, vii. 101, "Blynde and bedered." The modern corrupt form 'bedridden' occurs in Hampole's *Pricke of Conscience* (1340), "For when he is seke and bedreden lys." This term -*en* (which is not that of the past participle), Mr. Oliphant explains to be that of the agent, like the term -*a*, meaning 'one,' and compares 'thu gionga' = 'thou young un.'

581-583. *Judges*, xv. 19, "And he was sore athirst, and called on the Lord ... but God clave an hollow place that was in the jaw, and there came water thereout." The marginal reading for 'jaw' is *Lehi*, and means the *place* of that name. Chaucer, however (*Monkes Tale*), takes 'jaw' literally, and says, "And of this asses cheke, that was dreye, | *Out of the wang-toth* ('grinder') sprang anon a welle" (3233, 4). He has the authority of the *Vulgate* on his side. **battle**, rather the 'slaughter' at Ramoth-lehi; see l. 145. **brunt**, the word usually means 'shock' of battle. It may well be taken here in its literal sense of 'heat' of battle, from Icel. *bruni*, 'heat,' Eng. 'burn.'

583. **easy**, adv., as in the expression 'his honours sit easy on him.'

584. **spring**, the word embodies a metaphor from 'a fountain,' l. 581.

586. **me**, reflex. 'myself.' **so**, 'that it will be so.'

588, 589. These lines forward the action by raising expectation of *some* great exploit Samson is destined yet to perform. He does perform a great exploit, but one whose tragic end was not dreamt of when these words were spoken. This mode of raising expectation in order partly to fulfil and partly to disappoint it, is frequently resorted to by Sophocles, and is called after him the *Irony of Sophocles*. **not for naught**, a play upon words (*paronomasia*). **frustrate**, 'rendered fruitless.' Cf. *P. R.* i. 180, "Be frustrate all ye stratagems of hell"; *P. L.* ix. 944, "So God shall ... be frustrate"; Shak. *Temp.* iii. 3. 10, "Frustrate search"; Hooker, *Eccl. Pol.* i. 11. 4, "It is an axiom of nature that natural desire cannot utterly be frustrate." The modern pt. adj. 'frustrat*ed*' has a double or pleonastic term., '-*at*' and '-*ed*.'

590-598. The deep pathos of these lines, and their touching application to Milton himself, make this the most affecting passage in the drama.

590. **All,** adv. ' quite,' ' entirely.'

591. **dark,** ' darkened,' ' blind.'　Tasso conversely uses blind '
for ' dark ' ;　*Ger. Lib.* iv. 3, " L' aer cieco."　**treat,** ' converse '
(metaphorically), ' be open to the sensation of.'　The lit. sense of
' converse ' occurs in *P. L.* ii. 588, " And now of love they treat " ;
Wyclif, *Mark*, ix. 32, " What tretiden ye in the weie ? " (A.V.
" What disputed ye among yourselves by the way ? ") ; Lat.
tractare, to handle, *trahere*, to draw.

592. **light of life,** see l. 90, n.　The ' of ' is appositive ; ' the
other light which is life ' ; see Abbott, § 172.

593. **double darkness,** namely blindness and death.

595, 596.　Prof. Masson compares Shak. *Haml.* i. 2. 133, "How
weary, stale, flat and unprofitable seems to me all the uses of this
world," and draws attention to the singularly sorrowful cadence
of the last five lines of this speech, and the deep melancholy of
the last line.

598. **with them that rest,** cf. *Job*, iii. 17, "There the wicked
cease from troubling, and there the weary be at rest " ; Soph.
Trach. 1173, τοῖς γὰρ θανοῦσι μόχθος οὐ προσγίγνεται, "For the dead
rest secure from toils."

599. **suggestions,** ' promptings' in a bad sense, as in Shak. *Macb.*
i. 3. 135, " Why do I yield to that suggestion whose horrid image
doth unfix my hair?"　*Lear*, ii. 1. 75, "I 'ld turn it all to thy
suggestion, plot and damn'd practice."

600. **humours black**, ' melancholy.'　According to the physi-
ology of those days set forth in the Induction to Ben Jonson's
Every Man out of His Humour, the human body contained four
humours—choler, melancholy, phlegm, and blood—continually
flowing through it.　The due tempering of these constituted per-
fect health, and the preponderance of any one of them rendered a
man's disposition ' humorous.'　Samson's despondency, says
Manoah, is the ' humorousness ' caused by the preponderance of
' melancholy ' or ' black bile ' (the *atra bilis* of Celsus).　How this
was brought about is shown by Burton, *Anat. of Mel.* quoted
by Todd : " ...The *mind itselfe* by those darke obscure grosse
fumes ascending from *black humors*, is in continual darknesse,
fear and sorrow ; divers terrible monstrous *fictions* in a thousand
shapes and apparitions occurre...by which the braine and *phantasy*
are troubled and eclipsed."　Dunster quotes the similar language
of Oceanus to his nephew Prometheus, Æsch. *Prom. Vinct.* 333-335.

602. **timely,** ' taken early ' ; cf. *Comus*, 970, "Heaven hath
timely tried their youth"; Shak. *Com. of Err.* i. 1. 139, " Happy
were I in my timely death " ; Greene, *Friar Bacon and
Friar Bungay* (Dodsley, viii. 198), " For timely ripe is rotten,
too too soon."　Milton (*Death of Fair Infant*) uses ' timelessly'
for ' too early.'

604. or how else, 'or however else,' *i.e.* 'by whatever other means' (it can be prosecuted); the modern prose constr. would be 'or by any other means.' For this Latin use of the interrogative for the indefinite in a subordinate clause, see Abbott, § 46.

605. healing words, cf. *P. L.* ix. 290, "To whom with healing words Adam replied." Todd refers to Eur. *Hippol.* 478, εἰσὶν δ' ἐπῳδαὶ καὶ λόγοι θελκτήριοι, "Know there are charms and healing words (to cure this sickness of the soul)"; cf. also Æsch. *Eum.* 846, γλώσσης ἐμῆς μείλιγμα καὶ θελκτήριον, "The soothing and healing powers of my tongue"; *Prom. Vinct.* 386 (quoted in n. to l. 184).

606-651. *In this Promethean outburst of suffering Samson uses the language of bodily torment suggested by Manoah's parting words, but his thoughts run upon the agonies of mind and spirit. His disease is "despair and sense of Heaven's desertion." The greater part of this speech, like that portion of the first in which he bewails his blindness, is in Irregular metre, used where strong passion has to be portrayed (and not for fear of "growing tedious to the reader," as Thyer strangely says). In the latter part of the speech Samson agains reverts to the story of his cruel fate, evidently unable to tear himself away from the subject, and concludes with a prayer for speedy death—a prayer granted almost immediately.*

609. reins; the word is less commonly used now than in 16th and 17th century English (*e.g.* in the *A. V.*).

610, 611. A rhymed couplet. **inmost mind,** a Latinism for 'inmost parts of the mind.'

612, 613. his, 'its,' antecedent 'torment.' **her,** 'its,' antecedent 'mind.' The different genders here are due partly to grammar (in Lat. *tormentum* is neut., and *mens* fem.) and partly to sense, 'torment' and 'mind' being agent and patient—the wild beast and its prey. 'His' grammatically is neut. as it is in M. E. and A. S.; but in the metaphor it is masc **accidents,** 'symptoms,' cf. Bacon, *Adv. of L.* ii. 10. 2, "The diseases themselves with the accidents." The word literally means 'property,' 'something that befalls or accompanies.' The medical significa- tion of the word can be traced to this meaning, through its signification in logic In the Aristotelian logic *Ens* or *Being* was distinguished as *Ens per se* or Substance, and *Ens per accidens* or Accident or Property, of which there were nine; these with Substance making up the Ten Categories under which things could be predicated. On this doctrine Milton made an ingenious Allegory in the English part of his *Vacation Exercise,* in the course of which Ens, the father, tells his eldest son, Substance, that he "should still from eyes of mortals walk invisible" (l. 66), and the Sibyl informs Ens that his son, Substance, "shall subject be to many an accident" (l. 74). Sir T. Browne in

speaking of Guardian Angels says that light as visible in the sun
and elements is a "bare accident," but where it subsists alone
"'tis a spiritual substance": "conceive light invisible and that
is a spirit." These two references help to explain 'accident' in
the text:—'Torment' in itself is 'substance,' invisible, without
manifestation : but when it puts forth its 'accidents' or pro-
perties, and preys upon the spirit of man, it then becomes visible
in its effects, manifests itself in pain inflicted.

614. **entrails,** 'inward parts,' Low Lat. *intralia* (*intra*, 'within.')

615, 616. 'Mental anguish resembles bodily pain, but is
sharper, and unlike the latter is not *located* in the body.'
answerable, 'corresponding,' 'similar.' **corporal sense** implies
that bodily pains are 'localized,' that is, diffused all over the
body or felt in some particular part of it.

620. **wounds,** *sc.* 'of the body.' **immedicable,** 'incurable.'
Todd quotes Ovid, *Met.* x. 189, "immedicabile vulnus."

621, 622. The same sense is here repeated in different words
for the sake of emphasis, as in l. 631. **Rankle,** lit. 'to grow
rank' or 'foetid,' is the same as *fester* (etym. doubtful).
gangrene is the Greek word equivalent to the Lat. *mortification*.
Note the harsh rhythm of these two lines.

624. **apprehensive,** 'able to seize or apprehend impressions';
cf. Shak. *Jul. Caes.* iii. 1. 67, "And men are flesh and blood and
apprehensive"; Fisher, *Fuimus Troes* (Dodsley, vii. 430),
"Grateful revenge, whose sharp-sweet relish fats my apprehensive soul." The word here refers to 'susceptibilities'; in
Shak. 2 *Henry IV.* iv. 3. 103, and Beau. and Fl. *Philaster,* v. 1
(Dyce, i. 308), it refers to 'intelligence.' **apprehensive tenderest
parts,** 'the most sensitive part of my mind.'

627. **méd'cinal,** so accented in *Comus,* 636; and spelt 'medcinal'
repeatedly, according to Todd, in the Prose Works. This is an
instance in which Milton departs from the Latin accent, which
occurs in Shak. *Othello,* v. 2. 351, 'mèdìcìnàl.'

628. **Alp;** common noun, 'a mountain'; cf. *P. L.* ii. 620,
"O'er many a frozen, many a fiery Alp." In Gaelic 'alp' means
'a high mountain' according to Servius, note on Virg. *Georg.* iii.
474 ; so in Silius Italicus *gemini alpes* is 'two mountain ranges.'
Probably from Lat. *albus* 'white,' hence 'snow-capped.' Cf. *P.
L.* iv. 264, "Airs, vernal airs, | Breathing the smell of field and
grove."

629. **forsook;** see note on 'forgot,' l. 479.

630. An Alexandrine ; see l. 146 n.

631, 632. See note on ll. 621, 622.

632. Although there are instances (e.g. *Il Pens.* 54, "contem

platiön ") of Milton's use of the term. ˑᴗᴊon as a dissyllable (as it very frequently is in Spenser), the present is not one. The sense is better echoed by taking the line as one with a broken rhythm—tetrameter catalectic (seven syllables).

634. **His destined,** 'destined to be his,' 'consecrated to him.' **from the womb**; so were Samuel and John the Baptist, 'perpetual Nazarites,' (*Nazaraei nativi*).

635. **message**; by *metonymy* for 'messenger.' The usage is old; cf. Chaucer, *Man of Lawes Tale*, " Geven by Godes message, Makomete"; Early English Allit. Poems, *The Deluge* (1360), " A message from the meyny," said of the raven sent out by Noah.

637. **Abstemious,** 'temperate,' 'abstaining from wine': from Lat. *abs*, from, *temetum*, strong drink. **amain,** 'vigorously,' lit. 'on main'; 'main,' 'strength,' is from the root MAG, whence 'may,' 'might'; the expression 'might and main' (which occurs as early as in the *Tale of Gamelyn*, " Ne had I mayn and might in myn armes ") is pleonastic. The adv. 'amain' is not of very old use. Oliphant traces it back to a play of *circ.* 1530, in Dodsley's Collection.

639. **nerve,** 'strength'; cf. Shak. *Hamlet*, i. 4. 83, " Hardy as the Nemean lion's nerve "; used in the same sense in the pl. in *Comus*, 797, " The brute Earth would lend her nerves."

641. **as never known,** 'as never having distinguished myself in his service.'

643. **provoked,** see l. 466, n.

644. An Alexandrine. **irreparáble,** Latin accent.

645. **repeated**; the constr. here is either (1) adv. 'repeatedly,' or (better) (2) pass. pt., with 'as' understood, meaning 'made again and again.' The otherwise strange omission of 'as' can be accounted for by taking (2) as a *synesis*, the constr. being such as if Milton had used instead of 'repeated' its equivalent in sense, 'made over and over.'

649. **might I,** 'if I might,' subjunctive, not optative.

650. This line adds another link to the chain of the action. The reply to this petition for death is the sudden inspiration Samson feels prompting him to accompany the Officer (ll. 1381 *sq.*). Job in his despair makes a similar petition (*Job*, vi. 9).

651. Cf. Æsch. *Fragm.* ὦ θάνατε παιὰν ... μόνος γὰρ εἶ σὺ τῶν ἀνηκέστων κακῶν ἰατρός; ἄλγος δ' οὐδὲν ἅπτεται νεκρῶν, " O Death the physician ! ... for thou alone art the healer of incurable ills ; no sorrow reaches the dead."

652-709. *The Chorus wisely abstains from inflicting on Samson saws, ancient or modern, in praise of patience, but taking up his despairing cry that God has cast him off* (l. 641), *they find that others, too,—gifted and favoured servants of God—have in the midst of prosperity felt His heavy hand regardless of past services. The gloomy conclusions at which they arrive regarding the justice of God, and the inscrutableness of His ways, find a parallel in the reflections in the earlier part of the Book of Job, and correspond to the unsolved enigma of human life so frequently the subject of the Greek dramatists. But in the case of Samson (as in that of Job) the Christian dramatist does not leave the enigma unsolved, and the Chorus that here bitterly complains that "just or unjust alike seem miserable," at the conclusion of the drama (l. 1749) is made to acknowledge reverentially that "all is best, though oft we doubt." The Chorus concludes with a prayer that the end for which Samson has prayed may be peaceful.*

653. **antient**; for example, the *Consolatory Treatises* of Seneca to his Friends, the *Consolations of Philosophy* of Boethius, the *Consolatory Letter* (Παραμυνθητικὸς) of Plutarch to his Wife. **modern**; for example, the many English translations and adaptations of Boethius from King Alfred's and Chaucer's down to the *Boke of Comfort* (1525); Eccard's *Consolation of the Monks* (12th century), Gerson's *Consolation of Theology* (15th century), both being Latin imitations of Boethius; the *Inconstancy of Fortune*, in French, by Simon du Fresne; Petrarch's *Sonnets and Canzone on Laura's Death*. Of course this Chorus, supposed to have lived somewhere about 1100 B C., could scarcely speak of 'ancient and modern' literature, or call such literature as they possessed 'ample.' It is Milton who really speaks. **enrolled**; books were written on rolls of skin or parchment among the Hebrews; thus Baruch wrote the prophecies of Jeremiah upon a 'roll of a book' (*Jer.* xxxvi. 4). Cf. the Latin word *volumen*, 'volume,' from *volvo*, 'to roll.'

654. Cf. *P. L.* ix. 31, "The better fortitude | Of patience and heroic martyrdom | Unsung." Such was the Stoic doctrine that defined Fortitude or Courage to be "practical wisdom in matters that have to be suffered or endured " (Plut. *Virt. Mor.* ii.).

655. **to**, 'for.'

657. **Consolatories**, 'books professing to afford consolation'; for the word cf. Cic. *ad Att.* xiii. 20 (init.) *literae consolatoriae.* For example see l. 653, n. **writ**, *i.e.* 'are written.'

658. Various constructions have been proposed for this difficult passage:—(1) 'Consolatories are writ and much persuasion is sought'; or (2) 'Consolatories are writ and are sought with much persuasion'; or (3) 'Consolatories are writ with studied argument and with much sought persuasion.' In (1) and (2) 'sought' is a verb, and means 'collected studiously or with pains'; in (3) it is a pt. adj., and means 'far-sought,' 'over-refined,' Fr. *recherché*. I prefer the last constr. **persuasion,**

'persuasive or hortatory arguments.' Milton here borrows the language of Roman rhetoric. He has in view the twofold division of Oratory by Quintilian into '*Controversial*' and '*Suasory*' (*Inst.* ii.), when he distinguishes 'argument' from 'persuasion' in the text, meaning by the one an appeal to the reason, and by the other an appeal to the feelings. This, however, is not quite Quintilian's own distinction. Seneca wrote both *Controversiae* and *Suasoriae*.

659. **Lenient of**, in the Latin sense of 'lenitive of,' 'soothing.' Newton quotes Hor. *Ep.* i. 1. 34, "Sunt verba et voces, quibus hunc lenire dolorem | Possis."

660. **sound**, implies that to the ears of the afflicted they are but empty sound, sound without meaning.

661. **prevails**, 'avails,' 'is of effect.' Cf. Wither, *Fidelia*, "Nor any service may prevail me now"; Shak. 1 *Henry VI.* iii. 1, "I would prevail if prayers might prevail to join your hearts"; Marlowe, *Dido, Queen of Carthage*, v. 1, "What can my tears or cries prevail me now"; Beau. and Fl. *Valentinian* iii. 1, "This prevails not, nor any agony you utter, lady."

661, 662. Thyer quotes from the *Apocrypha* (*Ecclus.* xxii. 6, "A tale out of season is as music in mourning"). **mood**, 'mode,' a musical term which may be popularly rendered by 'key,' each mode having a distinctive character of its own. Thus in *P. L.* i. 550, the "Dorian mood" is mentioned as breathing "deliberate valour"; in *L'All.* 136, we have "soft Lydian airs," this mood being associated with tenderness; Euripides (*Orest.* 1426) and Horace (*Epod.* ix. 5) both speak of the 'barbarian' strains of the Phrygian mode.

667. **what is Man!** Cf. *Heb.* ii. 6, "What is man, that Thou art mindful of him? or the son of man, that Thou visitest him?"; *Ps.* cxliv. 3, "Lord, what is man that Thou takest knowledge of him! or the son of man that Thou makest account of him!"

668. **various**, 'changeful,' 'interchanging adversity and prosperity.' This and the next line make a rhymed couplet.

669. **contrarious**, 'adverse,' 'punishing instead of rewarding merit.' The word occurs in Shak. 1 *Henry IV.* v. 1. 52, "Contrarious winds"; Chaucer, *Legend of Good Women* (Dido), "Sens that the goddes ben contrarious to me." Cf. Eur. *Hel.* 710, ὦ θύγατερ, ὁ θεὸς ὡς ἔφυ τι ποικίλον καὶ δυστέκμαρτον, "O my daughter, how God assigns to different men fortunes as different, and how inscrutable are His ways!"

670. **temperest**, 'regulatest,' 'moderatest.' Cp. *P. L.* x. 77, "Yet I shall temper so justice with mercy"; xi. 361, "To temper joy with fear and pious sorrow." **his short course**, 'man's life on earth.'

671. **evenly,** 'uniformly,' opposed to 'with various hand,' l. 668.

672. **angelic orders.** The hierarchy of the angels is frequently alluded to in Milton. See esp. *P. L.* v. 748, "Seraphim and Potentates and Thrones in their triple degrees." Keightley traces this gradation through Drayton's *Man in the Moon* to Tasso, to Dante, and even to St. Paul. Spenser (*F. Q.* i. 12. 39) alludes to the same gradation under the expression "trinal triplicities" after Aquinas. **creatures mute.** Cf. *Ps.* civ. 24-30, and Sterne's line, "God tempers the wind to the shorn lamb." This line and the next, and the next two lines, make a pair of rhymed couplets.

674. **rout,** see l. 443, n.

676. **summer fly,** 'may-fly,' the ἐφημέριοι of Pindar, Aristophanes, and Æschylus. The expression occurs in Shak. 3 *Henry VI.* ii. 6. 8, "The common people swarm like summer flies"; *Othello*, iv. 2. 66, "As summer flies are in the shambles, that quicken even with blowing."

677. **Heads without name,** 'obscure persons.' Cf. *Liv.* iii. 7, where *ignota capita* is opposed to *clari viri.* 'Caput in Latin, κάρα, κάρηνον, κεφαλή in Greek, are frequently used by *synecdoche* for 'person' (*e.g. carum caput* and φίλη κεφαλή ("dear head") are common forms of addressing persons; πυκνὰ καρήατα, *Il.* xi. 309; κάρηνα Τρώων, *Ib.* 158 ; τοίην κεφαλήν *Od.* i. 343). **no more remembered,** *sc.* 'after they perish.' This expression is very frequent in Homer's *Odyssey* for the 'forgotten dead,' νεκύων ἀμενηνα κάρηνα.

678. With this line commences the allusion to the Puritan Republicans.

680. **To,** 'for the performance of.' Cf. the expression 'to this end.'

681. **in part.** The Monarchy had been overthrown, but the Puritan Republic had not had time to take root. Warburton and Newton worked out the details of the allusions in this and the following lines. See Todd.

683. **Their** by *hypallage* belongs to 'noon.' The allusion is to the ascendancy of the Independent Republican party on the abdication of Richard Cromwell (1659). **noon,** 'fame,' 'great work' (l. 680). **highth of noon,** 'high noon,' 'zenith of their fame.' Todd quotes from Sandys' *Paraphrase of Job,* "When men are from their noon of glory thrown."

684. **thy countenance and thy hand,** 'thy favour and thy gifts.' There is no need to suppose a zeugma in 'changest,' since both words occur in opposite senses in Scripture. Cf. *Ps.* lxxxix. 15, "the light of thy countenance"; *Ps.* lxxx. 16, "The rebuke of thy countenance"; so *Job,* ii. 10, "receive good at the hand of God"; 1 *Sam.* v. 11, "The hand of God was very heavy there."

685, 686. or them, 'or *from* them.' **favours.** The allusion is to the success of Milton's party against the superstition of the Established Church and the tyranny of the Monarchy. **service.** The allusion is to the efforts of that party to establish Independency in religion, and a Republic in politics.

687. remit, in the lit. Latin sense of 'send back,' *sc.* 'to their *former* obscure life.'

688-691, a rhymed stanza. Cf. ll. 303-6.

688, 689. obscured, 'rendered obscure,' *sc.* 'by the withdrawal of the light of Thy countenance,' 'caused to be forgotten.' **which were**, 'which would be,' *sc.* 'if thou didst not throw.' ... **fair dismission**, 'just and merited dismissal.' Cf. Hom. *Od.* xvi. 212, ῥηίδιον δὲ θεοῖσι, τοὶ οὐρανὸν εὐρὺν ἔχουσιν, | ἠμὲν κυδῆναι θνητὸν βροτὸν ἠδὲ κακῶσαι, "'Tis easy for the gods that dwell in the wide heaven, either to honour mortal man or to injure him." Hor. *Od.* i. xxxiv. 12, "Valet ima summis | Mutare et insignem attenuat deus | Obscura promens," "God can raise the lowest to the place of the highest, and He humbles the exalted, and exalts the obscure."

690. Unseemly, 'unbecoming,' because undeserved. Cf. Greek, ἀεικής, similarly used.

691. trespass, 'overstepping the bounds of duty.' **omission**, 'falling short of these bounds,' 'faults of commission and omission.' The allusion in 'trespass' is to the disunion and quarrels among the Puritan leaders, and in 'omission' to their neglect to new-model the law and constitution according to Ludlow's advice.

693. heathen and profane. The members of the Established Church were so in Milton's eyes; see l. 1463, n.

694. carcasses ... prey. Cf. Hom. *Il.* i. 4, αὐτοὺς δὲ ἑλώρια τεῦχε κύνεσσιν οἰωνοῖσί τε πᾶσι, "They (on the battle plain | Unburied lay,) a prey to ravening dogs | And carrion birds." On the anniversary of the execution of Charles I. the remains of Cromwell, Ireton, and Bradshaw were desecrated; see ll. 368-372, n. **captíved**, Latin accent as in l. 33. The allusion is to the trial and condemnation to perpetual imprisonment of Lambert and Martin, two of the Parliamentarian leaders (1662).

695. unjust tribunals. Sir Harry Vane (to whom Milton's fourteenth sonnet is addressed) was brought to trial on a charge of treason, condemned, and executed in 1662, in violation of the spirit of the law, and of the king's pledge to the Convention parliament. **the ungrateful multitude.** Milton's high opinion of what the country owed to Vane may be gathered from his calling him the "eldest son of religion," and one to whom the country owed the "bounds of either sword" (the spiritual and civil power).

697-702. The allusion in these lines is to Milton himself.

699. Painful diseases. Dr. Wright, a clergyman who visited Milton during the last five years of his life, described him as "pale but not cadaverous, his hands and fingers gouty, and with chalk stones." To him Milton "expressed himself to this purpose, that was he free from the pain this gave him, his blindness would be tolerable." (Richardson quoted by Masson.)

700. In crude old age. Dunster pointed out that the expression occurs in Hesiod, *Erga*, 703, ὠμῷ γήραϊ δῶκεν, "Consigns him to premature old age," and Hom. *Od.* xv. 356, ἐν ὠμῷ γήραϊ. **crude,** 'premature,' Latin use as in Statius, *Theb.* ix. 391, "Cruda funera nepotis," "The premature obsequies of a grandchild." Its commoner meaning of 'immature' occurs in *Lycidas*, 3, "Berries harsh and crude."

701. disordinate, 'leading irregular lives,' qualifies 'them' (l. 698).

702. of dissolute days, 'which should only befall those that have lived dissolute lives.' Milton's way of living was sober, whereas gout is a disease common among the intemperate.

703, 704. Sympathy for Samson is the only explanation of this bitter charge against the justice of God. Hurd thought that these lines were not meant "to calumniate Providence, but to soothe the unhappy sufferer." But, if Samson derives any consolation from these lines, it is that of finding another being that has felt as heavily as himself the hand of God. It is not the ideal chorus of Greek dramatic art, but the living and suffering Milton, that here speaks. Cf. for the sentiment Eur. *Suppl.* 226, κοινὰς γὰρ ὁ θεὸς τὰς τύχας ἡγούμενος | τοῖς τοῦ νοσοῦντος πήμασιν διώλεσε | τὸν οὐ νοσοῦντα (var. τὸν συννοσοῦντα) κοὐδὲν ἠδικηκότα, "For round us waits | One common fortune; and full oft the gods | Crush in the ruins of the falling guilty, | Entangled in their fall, the innocent"; Theognis, *Eleg.* 377, πῶς δή σευ Κρονίδη τολμᾷ νόος ἄνδρας ἀλιτρούς | ἐν ταὐτῇ μοίρῃ τόν τε δίκαιον ἔχειν; "How, pray, son of Saturn, canst thou reconcile it to thy sense of right and wrong to treat the wicked and the good in the same way?"

705. So, 'in like manner.'

706. image of thy strength. 'Image' is a very bold epithet for the superhuman strength of Samson; but although applied to the Messiah (*P. L.* iii. 63), it is also applied to Adam (*P. L.* iv. 292). **minister,** 'the servant of God.'

709. This line is also a prayer offered by Milton for himself.

710-731. *The pomp of Delilah's approach attracting notice from far, and the studied gracefulness of her affected sorrow, are a striking contrast to the humiliation and wild grief of Eve when seeking Adam's pardon.* "*But Eve, not so repulsed, with tears that ceased not flowing, and tresses all disordered, at his feet fell humble, and, embracing them, besought his peace.*" P. L. x. 910 sq.

710, 711. thing … it. The neuters imply the difficulty of discerning the person or sex. **what thing of sea or land**? 'what strange or wonderful creature?' The expression occurs in Greek poetry in connection with women, as here; cf. Eur. *Hec.* 1181, (γυναῖκας) … γένος γὰρ οὔτε πόντος οὔτε γῆ τρέφει τοιόνδε, "(Women) …'Tis a breed which neither sea nor land produces the like." Menander, *Fragm.* πολλῶν κατὰ γῆν καὶ κατὰ θάλατταν θηρίων ὄντων, μέγιστόν ἐστι θηρίον γυνή, "Of all wild things on land or in the sea, the greatest is woman."

715. ship Of Tarsus. These ships, frequently mentioned in the Bible (cf. *Is.* ii. 16; *Ezek.* xxvii. 25), were large sea-going vessels like the East-Indiamen before the introduction of steam-ships. Hence the epithet 'stately.' **Tarsus, the Tarshish of Scripture, is** generally identified with Tartessus in southern Spain; but sometimes with a port or country accessible from the Red Sea, probably India, and sometimes with Tarsus in Cilicia in Asia Minor. This last identification is grounded on the statement (*Gen.* x. 4, 5), that the "Isles of the Gentiles" were divided among the sons of Javan, one of whom was Tarshish. Milton adopts it.

716. isles Of Javan, 'islands of the Ionians,' *i.e.* the isles of Greece. 'Javan' is the Gr. Ion, the fabulous ancestor of the Ionians, and grandson of Hellen. **Gadire,** Gr. Γάδειρα, Lat. *Gades,* modern Cadiz. Milton uses the Lat. form in *P. L.* iv. 77.

717. bravery, 'finery.' Cf. *Is.* iii. 18, "The bravery of their tinkling ornaments about their feet"; Ben Jonson, *Every Man in his Humour,* i. 1, "Nor would I you should melt away yourself in flashing bravery"; Beau. and Fl. *Wit at several Weapons,* iv. 1, "(Enter Pompey dressed as a gallant), *Cunn.* How now! ha! what prodigious bravery's this? A most preposterous gallant!"; Bacon, *Essays,* xxxvii. "The glories of them are … in the bravery of their liveries." This was the original meaning of the word. It occurs in Dunbar (1503) as an adv. (a hat is trimmed "richt bravelie"); and still survives in the Lowland Scotch 'braw,' 'fine.' The next meaning was that of 'ostentation,' 'boastfulness,' as in l. 1243. This sense occurs as early as 1548 in Patten (*Arber's English Garner*). Cf. Shak. *Hamlet,* v. 2, 79, "But sure the braverie of his grief did put me into a towering passion." This sense still survives in the phrase 'to brave it out.' The present meaning of 'courageous' occurs as early as in Puttenham's *Art of Poesie* (1585). (The word 'gallant' has run through a similar history.) **tackle trim,** 'all her gear adjusted.' 'Tackle' lit. is what 'takes' or holds the masts, etc., in their proper places. Keightley points out that Milton uses the same simile sarcastically of the bishops in his *Reform in England,* ii. … "to see them (the bishops) under sail, in all their lawn and sarcenet, their shrouds and tackle, with geometrical rhomboides upon their heads."

719. hold them play, 'sport with them,' 'entertain them.
Cf. Shak. *Henry VIII.* v. 4. 90, "I'll find a Marshalsea shall hold
ye play these two months." From the analogy of such passages as
"Hold you a penny" (*Tam. of the Shr.* iii. 2. 85), "Hold me pace"
(1 *Henry IV.* iii. 1. 49), "Hold thee any wager" (*Mer. of Ven.* iii. 4.
62), the constr. is 'hold play to them,' *i.e.* 'offer pleasure to them.'
In A.S. *plega* ('play') means 'pleasure.' The word is from the
same root as the Lat. *plaga*, 'a stroke,' 'blow,' whence 'sword-
play.' (I can find no analogy for taking the constr. here to be
'hold them in play.') **Courted by all the winds.** Todd points
out that this expr. is applied to Eve in the *Adamo* of Pona,
"corteggiata da' venti."

720. amber scent, 'scent of ambergris.' Cf. Beau. and Fl.
The Honest Man's Fortune, iii. 3. "You that smell of amber at
my charge," as a verb ; Id. *The Custom of the Country,* ii. 2, "Be
sure the wines be lusty, high, and full of spirit, and amber'd all."
This perfume is a different thing from the resin amber (electrum),
but both words are of the same derivation (Arabic). In *P. R.* ii.
344, Milton uses "Gris amber," and in *L'All.* 61 ("Amber light"),
and *Comus,* 333 ("Amber cloud"), he uses the word as an adj.
(as here), but as referring to colour.

721. Her harbinger, 'her herald,' 'wafted before her.' Cf.
P. R. i. 71, "Before him a great prophet, to proclaim His coming
is sent harbinger." The original meaning was 'a provider of
lodgings' (harborage), who went before a great man when travelling. His method of procedure is seen in Tomkis's *Albumazar,*
i. 2. (Dodsley, vii. 114), "Love's harbinger hath chalk't upon my
heart, | And with a coal writ on my brain, 'For Flavia.'" The
original spelling is seen in Chaucer, *Man of Lawes Tale,* "By
herbergeours that wenten him biforn." The word is derived from
'harbour' (see l. 459, n.), and the 'n' is adventitious, as in
'messenger.'

722. may seem, 'would seem to be.' The use of 'seem' alone
weakens the assertion, which is further weakened by the
potential.

723. certain, adv. 'certainly'; so 'sure' is now frequently
used as an adv.

725. The *caesura* falls on the third foot, and the fourth is an
anapaest— | 'hèr nòt cóme'|.

726. eyes thee fixed, 'gazes at thee fixedly.' This verb is frequently used in Shakspere. Cf. *Temp.* iii. 1. 40, "Many a lady I
have eyed with best regard."

727. spoke ; see l. 629, n.

728. For this beautiful simile Todd refers to Hom. *Il.* viii.
306, μήκων δ' ὡς ἑτέρωσε κάρη βάλεν, ἥ τ' ἐνὶ κήπῳ | καρπῷ βριθομένη
νοτίῃσί τε εἰαρινῇσιν, "Down sank his head, as in a garden sinks|

A ripened poppy charged with vernal rains." Cf. also Virg. *Æn.*
ix. 436, " Lassove papavera collo | Demisere caput, pluvia cum
forte gravantur," " Or (as when) poppies droop the head from tired
stem, when heavily charged with rain."

729. addressed, 'prepared,' ' made ready ' (for utterance) ; cf.
P. L. vi. 296, "And both for fight addrest unspeakable." Shak.
M. N. D. v. 1. 107, " So please your grace, the Prologue is address'd."
The lit. meaning is ' to direct ' (Lat. *ad, dirigere*) as in *P. L.* ix.
496, "And towards Eve addrest his way." It is the same as the
word ' dress ' (used in this sense by Chaucer, *Clerkes Tale,* " But
to Griseld agayn wol I me dresse ").

731. makes address, ' prepares ' ; see above.

732-765. *Delilah announces her purpose in coming to be ' to see
his face,' ' to make amends,' to offer her services. Contrasted with
the burning anguish of Eve's speech (P. L. x. 914 sq., " Forsake
me not thus, Adam !" sq.), all this has a ring of hollow insincerity
which well deserves the cynicism of Samson's reply. The general
tone of this reply and of Samson's other speeches to Delilah is
strongly Euripidean ; and in particular passages (e.g. ll. 753, 905,
906, 955-957) it descends to undignified sarcasm. The contrast
between the artful persuasiveness of Delilah, and the stern, savage
firmness of Samson, is as remarkable as that between Delilah's
decorous sang froid and Eve's wild passion. It is observable that
Delilah always takes care to palliate her guilt by calling it mere
' rashness ' (l. 746), ' a common female fault ' (l. 777), as due to the
' jealousy of love ' (l. 791), and so forth.*

734. without excuse, ' fully,' ' without having as excuse to
advance.' Join with ' acknowledge ' in next line. Note the
hypocrisy of this : her speeches contain quite a string of excuses.

736. fact, ' act ' ; see l. 493, n.

737. perverse event. ' untoward result ' ; cf. *P. L.* ix. 405,
" Event perverse !" Latin use of ' event,' see l. 1454, n.

738. penance, ' penitence.' The word is now used for the *act*
not for the *feeling,* as here. **pardon,** *sc.* ' is,' understood from the
preceding ' hath.'

742. estate, ' state,' ' condition,' see l. 170 ; cf. *Ps.* cxxxvi. 23,
" Who remembered us in our low estate " ; freq. in Shakspere,
e.g. 3 *Henry VI.* iv. 3. 18, "If Warwick knew in what estate
he stands."

745. The constr. is ' *whatever* amends *it* is in my power,' *sc.*
' to make.' It is necessary to make ' is ' impersonal, as ' amends '
is a true pl., and the sing. is not used in English as it is in
French. The prefix ' *a-* ' is unusual for ' *e-* ' (Lat. *ex-,* ' out of,
mendum,* ' a fault ') : the proper form ' emend ' occurs as a verb
only.

746. in some part, 'in part,' 'partly.' **recompense,** 'compensate for'; cf. *P. L.* iv. 893, "Soonest recompense | dole with delight": lit. 'to repay,' 'requite,' as in *Rom.* xii. 17, "Recompense no man evil for evil."

747. 'The misfortune entailed on you by my deed was greater than the rashness that prompted me to it.' Delilah urges that she never expected so great a misfortune would result from her act, see l. 736. **rash,** 'thoughtlessly imprudent,' as opposed to 'deliberately wicked.'

748. hyæna. Pliny, *Hist. Nat.* viii. 44 *et al.*, gives many instances of this animal's cunning and its power for evil. He says it imitates 'vomitionem hominis' to attract dogs on which it then preys, that dogs are struck dumb when touched by its shadow, that it possesses a certain magical power by which any animal round which it has walked thrice loses the power of motion, and, lastly, that "hee will counterfet man's speech, and comming to the shepheard's cottages, will call one of them forth, whose name he hath learned, and when he hath him without, all to worrie and teare him in peeces" (Holland's transl.). Todd adduces Greene, *Never too Late*, "She weepes with the crocodile, and smiles with the hiena, and flatters with the panther"; and Ben Jonson, *Volpone*, iv. 6, "Out, thou chameleon harlot! now thine eyes vie tears with the hyaena." The word is the Gr. ὕαινα, 'the sow-like animal' (ὗς).

750. Literature, unhappily, abounds with this sentiment; cf. Hom. *Od.* xi. 456, ἐπεὶ οὐκέτι πιστὰ γυναιξίν, "Since there is no faith in women." Aristoph. *Eccl.* 238, αὐταὶ (γυναῖκες) γάρ εἰσιν ἐξαπατᾶν εἰθισμέναι, "For they are wont to deceive." Eur. *Iph. in Taur.* 1298, ὁρᾶτ᾽, ἄπιστον ὡς γυναικεῖον γένος, "See, how faithless is woman's race." Propert. *El.* ii. 9. 31, "Sed vobis facile est verba et componere fraudes; | hoc unum didicit femina semper opus, "But 'tis easy for you to counterfeit words and actions; this one work has woman ever learnt." So Plaut. *Mil. Glor.* ii. 2. 34.

752. move, 'urge,' 'propose'; cf. Shak. *Othello*, iii. 4. 166, "If I do find him fit, I'll move your suit."

753. promise ... change, 'promise a complete or wonderful change.' There is an unpleasant ring in this and similar cynical remarks of Samson.

754. chief, 'chiefly'; cf. *P. L.* iii. 29, "But chief thee, Sion, ... nightly I visit."

755. bears, 'may bear, 'will bear.'

756. virtue or weakness; a virtue becomes a weakness when it is no longer able to resist temptation.

757. instructed skill; 'instructed' is a comparative, and the meaning is the Latin one of 'prepared,' 'designed' (cf. **Lat.**

instruere fraudem, instruere orationem) ;—'skill more carefully or artfully designed.' Halliwell notices this rare meaning ; and Ben Jonson uses it in this sense in *The Silent Woman* (Gifford, iii. 438), "O my cursed angel, that instructed me to this fate !" Cf. also *Two Noble Kinsmen*, i. 1, "To instruct me 'gainst a capital grief indeed." The word lit. means 'built,' as in Dryden, *Annus Mirabilis*, "Instructed ships."

758. **submits**, 'repents.'

759-763. The allusion is to Milton's forgiveness of Mary Powell (in 1645) (see l. 219, n.). Describing the incident Phillips says "... He might at first make some show of aversion and rejection ; but partly his own generous nature, more inclinable to reconciliation than to perseverance in anger and revenge ... soon brought him to an act of oblivion." Prof. Masson has collected facts that go to show that their subsequent married life of seven years was not happy. This is alluded to in ll. 762, 763.

760. **With goodness principled not**, 'whom the principle of goodness prompts not to.' **principled**, 'instructed in the *principia* or elements of '; cf. *Comus*, 357, "So unprincipl'd in Virtue's book."

763. **Entangled with**, ' caught in the folds of,' ' unable to shake off.' For this use of ' with ' for ' by ' see Abbott, § 193 ; and cf. Shak. *Wint. Tale*, v. 2. 68, "He was torn to pieces with a bear." **bosom-snake.** Cf. Æsch. *Choe.* 240, πατρὸς θανόντος ἐν πλεκταῖσι καὶ σπειράμασι δεινῆς ἐχίδνης (said of Clytaemnestra), "The parent eagle, that, inwreathed | In the dire serpent's spiry volumes, perished "; Soph. *Antig.* 531, σὺ δ', ἢ κατ' οἴκους ὡς ἔχιδν' ὑφειμένη λήθουσά μ' ἐξέπινες, "Thou, like a viper creeping through my house | With wily secrecy to drain my blood "; Shak. *Rich. II.* iii. 2. 131, "Snakes in my heart-blood warm'd, that sting my heart." The idea of a snake cherished in one's bosom is as old as Æsop's fable on the subject.

65. **example**, 'warning.'

766-842. *Delilah shifts her ground from insincere penitence to cunning excuse-making. She tries to persuade Samson that she was not more to blame than himself, for he was the first to divulge a secret, nor more to blame than the rest of her sex, curiosity to know and inability to retain secrets being "common female faults"; that it was the jealousy of love that prompted her to get Samson into her power ; that she had been deceived by false promises of Samson's safety made by her enemies. Samson at once discovers her purpose—it was "malice not repentance" that has brought her hither—and taking her at her own word, sternly points out that her fault having been, as she affirmed, the same as his (namely, weakness in both), he forgives her just as much as he forgives himself.*

766. not that, ' it is not that.'

769. aggravations. Delilah deprecates Samson's painting her offence blacker than it is, as she, on her part, had abstained from trying to whiten it.

770. just allowance. Note how subtly Delilah pleads for that extenuation of her fault which she has but just professed to decline. The same undercurrent of false reasonings and self-contradictions that runs through Delilah's speeches is more plainly perceptible in the sophistries of Comus in his speeches to the Lady.

771. I may ; to be joined in constr. with ' but that' (l. 768). **thy pardon find The easier,** i.e. 'find thee more readily inclined for pardon.'

773. granting ; there is an *anacoluthon* in this unrelated participle : '*granted*' would be better grammar.

775. Scan thus :—" Cùriós | ìtỳ ìn | quísì | tìve ím | pòrtúne " (Masson) ; instead of the tribrach in the second foot we may have an iambus, | itý ìn |, by *synizesis*. **importúne,** Latin accent, 'troublesome.' Milton uses this, the correct form (from Lat. *importunus*) twice again : *P. R.* ii. 404, "The importune Tempter "; and *P. L.* x. 933, "Me thus, though importune." Chaucer uses it in the same sense, *Rom. of the Rose*, "For he will be importune unto no man " ; Spenser in that of ' violent,' *F. Q.* i. 11. 53, "Importune might "; ii. 11. 7, "Importune toyle." The original idea was ' difficult of access ' (Lat. *in*, not, *portus*, harbour). Similarly ' opportune ' lit. means ' easy of access ' (*ob*, lying over against). The coined form ' importunate ' occurs, side by side with the correcter form, in Berners' *Golden Boke* (1533), "I am importune on you that ye be not importunate on me."

776. Of, i.e. ' to get at,' ' to learn.' **then,** i.e. ' when the secrets have been learnt.' **like ;** because both kinds of weakness are due to the same cause—want of self-restraint. The constr. is an *anacoluthon*. The sense requires the sentence " then with like informity," etc., to be co-ordinate with the preceding sentence " it was a weakness, curiosity," etc. This co-ordination may be expressed thus :—" It was a weakness in me *to be curious, ... to learn* secrets ; *it was*, then, *a similar weakness* to publish them." The constr. in the text does not bring out this co-ordination.

778. Was it not weakness, *sc.* ' in thee.' This is the principal sentence after ' granting,' etc., l. 773. Prof. Masson points out that the strain here resembles that of Eve's speech, *P. L.* ix. 1155, where in their mutual accusations Eve tries to throw the blame partly on Adam.

779. For importunity, *i.e.* 'giving way to, yielding to importunity.' **for nought,** 'for no good reason,' 'for no solid consideration.' The expr. is frequent in Scripture: *Job*, i. 9, "Doth Job fear God for nought?"

780. This line is the object of 'make known' above.

782. But I, 'but *you will say that I* '; for similar omissions of the verb 'to say,' see ll. 836, 895, 1205. The emphatic word here is 'enemies,' the point Delilah states being 'You say that I revealed your secret to enemies, whereas you revealed it only to me your wife.'

783. Nor should'st thou, 'neither should'st thou.' Delilah proceeds to refute the point she had stated as a probable objection raised by Samson. Cf. Shak. *Hamlet*, i. 2. 146, "Frailty, thy name is woman." For the sentiment cf. *Micah*, vii. 5, "Keep the doors of thy mouth from her that lieth in thy bosom"; Hom. *Od.* xi. 441, τῷ νῦν μήποτε καὶ σὺ γυναικί περ ἤπιος εἶναι· | μηδ᾽ οἱ μῦθον ἄπαντα πιφαυσκέμεν, ὅν κ᾽ ἐὺ εἰδῇς, | ἀλλὰ το μὲν φάσθαι, τὸ δὲ καὶ κεκρυμμένον εἶναι, "Wherefore in this present case do thou never be gentle even towards thy wife, nor tell her everything that thou knowest; but unfold some (trifle), and conceal the rest"; Seneca, *Hippol.* 876, "Alium silere quod voles, primus sile," "If thou wishest another to be silent about a thing, be thou silent about it thyself"; La Bruyère, *Caractères*, v., "Toute révélation d'un secret est la faute de celui qui l'a confié," "Every revelation of a secret is the fault of him who imparts it"; La Rochefoucauld, *Maximes*, "Comment prétendons-nous qu'un autre garde notre secret, si nous n'avons pas pu le garder nous-même?" "How can we expect another to keep our secret, if we have not been able to keep it ourselves."

785. Note the insidious address with which Delilah places herself on the same level with Samson with regard to degree of guiltiness. **parle,** 'negotiation with a view to reconciliation'; cf. *P. R.* iv. 529, "By parle or composition, truce or league | To win him." Shak. *K. John*, ii. 1. 205, "Our trumpet called you to this gentle parle." The word lit. means 'conversation,' as in Shak. *L. L. L.* v. 2. 122, "to parle, to court, to dance." For derivation, see l. 500, n.

787. Thine, 'let thy weakness,' *i.e.* 'let the consideration that you yourself were weak induce you to forgive me also for having been weak.' **censure,** 'judge,' in the Latin sense, very frequent in Elizabethan English both as a noun and as a verb; in this sense cf. Shak. *Jul. Caes.* iii. 2. 16, "Censure me in your wisdom"; *Hamlet*, i. 3. 69, "Take each man's censure, but reserve thy judgement"; Bacon, *Adv. of L.* ii. 23. 49, "Erudition of law is to be censured and governed."

790. what if; see l. 44, n.

791. Cf. Eur. *Androm.* 181, ἐπίφθονόν τι χρῆμα θηλειῶν ἔφυ, καὶ ξυγγάμοισι δυσμενὲς μάλιστ' ἀεί, "Our sex to jealousy by nature prone, | Brooks not a rival in the nuptial tie."

793. mutable. So Dejanira fears that her husband Hercules will forget her for the youthful Iole, and prepares what she thinks to be a love charm, to bind him to her, but which has the "perverse event" (l. 737) of causing Hercules's death" (Soph. *Trach.*; also see l. 1073, n.).

796. endear. The constr. grammatically is ' endear thee to me' from the next sentence; but the sense of course is ' endear myself to thee.'

802. hold, ' check,' ' control.'

803. That made for me, ' that was to my advantage'; cf. *Rom.* xiv. 19, "Let us therefore follow after the things which make for peace "; Bacon, *Essays*, xvi., "For none deny there is a God, but those for whom it maketh that there were no God." Sir T. Browne, *Rel. Med.* i. 27, "Writers whose testimonies we do not controvert in points that make for our own opinions." **liberty,** *i.e.* ' continued liberty.'

806. widowed. So Duessa in her letter to the king of Eden calls herself "widow sad," though the Red Cross Knight, of whose desertion of her she complains, was still alive. Spenser, *F. Q.* i. 12. 27. ' Widow' is from the root VID, ' to separate.'

809. unhazarded, *sc.* ' by me.' The passive here has a peculiar force. Delilah speaks of Samson as a precious possession whose loss she would not hazard by permitting him to go abroad.

811. for good, ' as valid.' In modern prose the expression has an entirely different meaning—' for ever.'

812. fond, ' foolish '; see l. 228, n.

813. well meaning, ' when its purpose was blameless,' ' with good intentions '; see l. 793, n.

815. not austere. Unless we choose to take the constr. to be "be not unlike all others; *be* not austere," we should omit the second ' not '—"be not, unlike all others, austere," etc. For the double negative cf. *P. L.* iv. 21, "*Nor* from Hell | one step, *no* more than from himself can fly "; so *P. L.* v. 548. The modern rule that two negatives amount to an affirmative was not observed in M.E. (*e.g.* the *Owl and Nightingale* concludes with "*Ne* can ich eu *namore* telle : | ther *nis na* more of thisse spelle "; Chaucer has " *Nis non, no, nouther* he *ne* she "), or in Elizabethan English whenever emphasis was required. Even now it is not observed in " vulgarisms," which often preserve in disguise purer forms of idiom than the literary or written language (*e.g.* " **Oh no,** not by no means, I never said no such a thing ").

818. uncompassionate, 'pitiless'; used again by Milton in *Tetrachordon*—"God was not uncompassionate of them in the framing of this law." The older form of the verb was periphrastic, 'to have compassion'; it occurs in Dan Michel's *Ayenbite of Inwit* (1340), and, shortly afterwards, in Chaucer and Wyclif. The form 'to compassionate' appears in the *Mirror for Magistrates* (1557), but before it was quite established a short-lived variant 'to compassion' occurs in Bp. Hall and Shakspere (*Tit. Andr.* iv. 1. 124).

819. displays, 'makes a show of acknowledging.'

820. upbraid me mine ; 'me' is the indirect object—'to me'; the modern constr. would be 'to upbraid me (direct object) *with* my transgressions.' The direct object of the thing (as here) occurs in Shak. *Macb.* v. 2. 18, "Minutely revolts upbraid his faith-breech"; *Tr. and Cr.* iii. 2. 198, "Yet let memory upbraid my falsehood"; Spenser (with the coined form 'upbray'), *F. Q.* ii. 4. 45, "And knighthood dost with shams upbray." The A.S. verb is *braegdan*, 'to draw' (*e.g.* a sword, "heorugrimm hring-mael gebraegd," "Savagely fierce drew (it) adorned with rings," (Beowulf); the 'g' was lost as early as in Layamon's *Brut* (1205). Hence 'upbraid' is lit. 'to draw up' a person, 'to haul him up,' in familiar language. The same A.S. word gives the M.E. 'abraide,' 'to start,' and mod. E. 'to braid' ('weave ').

822. gave, 'set.' The French idiom is similar, *donner un exemple.*

825, 826. This striking utterance of Samson turns Delilah's own weapon of special pleading against herself; at the same time it exemplifies that 'over-justice' (l. 514) for which Manoah had reproved him. This excessive rigour of self-condemnation is the natural reaction from that excessive pliancy to Delilah's wishes that had worked his fall. No other presentment of Samson's character in this place would have been consistent.

826. Take to, 'receive for'; for this use of 'to' cf. the *Litany*, "To give and preserve *to* our use the kindly fruits of the earth." **which,** *sc.* 'pardon,' from the preceding line.

829. feigned, predicative—'to be feigned.'

831. Philistian gold ; see l. 389, n.

834. All wickedness is weakness, 'all vice is the result of want of self-control.' The two qualities are united, but in a different sense, in *P. L.* iv. 856, "Thee wicked and thence weak." According to the Stoics 'Self-control' was one of the components of Virtue. Such too was Descartes' view ; so the Greek word κακότης, lit. 'wickedness,' means 'cowardice,' 'weakness.' Note the contemptuous emphasis with which the word 'weakness' is repeated thrice, within a few lines. **plea,** 'excuse,' from Lat. *placitum*, 'opinion.' Among the Romans *placet* ('it pleases')

was used of the decrees of the Senate, as the corresponding
expression is now used of royal decrees. From this the French
obtained two forms *plait* and *plaid*, both meaning a court of law,
a tribunal, and thence, the counsel's speech before the court.
Both forms passed into English. They occur frequently (as may
be expected from the subject of the poem), both as noun and
verb, meaning 'dispute,' in the *Owl and Nightingale*. Both
forms continue to occur in *Piers Plowman* and Chaucer, and
'plete' occurs as late as in Skelton, "To plete a trew tryall
within Westmynster Hall":—*Why come ye nat to Courte* (1522).
The modern form 'plea' occurs as 'plee' as far back as the
Paston Letters (1465) in the sense of 'law-suit.'

836. **But love**, ' but *thou sayest* love '; see l. 782.

837. **to have love**, *sc.* 'in return'; cf. Dante, *Inf.* v. 103,
"Amor che a nullo amato amar perdona" (explained as ' che
vuole che ogni amato riami'), "Love that denial takes from
none beloved"; Seneca, *Ep.* ix. "Si vis amari, ama," "Love, if
thou wishest to be loved"; Martial, *Epigr.* vi. 11. 10, "Ut ameris
ama," "Love, that thou mayest be loved."

838. **hope**, 'hope for,' 'expect'; used transitively also in Shak.
All's Well, ii. 1. 163, "Within what space hopest thou my cure?"
took'st the way, ' didst adopt the means.'

840. The use of a participle after verbs of knowing, seeing,
remembering, etc., is a Graecism. The English constr. would
be ' knowing *myself ... to be* betrayed by thee '; cf. *P. L.* ix. 792,
"And knew not eating death."

841. **to cover shame with shame**, ' to palliate thy shameful act
by shameful excuses.'

842. **For.** This is the reading of Milton's own edition. It was
altered to ' or ' by Newton, whom subsequent editors have followed. The objection to Newton's emendation is that it makes
' in vain ' from the preceding line an adverb to ' uncover'st,' while
the sense does not require the adverb ; indeed, does not admit of
it. The objection to the original reading is that ' thou ' the
nominative to ' uncover'st ' should in this case have been expressed. This objection is met by the parallel of *P. R.* i. 85,
"This is my son belov'd, in him am pleas'd," where ' I ' is similarly omitted. The reason of such omissions is obvious; namely,
whenever the inflection of the verb implies the nom. clearly
enough, the nom. can be safely omitted. They occur in Elizabethan poetry, see Abbott, § 399. The sense is quite plain. The
sentence introduced by ' for ' explains ' in vain ' in the preceding
line. **by evasions ... more**, 'you make your crime clearer than
ever by trying to elude the charges I bring to prove it.'

843-902. *Delilah again shifts her ground, and abandoning the
plea of weakness, takes up the higher ground of patriotism. She*

urges that the magistrate and the priest—both civil and religious authority—combined to press on her the betrayal of Samson, till love—her only defence against such powerful attacks—gave way to sense of duty; 'private respect yielded to public good,' and she espoused the cause of 'virtue, truth, and duty.' To this Samson replies that having been chosen by him in preference to his own countrywomen, she became his, and his country hers. He meets her double plea by showing that as the magistrates of her country sought his life by foul means, it was not patriotism in her to aid and abet them; and that as her gods and their priests sought to overcome him by like foulness, they deserved not to be obeyed and feared by her—the wife of him whom they plotted against.

843. **determin'st**, 'judgest,' 'decidest'; cf. Shak. *Com. of Err.* v. 1. 167, "I will determine this before I stir." Also used by Shakspere with 'of' in this sense; *Rom. and Jul.* iii. 2. 51, "Brief sounds determine of my weal or woe." The lit. meaning is 'to limit,' 'to put an end to,' which occurs in *P. L.* ii. 330, "War hath determin'd us." **for**, 'to be,' 'as,' very frequent in Shakspere, *e.g. Cor.* iii. 1. 196, "Named for consul"; 3 *Henry VI.* v. 7. 6, "Renowned for hardy and undoubted champions."

844. **though to ... condemning**, 'though it tends to, results in, your own condemnation.' Another expression common in Shakspere; cf. *Com. of Err.* iv. 1. 84, "To your notorious shame"; *Cymb.* i. 1. 120, "To your so infinite loss"; *Rich. III.* iii. 1. 98, "To our grief."

845. **I had**, 'I received,' 'I was exposed to.'

847. **best-resolved**, 'of the strongest and firmest resolution.' **men**, emphatic, *sc.* 'much more a weak woman like me.'

848. **without blame**, 'without being blamed for doing so.'

850. **wrought with**, 'wrought upon,' 'influenced'; cf. Shak. *Rich. II.* iv. 1. 4, "Who wrought it with the king." **magistrates and princes.** *Judges*, xv. 5 merely mentions "lords of the Philistines," but Josephus says, "those that administered the public affairs of the Philistines"; see ll. 251, 981, nn.

854, 855. **just ... honourable ... glorious.** A climax is here meant.

856. **common**, 'national,' 'to the community at large.'

857. **the priest.** The Bible account mentions no priests, nor does Josephus. For the allusion probably in Milton's mind in thus introducing a mention of the priest, see Introd. p. xli.

858. **Was not behind**, 'was equally active.' **ever at my ear**, an action characteristic of the tempter. So Satan sits "close at the ear of Eve" (*P. L.* iv. 800).

859. **with**, 'in the eyes of'; cf. Shak. *Ant. and Cl.* i. 1. 56, "Is Caesar with Antonius priz'd so slight?"

863. **debate,** not 'discussion or deliberation' as now, but in the older sense of 'fight,' 'struggle'; cf. *P. L.* vi. 122, "That he who in debate of truth hath won | should win in arms, in both disputes, victor"; Spenser, *F. Q.* vi. 8. 13, "The villaine ... himselfe addrest unto this new debate, | and with his club him all about so blest."

865. **contést,** Latin accent; so in *P. L.* xi. 800. **grounded maxim,** 'well-established principle'; cf. Bacon, *Adv. of L.* ii. 6. 1, "But the sober and grounded enquiry." A 'maxim' is lit. 'a saying of very great importance,' being the Lat. superlative degree of *magnus.*

866. **rife,** 'prevalent. For this wider use of this adj. cf. *Will. of Palerne,* "There was sorwe rife"; Gower, *Conf. Am.* "Whose fame yet in Grece is rife"; Shak. *M. N. D.* v. 1. 42, "Sports are rife." The present use of the word is much more limited, being confined to a few subst. like 'sickness' and 'rumour.'

867, 868. Cf. Ovid, *Trist.* iv. 2. 74, "Causaque privata publica major erit," "The public good is greater than private interests"; Plin. *Ep.* vii., "Sed oportet privatis utilitatibus publicas, mortalibus aeternas anteferre," "But we ought to place public interests before private, eternal welfare before earthly." **respects,** 'considerations'; cf. Bacon, *Adv. of L.* ii. 23. 12, "The worthiest men do abandon their fortune willingly for better respects"; *Essays,* xi. "But if importunity or idle respects lead a man."

869. **Took ... me,** 'enlisted me entirely in their service.' **prevailed,** 'overcame my opposition.' In the order of thought the sentence would be reversed thus, "prevailed and took full possession of me."

870. **so enjoining,** 'bidding me act so.'

871. **circling wiles.** Another and perhaps commoner metaphor would be '*crooked* wiles,' by which Delilah tried to evade confessing her guilt. According to the metaphor in the text, she completes the 'circle' by taking refuge in religion. In ordinary language we speak of a person 'going round and round the point without coming to it.'

873. **still odiously pretended.** Samson implies that Delilah with hateful art steadily ('still') maintained the mask of love for him, while all the time she was plotting his betrayal. **still,** 'always,' as in l. 807 ; see l. 77, n.

876. **before,** 'in preference to,' like the Lat. *prae,* which primarily means 'before,' 'in front of.'

877. **from among.** In such double prepositions the second has partly the character of a substantive governed by the first preposition, and partly that of a preposition governing the sub-

stantive following. Thus in the text 'from' governs 'among,' which in its turn governs 'enemies.' An analogous case is that of the present participle governed by a preposition and governing an object, *e.g.* "of (well) pronouncing Shibboleth" (l. 289).

878. **too well.** It is an interesting little task, in a particular context, to find out the exact shade of meaning of the word 'too,' out of the great variety clustering round its ordinary one of 'more than enough.' Here it means that Delilah's knowledge of Samson's love for her was more than it should have been, *because she turned it to an evil purpose.*

879. **Too well** : supply "loved thee" from the preceding line. The pathos of this repetition is entirely lost by putting a comma after 'knew'st' (as some editions have it), and making 'too well' qualify 'loved thee' in l. 878—a most flat and feeble construction. Dunster perhaps makes too much of a supposed inconsistency between these two lines and ll. 232, 422, where 'divine impulsion' to 'oppress Israel's oppressors' (and not 'an unwise love') was stated to be Samson's motive in his marriages. There is nothing in Scripture, or in human nature, to prevent the two motives from acting together.

880. **levity,** *i.e.* the impiety that makes light of revealing the secrets of God ; cf. ll. 497, 498.

881. **who,** antecedent 'I,' l. 876. This is the causative use of the relative 'I unbosomed ... who,' being equivalent to 'I unbosomed ... *because I* ' ; see l. 984.

882. **now,** namely in Delilah's speech, l. 856.

885. **thou wast to leave.** 'it was thy duty to leave.' For this use of 'was to' for 'should,' 'ought to' (duty), see Abbott, § 324. Similarly 'have to' stands for 'must' (compulsion). In ordinary Lowland Scotch there is a modified use of this expr. 'are to,' softened into meaning 'are requested to.'

886. **leave Parents and country.** Perhaps *Gen.* ii. 24 (quoted in l. 929, n.) is here made reciprocally applicable to the wife. It is noticeable, however, that Samson probably lived in the Philistine country [Sorek (l. 229) perhaps] after marrying Delilah, so that the latter had no occasion to leave her country ; neither does Samson here say anything about Delilah's religion. As a matter of fact, when an Israelite married a foreign woman, the latter could retain her religion, and often converted her husband to it, as in the cases of Solomon and Ahab. **nor was I their subject.** Samson contrasts his case with that of Israelites who had emigrated to Canaan, married Canaanitish women, and adopted the Canaanitish religion (see *Judges*, iii. 5-8). A similar case was that of Ruth's husband (*Ruth*, i. 4, 16).

888. **Thou ... theirs,** 'thou wert *my subject* (as wife), not their subject (as child and fellow-countrywoman).' Cf. *Eph.* v. 24,

"Therefore as the church is subject unto Christ, so let the wives be to their own husbands in every thing."

889. **Thy country**, 'thy countrymen,' by *metonymy*, as in l. 891. **of**, 'from.'

890. **Against ... nature**, 'unnatural,' namely, in asking a wife to betray her husband. The **law of nations** ; the Mosaic law was explicit on this point : *Exod*. xxii. 21, "Thou shalt neither vex a stranger, nor oppress him : for ye were strangers in the land of Egypt." *Lev*. xix. 33, 34, repeats this, and adds, "But the stranger that dwelleth with you shall be unto you as one born among you, and thou shalt love him as thyself."

891. **crew**, 'crowd,' used contemptuously ; cf. *Comus*, 653, "curst crew," and l. 443, "rout." Formerly the word was not confined to sailors. In the Rolls of Parliament for 1455 and 1520 'crew' is used of soldiers, and in Lyly's *Euphues* (1579) we read of a "crew of gentlemen." In Stanyhurst's *Description of Ireland* (1577) the word acquires the bad sense of 'robbers.' In Shakspere it occurs in both senses, *e.g. Rich. III*. iv. 5. 12, "Valiant crew" ; *Lucrece*, 1731, "Lordly crew" ; *M. N. D*. iii. 2. 9, "A crew of patches" ; *Macb*. iv. 3. 141, "Crew of wretched souls."

895. **But zeal**, 'but *thou sayest* zeal' ; see l. 782, n.   **zeal**, 'religious zeal.'

897. **acquit**, 'vindicate' ; cf. 'assert,' l. 467, and l. 509, n. Originally the word meant to 'free,' 'release,' as in Spenser, *F. Q*. i. 7. 52, "Till I have acquit your captive knight" ; the present reflexive use meaning 'to clear one's self' occurs in Shak. *Rich. III*. i. 2. 77, "Of these supposed evils to acquit myself." The modern sense 'to discharge one's duty' is readily derivable from the above.

899. **deity**, abstract noun ; see l. 464, n.

900. **to be**, 'deserving to be.'

901. **varnish'd**, 'false,' 'specious' ; cf. Shak. *Mer. of Ven*. ii. 5. 33, "Christian fools with varnish'd faces" ; *Timon of Ath*. iv. 2. 36, "But only painted like his varnish'd friends."

902. **Bare**, 'laid bare, 'exposed.'

904. **Goes by the worse**, 'fares the worse,' 'gets the worst of it,' in modern familiar language.

906. **Witness when**, 'let the occasion when I was, etc., witness.' 'Occasion' is understood as equivalent in sense to 'then' or 'the time' contained in the compound 'when,' which stands for 'then when' or 'or the time when.'   **peals** ; see l. 235, n.

907-959. *Finding that Samson, unlike her former experience of him, is proof against her wiles, Delilah at length abandons them, and displays for once a touch of natural feeling that for a short while relieves her artful character. She unreservedly asks Samson's pardon, and offers, as Manoah had done, to effect his release, that he may abide with her and in his helplessness be tended and nursed by her, now and when old age comes. Samson is sensibly softened at this touch of sincerity, but, as a burnt child dreads the fire, he, who had been deceived when strong and free, fears he might be treated worse, now that he is blind and helpless. In curt language, that contrasts strongly with his desponding tones when refusing Manoah's offer, he tells her his feet will never again cross her threshold ; and saying he forgives her ' at a distance,' dismisses her.*

908. In what, namely, in the method she had adopted of trying to persuade Samson to forgive her.

910. place, ' opportunity'; cf. *Heb.* xii. 17, "He found no place of repentance"; so Wyclif's version, "He found not place of penaunce." **recompense,** 'reparation,' 'compensation'; see l. 746, n.; cf. Spenser, *F. Q.* i. 3. 30, "His lovely words her seem'd due recompence | Of all her passed paines." The modern use of the word is confined to a 'reward for services rendered.'

911. intend, transitive; see l. 1259, n. **misdone,** 'done amiss,' 'done wrong'; the prefix occurs now only before the substantive ('misdeed').

913. sensibly, 'sensitively,' the French use of the word (*sensiblement*); cf. Shak. *Hamlet*, iv. 5. 150. "Am most sensibly in grief for it." **insist to afflict,** 'persist in afflicting.'

915. enjoyed, 'enjoyable'; for this use of the term. *-ed* for *-able,* see Abbott, § 375.

916. want not, 'are not without'; see l. 315. This meaning is very common in Shakspere.

918. Exempt ; see l. 103, n.

920. I to the lords will intercede. Although Richardson gives an instance of the use of this word with the prep. 'to' ("He besought the lorde hys God and made intercession *to* hym," 2 *Chron.* xxxiii. 13, Bible of 1551), it is preferable to take the present case as an instance of a *verbum praegnans,* of which other examples occur in ll. 977, 1055, 1089, 1343. The full expression is, 'I will *go to* the lords and intercede *with* them'; cf. Shak. 2 *Henry IV.* ii. 1. 70, "I beseech you stand *to* me," *i.e.* '*come to* me, and stand *by* me.' The omitted verb in such cases is frequently a verb of motion. See Abbott, § 187.

922. From forth, 'forth from'; so "from off," l. 26.

924. nursing diligence, 'diligent nursing': an example of *double enallage* or interchange of parts of speech. **glad office,** 'pleasant task.' 'Glad' is here causative for 'gladsome,' 'gladdening'; see l. 144, "glad news," and cf. the common expr. 'glad tidings.' Earlier the verb was similarly used in a causative sense, *Ps.* xxi. 6 (marginal reading), "Thou hast gladded him with joy"; Wyclif, *Luke*, i. 47, "And my spirit hath gladid in God my helthe" (reflexively, 'gladded itself').

925. to old age, 'till old age comes,' *i.e.* 'during old age when it comes.'

928. Samson is evidently moved by Delilah's offer, but, recalling the past, he quickly recovers his former sternness of purpose. This fine picture of Samson refusing Delilah's offer, adds a noble touch to his character: Samson in adversity rises superior to the temptations of one whom in prosperity he had been unable to resist.

929. fits not, 'is not befitting'; see l. 1318. **are twain**, 'have been separated.' The reference is to *Gen.* ii. 24, "Therefore shall a man leave his father and his mother, and shall cleave unto his wife ; and they shall be one flesh."

931. To bring, 'as to bring'; cf. Shak. *Mer. of Ven.* iii. 3. 9, "So fond to come abroad"; and see Abbott, § 281.

932. trains ; see l. 533, n.

933. gins, 'snares'; cf. Shak. *Twelfth N.* ii. 5. 92, "Now is the woodcock near the gin." The derivation, commonly given, from Lat. *ingenium*, through Fr. *engin*, is doubtful. The use of 'ginn' by so pure a Saxon writer as Ormin (in the *Ormulum*, *circ.* 1200) for the A.S. *craeft*, 'contrivance,' points to the Scandinavian *ginna*, 'to deceive,' as the true derivation. The word is used in the sense of 'artful contrivance' in *King Horn*, *circ.* 1300 ("Ne mai ther come inne, no man with none ginne"). In Chaucer, however, appears a new meaning—'a skilful contrivance,' 'piece of ingenuity'—*Squieres Tale*, "Bidde him (the Horse of Brass) descende, and trille another pin, | For ther-in lyth the effect of al the gin." Here the derivation evidently is from Fr. *engin*. So, later, in Surrey's transl. of the *Æneid* (1540) the Trojan Horse is alluded to as "This fatall gin thus over-clambe our walls." The word has this meaning repeatedly in Beau. and Fl. (This early instance of confusion of etymologies was reversed when the Latin 'engine' was used like the old Scandinavian 'gin' to mean 'subtilely' in Elyot's *Governor*, 1533.) **toils**, 'snares'; lit. 'a hunter's nets'; from Lat. *tela*, 'a web,' *texo*, 'to weave.' It is a different word from 'toil,' 'labour.'

934. Another *anachronism.* The allusions are: (1) to the enchanted cup of Circe, daughter of the Sun, dwelling in the island Aeaea. This cup turned those of the companions of Ulysses that drank of it into swine (Hom. *Od.* x.) : (2) to the songs of the Sirens, who dwelt on an island between Aeaea and the rock of Scylla, near the south-west coast of Italy. They attracted mariners with the sweetness of their singing, and then devoured them. Milton makes Circe to be the mother of Comus. The

Sirens also are alluded to in *Comus*, and in a different sense in *Arcades*. **charms ;** in a double sense, 'songs' and 'magic incantations': the Lat. *carmina* has both these senses; for the first cf. *P. L.* iv. 642, "Charm of earliest birds." The anachronism here seems to have particularly offended 18th century purism, but it is impossible to get rid of it. It is true that a 'magic cup' (Joseph's) is mentioned in Scripture, and it is not difficult to connect 'magic incantations' with the witch of Endor, Egyptian magic, Laban's teraphim, etc.; but the allusion to the Greek myths is too palpable to admit of any forced allusions to Hebrew or Biblical sorcery.

935. their force is nulled ; as in the case of Ulysses who escaped Circe by using the herb 'moly,' and the Sirens by getting himself tied to the mast of his ship. **nulled,** 'annulled.' This rare form of the verb is also used by Milton's contemporary, H. More, *Antidote against Atheism*, "There is a principle in the world that forcibly resists or nulls one common law of nature for the more reasonable exercise of another."

936. adder's wisdom ; cf. *Ps.* lviii. 4, "They are like the deaf adder that stoppeth her ear : which will not hearken to the voice of the charmers, charming never so wisely."

937. fence, 'guard,' 'fortify': cf. *Numb.* xxxii. 17, "Fenced cities."

938. flower of youth, 'prime of manhood'; this passage need not be taken as an indication that Samson had been long enough in prison to speak of 'youth' or 'manhood' as past. Like the Chorus (l. 1489) he refers here to *premature* old age. According to Usher's *Chronology* all the events, from Samson's marriage with Delilah to his death, are included within the space of one year (B.C. 1120).

939, 940. Note the bitterness of the reproach conveyed in the repetition of 'me,' and in the heaping up of the verbs into two antithetic groups. **could ;** this is the reading of the original edition, altered to *could'st* in subsequent editions. Masson has restored the original reading, which is perfectly grammatical, being the *subjunctive* after 'if.'

941. thereby, 'owing to that circumstance'; so **thence,** l. 943.

944. last, 'at last.' **insult,** *sc.* 'me'; this absolute use of the verb occurs in Shak. 3 *Henry VI.* i. 4. 124, "Hath that poor monarch taught thee to insult?" and in Daniel, *A Funeral Poem* (quoted by Richardson), "The lion being dead, even hares insult."

946. perfet ; this, Milton's euphonic spelling, is midway between the Lat. *perfectus*, and the Fr. *parfait ;* it resembles the M.E. *perfit*, which was from O. Fr. *parfit*. Cf. 'verdit,' l. 324.

947. Bearing, 'carrying or reporting as an informer.'

948. gloss upon, 'comment upon'; from Gr. γλῶσσα, 'the tongue,' 'a language,' hence 'a word needing explanation,' 'the explanation itself.' Cf. Chaucer, *Wife of Bathes Tale*, "Men may devine and glosen up and downe"; the subst. in this sense occurs in *P. L.* v. 435, "The common gloss of theologians." The next or transition meaning is that of 'giving a *false* explanation' as in *The Plowman Crede*, "Loveth no synne, and gloseth nought the godspell." The last meaning is 'deceive,' 'flatter,' as in *P. L.* ix. 549, "So glozed the Tempter," and Chaucer, *Wife of Bathes Tale*, "And therewithal he coude so wel me glose." **censuring**; see l. 787, n.

949. jail, also spelt 'gaol'; from Low Lat. *caveola*, 'cage' (*cavus*, 'hollow'). The history of this double spelling seems to be this:—The Low Lat. *caveola* or *gaveola* became (1) *jaiole* in O. Fr., which passed through *jeole* into *geôle*, the modern form ('g' soft); but (2) it gave another form *gaole*, retained in French as a law term. From (1) were obtained the English forms 'jailer' (*Piers Plowman*), 'gailer' (Chaucer), and 'geol' (all obsolete except the first). From (2) was derived the other English form 'gaol,' originally used in the Rolls of Parliament (1455). **count,** see l. 250, n.

950. To thine, 'compared with thine'; cf. *Comus,* 506, "Not all the fleecy wealth ... is worth a thought | To this my errand "; Shak. *Macb.* iii. 4. 64, " Imposters to true fear "; see Abbott, § 187.

951-953. This is Delilah's last resource. Where words have failed she hopes that her touch might succeed. That Samson feels the danger too, and promptly resolves to avoid it, is shown by the savage energy of the reply with which he warns her off.

952. Not ... life, 'approach me not if thou carest for thy life.' Mr. Oliphant notes an expression, " Protestants for their lives " (*i.e.* 'earnest Protestants'), in Gresham's *Letters* (*circ.* 1560). The idea in both passages is that of doing something on which one's life depends.

953. My sudden rage, *i.e.* 'sudden rage in me.' **joint by joint;** 'by' in such expressions means 'after,' 'followed by' (from its original meaning of 'near'). Dr. Abbott gives to this 'by' a distributive force, as in ' one by one.' 'Joint by joint' would thus be equivalent to 'joint-meal' coined on the analogy of 'piece-meal,' 'limb-meal.'

955-957. This unpleasant irony seems meant to indicate Samson's recovery of his stern cynical frame of mind as regards women. **pious** refers ironically to Delilah's profession of religious zeal (l. 895) ; so **illustrious** and **faithful** are ironical for 'infamous' and 'faithless.' The irony can, however, be reversed by applying it to **memorable** in the sense of 'notorious,' 'branded,' and taking these two words in their natural sense. In the first ᴏ𝐫 these two ways, **Among** means 'in the list of'; in the second, it means 'in the opinion of.' I prefer the first.

958. **hastened widowhood**, for Delilah had made herself a widow (see l. 806), while her husband was yet alive.

960·1009. *Whatever good feeling Delilah's last two speeches may have inspired in us towards her disappears at this self-satisfied panegyric on her own conduct. She retracts her late confession of guilt, and taking up Samson's ironical taunts reasserts them in their serious meaning—she shall be illustrious in the annals of her country, and enjoy the reward her patriotism has earned: she washes her hands of Samson—and thus departs. The Chorus delicately hints that they are not insensible of the danger to which Samson has just been exposed* (l. 1003), *but Samson's reply is firm and clear.*

961. **more deaf ... seas.** Cf. Æsch. *Prom. Vinct.* 1022, ὀχλεῖς μάτην με κῦμ' ὅπως παρηγορῶν, "You tease me to no purpose, for you might as well try to talk over a wave"; Shak. *Rich. II.* i. 1. 19, "In rage deaf as the sea." The "more than" in the text must be taken as a hyperbole for the sake of emphasis. A similar hyperbole occurs in Spenser's description of Una's fairness, *F. Q.* i. 4, "More white than snow."

962. **reconciled.** A storm in common metaphor is said to be 'a conflict of the elements,' and waves similarly are said 'to beat angrily on the shore.' Hence the idea of 'reconciliation' in the text.

963. **still,** 'unceasingly,' 'unabated'; see l. 77, n. For another shade of meaning in this word, see l. 1626.

965. **suing ... reap.** It would be too bold to suggest that a pun was intended here. But one cannot help being reminded of the frequent occurrence of metaphors in Scripture drawn from 'sowing' and 'reaping.' I am unable to find anything in Ellis in support of the present pun, if there is one.

967. **evil omen,** 'inauspicious words,' referring to Samson's ironical expressions (l. 956 *sq.*).

969. **concernments,** 'affairs'; this rare word is also used by Milton's contemporary, Jeremy Taylor, in the sense of 'importance' ("It is of great concernment," *Liberty of Prophesying*), and by Dryden in that of 'anxiety' ("This ambition is manifest in their concernment," Preface to *All for Love*).

970. **nor ... disapprove.** The *meiosis* shows that even Delilah herself cannot bestow an unqualified approval on her own conduct **my own,** *sc.* 'concernments,' *i.e.* 'the affairs with which I have been concerned,' 'the part I have taken in them.'

971. **double-faced,** like Janus, who is called '*bifrons*' in Virg. *Æn.* vii. 180. **double-mouthed.** This idea is a modified one

from Chaucer's *House of Fame* (iii.), where Fame's herald Æolus
is represented with two trumpets—one of gold, called "Cleare
laude" (glorious Praise), and the other of black brass, called
"Sclaunder light" (unscrupulous Infamy). There are two other
celebrated descriptions of Fame, one by Virgil (*Æn.* iv.), and the
other by Ovid (*Met.* xii.).

972. The sense is 'the same deed that is considered famous in
one country or age is considered infamous in another.' **contráry**,
Latin accent. **contrary blast**; the allusion is again to Chaucer,
House of Fame, iii. 536-546, where Fame commands Æolus to
take his trumpet "and blow hire loos (praise) that every wight |
Speake of hem **harme** and **shrewdnesse** | In stede of good and
worthinesse ; | For thou shalt trumpe *all the contrarie* | Of that
they han done wel and faire."

973. **his.** In making 'Fame' masculine, Milton identifies
Fame with *Rumour* (as in the Induction to Shak. 2 *Henry IV.*),
which means 'reputation,' whether good or bad. This Rumour
is described under the name of *Fama* in Virg. *Æn.* iv. 173 *sq.* ;
and under that of Φήμη in Hesiod, *Erga*, 763, 4. **wings ...white,**
Milton, as Dunster pointed out, puts together this idea from
Silius Italicus, who describes Infamy as flying on black, and
Victory on snow-white, wings (*Pun.* xv. 95 *sq.*).

974. **Bears greatest names.** So Chaucer's *Fame* is described :
" On her shoulders gan sustene, | Both armes and the name | Of
tho that had large fame." **wild aery flight.** So Virgil's *Fame* is
described, " Pernicibus alis ... Nocte volat coeli medio terraeque
per umbram | Stridens," " Swift of wing ... by night she flies | Mid-
way 'twixt heaven and earth the darkness through | Shrilling."

977. The construction fully expressed is 'will stand defamed
among the circumcised, and *will be transmitted* to all posterity.'
For this construction, see l. 920, n. **To all posterity** ; an adverbial phrase like 'to eternity,' 'for ever,' and meaning the
same.

978. **the blot**, governed by 'with' understood ; '*traduced*'
being co-ordinate with '*mentioned.*'

981. These are four of the five capital cities of the five Princi-
palities of the Philistines (l. 251, n., and *Joshua*, xiii. 3). The
fifth city was Askalon. It was the least known of the five, and
the only remarkable event associated with it was the exploit
referred to in l. 138 ; Samson selecting Askalon probably because,
being an obscure place, the outrage would pass unnoticed.

983. **sung**, 'celebrated in songs.' This transitive use of 'sing'
is chiefly poetic, and is in imitation of Lat. *cano* and Gr. ἀείδω.
Cf. *P. L.* vii. 259, "Creator Him they sung."

984. **recorded**, 'remembered.' Latin meaning, still occurring
in the reflexive in Italian, *mi ricordo ;* cf. Marlowe, *Tamburlane,*

2nd pt., v. 2, " When I record my parents' slavish life " ; Shak.
Twelfth N. v. 1. 253, " O, that record is lively in my soul ! " The
meaning here, however, may be the particular one of ' remembered or celebrated *in song.*' Cf. *P. L.* vii. 338, " So eve and
morn recorded the third day," where the context makes this
meaning clear ; so Shak. *Two Gen. of Ver.* v. 4. 6, " Here can I, to
the nightingale's complaining notes, | Tune my distresses and
record my woes " ; Kyd, *Spanish Tragedy,* ii. 2, " Hark, madam,
how the birds record by night " ; Beau. and Fl. *The Pilgrims,* v.
4, " Hark, hark ! oh, sweet, sweet ! how the birds record too ! " ;
Hence ' recorder ' (' flageolet ') in Shak. *Hamlet,* iii. 2. 303, *M. N.
D.* v. 123. The latter particular meaning is preferable. The
tautology that arises in consequence is not unusual in Milton.
who, ' as one who,' causative relative ; see l. 881, n. **to save,** etc.,
infinitive clause, object of ' chose.'

986. **Above the faith,** ' in preference to keeping inviolate the
faith.' **wedlock,** from A.S. *wed,* ' a pledge.' The termination
' -lock ' is the same as ' -ledge ' (in ' knowledge '), and is derived
from A.S. *lác,* ' sport,' ' a gift as a token of pleasure.' *Wed-lac*
thus compounded was at first used in the sense of ' a pledge'; but
in the *Ormulum* (1205) and the *Life of St. Juliana* (1210) it is
used for the older word ' wif-lac,' ' a marriage-pledge.' **my
tomb,** supply ' shall be ' from l. 982.

987. **visited ... annual ;** cf. *Judges,* xi. 40, " And it was a
custom in Israel, that the daughters of Israel went yearly to
lament the daughter of Jephthah, the Gileadite, four days in the
year." Similarly anniversary mourning for Josias is mentioned in
the Apocrypha (1 *Esdras,* i. 32). The custom existed also among
the Phoenicians, *e.g.* the yearly mourning for Thammuz (*Ezek.*
viii. 14, and *P. L.* i. 446), and that for Adonis at Byblus (Lucian,
de Syria Dea, 6 *sq.*) ; Lane says that the modern Egyptians
visit the tombs at stated periods ; Chardin asserts the same of
the modern Persians. **odours.** So among the Jews, " sweet
odours and divers kinds of spices prepared by the apothecaries'
art " were burnt on Asa's tomb (2 *Chron.* xvi. 14) ; this is stated
to be a general custom (*Jer.* xxxiv. 5). Pietro della Valle, a
traveller in the 17th century, mentions a custom among the Jews
of burning perfumes at the site of Abraham's tomb at Hebron.
Mr. James notices the same custom at the present day in
Manchuria (*Long White Mountain,* p. 141). **annual :** by *enallage,*
an adverb qualifying ' visited ' understood. **flowers ;** cf. Shak,
Cymb. iv. 2. 220, " With fairest flowers, | While summer lasts, and
I live here, Fidele, | I 'll sweeten thy sad grave."

988. **in Mount Ephraim ;** the sense here is peculiarly con-
densed ; fully expressed it is ' in the song of Deborah who dwelt
in Mount Ephraim.' Cf. *Judges,* iv. 5, " And she dwelt under
the palm tree of Deborah between Ramah and Bethel in Mount

Ephraim." The deed itself was performed by Jael at Haro-
sheth.

989, 990. *Judges,* iv. 18 *sq.* ; v. 24 *sq.* After the defeat of
Jabin's army by Deborah and Barak at Kadesh, Sisera, the
captain of the defeated host, fled and sought refuge in the tent
of Jael, the wife of a Kenite (a Canaanitish tribe). He exacted
from her a promise that she would keep secret the place of his
concealment, and, exhausted with fatigue, fell asleep. Then
Jael "took a nail of the tent, and took an hammer in her hand,
and went softly unto him, and smote the nail into his temples,
and fastened it into the ground." For this horrible act of
treachery, committed in violation of the sacred claims of hospi-
tality, Jael was celebrated in a song by Deborah, the prophetess
and judge of Israel, and Barak, her general.

992. reward, *i.e.* the bribe alluded to in l. 831.

993. piety, 'patriotism'; both this and the allied meaning of
'dutifulness towards parents' occur in Cic. *Rep.* vi. 15, "Pieta-
tem (cole), quae cum sit magna in parentibus et propinquis, tum
in patria maxima est," "(Cultivate) piety, which, great as it is
with regard to parents and those near and dear to us, is greatest
with regard to our country." The word here however has also
the ordinary sense of reverence for the gods, as it would be expected to have in those theocratic times when government was
identified with religion.

995. envies at, 'feels mortification at.' The strictly grammatical constr. would be 'whoever envies this or repines at it.'
In using 'envy' with a prep. Milton may be imitating the Latin
idiom, according to which *invidere* ('to envy') governs the dative
case; cf. Shak. *K. John,* iii. 4. 73, "I envy at their liberty"; *Henry
VIII.* v. 3. 112, "Whose honesty the devil and his disciples only
envy at."

996. his. Note the cold and distant tone implied by Delilah's
use of the *third* person and of the indefinite 'whoever' above,
when she really means to refer to Samson.

997. a manifest serpent, 'exposed as, proved to be, a serpent,'
from the Latin sense of *manifestus,* 'convicted of,' 'caught in the
act.' **sting.** Todd quotes from the Apocrypha, *Ecclus.* xxvi. 7,
"An evil wife ... he that hath hold of her is as though he held a
scorpion." It is not quite accurate to speak of the 'sting' of a
'serpent,' but Shakspere also frequently does so.

999. So, 'unmasked and exposed as she has been.'

1000. my folly who, Latinism for 'the folly of me who'; see
l. 881, n.

1001. viper; see note on 'bosom-snake,' l. 763.

1003-1007. This sentiment of the Chorus was exemplified in the case of Eve when she sought and obtained Adam's pardon, and in Milton's own life when he forgave Mary Powell.

1003. **though injurious**, 'though found to be injurious,' 'though it has inflicted an injury.'

1004. **returning**, ' coming back penitent ' ; qualifies ' beauty.'

1006. **passion**, ' violent grief ' (from its lit. sense of ' suffering ') : a meaning very common in Elizabethan poetry ; cf. Shak. *M. N. D.* v. 321, " Her passion ends the play " (said of Thisbe); *Tit. Andr.* i. 106, " A mother's tears in passion for her son " ; Beau. and Fl. *Fair Maid of the Inn*, iii. 2, " Oh, that I could as gently shake off passion, | For the loss of that great brave man."

1008. Newton quotes the familiar line from Ter. *Andr.* iii. 3, " Amantium irae amoris integratio est," " Quarrels of lovers but renew their love."

1009. **Not**, *i.e.* ' does not so end.'

1010-1060. *This attack upon women in one respect surpasses those of Euripides in virulence. The latter puts his invectives into the mouths of characters who, having suffered wrongs at the hands of women, may be expected to judge them with resentment; but Milton sets down his as the utterances of the Chorus, supposed on this, as on all occasions, to give expression to sober and deliberate opinions, carrying weight, because not dictated by personal feeling. These may be summed up thus :— Woman's love is not won by virtue or wisdom or valour or intellect or manly beauty. External graces are so lavishly bestowed on her, only to hide the poverty of mental gifts. With these she ensnares man into marriage, but then she becomes a clog upon his advance in the path of virtue, and drags him down the road to ruin. A virtuous wife is rare, and happy the man that finds one such. God, therefore, to lessen the evil, has given despotic power to the husband over his wife.—This is what may be called the statement and proof of Milton's doctrine of the Inferiority of Woman to Man.*

1010-1017. Note the persistence of the rhymes in these lines.

1010. **wit**, ' intelligence,' Fr. *ésprit*; cf. *L'Alleg.* 123, " And judge the prize of wit and arms " ; *P. L.* ix. 93, " As from his wit and native subtlety | Proceeding."

1011-1014. Landor says these lines state what is ' untrue ' and ' tautological.'

1012. **inherit**, ' possess ' ; cf. Shak. *Temp.* ii. 2. 179, " The king and all our company else being drown'd, | We will inherit here " ; *Rich. II.* ii. 1. 83, " Gaunt as a grave, | Whose hollow womb inherits nought but bones " ; Spenser, *Ruines of Time*, 382, " To highest heaven where now he doth inherite | All happinesse in Hebe's silver bowre." ' *Disinherit* ' in the sense of ' dispossess ' occurs in *Comus*, 334.

1014. to hit, ' to light upon,' ' to discover.'

1015. refer it, 'explain it,' 'in whatever relation or connection men look upon it '; 'refer' is from the same Latin verb as ' relate.'

1016, 1017. *Judges*, xiv. 12-14, " And Samson said unto them, I will now put forth a riddle unto you; if ye can certainly declare it me within the seven days of the feast, ... Out of the eater came forth meat, and out of the strong came forth sweetness." For the solution see l. 1191, n. The word 'riddle' has lost a final '*s*,' having been in M.E. *raedels* (sing.), from A.S. *raedelse* (*raedan*, ' to read,' 'interpret'); the constr. in 'read a riddle' is thus that of the cognate accusative. The final '*s*' was lost early, the form *raedel* being found in the *Cursor Mundi* (1290). The word is distinct in derivation from 'riddle,' 'a sieve,' and its derivative 'to riddle' (with shot), 'make holes in.' Richardson confounds the two. **in one day**; join with 'to hit,' l. 1013. **sit musing,** *sc.* ' over it,' as the sentence would be completed in prose.

1018. If any ... all; supply the ellipsis from l. 1012, " If *it was* any ... all, *that could win woman's love*." **these**, the qualities mentioned in l. 1010 *sq.*

1019. Had not, 'would not have.' **preferred**. Keightley, no doubt referring to *Judges*, xv. 2, remarks that it was not the bride herself, but her father that is said to have preferred him. Josephus, however, says that " the girl despised his anger " (*Antiq.* v. 8. 6); and Chaucer is still more explicit, *Monkes Tale*, 3218, " And she untrewe | Unto his foos his conseil gan bewreye, | And him forsook, and took another newe."

1020. paranymph, ' the friend of the bridegroom ' (*John*, iii. 29); from Gr. παρανύμφιος, ' one who rides by the side (παρά) of the bridegroom (νυμφίος) when going to fetch the bride '; this word is not to be confounded with παράνυμφος (παρά, and νύμφη, ' bride '), ' a bridesmaid,' such as figures among the dramatis personæ in Aristoph. *Acharn*. Jeremy Taylor, *Sermons*, incidentally describes the duties of the paranymph to be " to solicit the suit, make the contract, and join the hands " of the couple. On the fulfilment of this last function alone could the bridegroom speak to the bride. This is meant in the passage in *St. John's Gospel* above referred to, " the friend of the bridegroom ... rejoiceth greatly because of the bridegroom's voice." Such was the office performed for Abraham by Eliezer, " the eldest servant of his house," in securing a bride for Isaac.

1021. Successor, *Judges*, xiv. 20, " But Samson's wife was given to his companion, whom he had used as his friend " (*i.e.* ' as his paranymph ').

1022. Nor both; the constr. is ' nor *had* both *thy wives*' ('**had**' being potential as in l. 1019). **disallied,** 'dissolved'; for the prefix see l. 442, n.

1023. nuptials, 'nuptial bonds.' The pl. form is on the analogy of Lat. *nuptiae,* Fr. *noces,* Ital. *nozze,* and is not due merely to the pl. 'their.'

1023, 1024. nor this last ... Had ; the strictly grammatical order would be 'nor had this last.'

1025. Todd quotes Tasso, *Aminta,* iii. 1 (*init.*) " E tu, natura | Negligente maestra, perchè solo | Alle donne nel volto e in quel di fuori | Ponesti quanto in loro è di gentile, | Di mansueto e di cortese ; e tutte | L' altre parti obliasti ? " " And thou, Nature, careless artist, wherefore in the face and exterior alone of woman placest thou all that is gentle and mild and courteous in her, and forgettest all the rest?" (*i.e.* "her mind"). **for that,** 'because,' an *archaism*; cf. Shak. *Macb.* iv. 3. 185, "For that I saw the tyrant's power a-foot." M.E. was rich in forms compounded of 'for' to mean 'because' and 'therefore,' which were used indifferently to mean either, *e.g.* 'for than,' 'for that,' 'for thy,' and in their fuller forms 'for than the,' 'for that the,' 'for thy the.' Thus 'for that' fully expressed would be 'for this (or that) that,' *i.e.* for this (or that) reason that' (conj.) ; cf. Fr. *parce que.*

1026. that, 'that therefore'; the sentence introduced by 'that' is the correlative (denoting consequence) to the sentence introduced by 'for that' above.

1027. for, 'through,' 'by reason of'; cf. the expression 'for fear' (lest). **judgment scant,** cf. Eur. *Hippol.* 644, γυνὴ γνώμη βραχείᾳ, "Woman of short sense." Supply 'was left' before 'scant.'

1030. affect, 'to like,' 'incline towards'; cf. *P. L.* vi. 421, "But what we more affect"; Bacon, *Essays,* xiii. "I take goodness in this sense—the affecting of the weal of men, which is that the Grecians call philanthropia." *Gal.* iv. 17, "They zealously affect you, but not well" (where Wyclif has "Thei loven not you wel"); Beau. and Fl. *Thierry and Theod.* ii. 1, "How 'tis possible | You can affect me that have learn'd to hate | Where you should pay all love."

1031, 1032. These lines make a rhymed couplet.

1033. The awkwardness of supplying the ellipsis 'or *love* not *anything* long ' in the second clause, from *nothing* in the first, is obviated by taking ' nothing ' to be an adverb, meaning ' not at all,' and ' love ' to be used absolutely ; cf. *P. L.* x. 1010, " But Adam with such counsel nothing sway'd " ; ix. 1039, " Nothing loth " ; 1 *Kings,* x. 21, " None were of silver ; it was nothing accounted of in the days of Solomon " ; Shak. *Coriol.* i. 3, " They nothing **doubt.**" Similarly the substantive 'nought has passed into the more common adverb 'not.' Ariosto illustrates the sentiment by the metaphor of ' leaves in autumn ' ; *Or. Fur.* xxi. 15, " Ma costei più volubile che foglia, | Quando l' autunno è più priva d'umore | Che 'l freddo vento gli arbori ne spoglia | E le soffia dinanzi al suo furore," " But she more volatile than leaf, when breeze | Of autumn most its natural moisture dries, | And strips the fluttering foliage from the trees, | Which, blown about, before its fury lies " ; Sannazzaro, by three most striking figures—*Ecl.* viii. " Ne l' onde solca, e ne l' arena semina | E 'l vago vento spera in rete accogliere | Chi sue speranze fonda in cor di femina," " He ploughs the waves, sows in the sand, and hopes to gather the wandering wind in a net, who builds his hope in the heart of woman." Contrast the sentiment in the text with the familiar line on constancy, " Love me little, love me long " (Heywood's *Proverbs,* Marlowe's *Jew of Malta,* Herrick's Song.

1034-1037. Masson quotes from *Doct. and Disc. of Divorce,* " The soberest and best governed men are least practised in these affairs ; and who knows not that the bashful muteness of a virgin may oft-times hide all the unliveliness and natural sloth which is really unfit for conversation." Also see l. 210.

1035. An Alexandrine. Besides the obvious metaphor. the allusion is to the Hebrew custom of virgins veiling themselves ; thus Rebecca " took a veil, and covered herself " when she met Isaac, her betrothed.

1036. demure, in the older sense of ' modest,' ' sober ' ; from the Fr. *de* (*bonnes*) *mœurs,* ' of good manners.' So Spenser in describing the virtues of faith and hope in the sisters Fidelia and Speranza speaks of their " countenance demure and modest grace " (*F. Q.* i. 10. 12). The word afterwards degenerated into meaning " pretending modesty," as in Gray's description of the cat, " demurest of the tabby kind "

1037, 1038. thorn intestine, ' a source of internal domestic unhappiness ' ; cf. for the expr. 2 *Cor.* xii. 7, " There was given to me a thorn in the flesh." **within defensive arms,** ' too near to him to be warded off.' The close and indissoluble tie of marriage makes him powerless to defend himself against this enemy. The metaphor is from fencing—a swordsman is helpless when his adversary gets *within his guard.* **defensive** in the original sense of ' warding off ' ; cf. the Latin expr. *defensor necis,* ' one who wards off death ' ; Spenser, *F. Q.* ii. 12. 63, " Set | With shady laurel trees, thence to defend | The sunny beames " ; iv. 3. 32, " Himselfe to save and daunger to defend " ; so Shakspere frequently uses the expr. " which God defend," in the sense of ' avert,' ' forfend ' (*Rich. III.* iii. 7. 81, *Much Ado,* iv. 2. 21). Berners' *Golden Booke* contains the same idea as the text—" Thei that be ill, been alwaies double ill, bycause thei beare *armour defensive* to defend their own yvels, and armes offensive, to assaile the good maners of other."

1039. cleaving mischief, 'an evil that cannot be shaken off.' Cf. *Doct. and Disc. of Divorce*, i. pref. "As yet the misinterpreting of some scripture, directed mainly against the abusers of the law for divorce given by Moses, hath changed the blessing of matrimony not seldom into a familiar and coinhabiting mischief"; the same idea is conveyed by the expr. "cleaving curse," occurring in the pamphlet, *Of Reformation*, ii. Cf. also Hesiod, *Erga*, 704, ἥτ' (κακὴ γυνή) ἄνδρα καὶ ἴφθιμόν περ ἐόντα εὕει ἄτερ δαλοῦ, "An evil wife roasts her husband, stout-hearted though he may be, without a fire." **mischief**, from Lat. *minus*, 'less,' *caput*, 'head,' has a stronger meaning in Milton than now; thus in *P. L.* ii. 141, it is used of a proposed invasion of heaven by Satan; and in xi. 450, of Abel's death. A mistaken etymology, from Lat. *malus*, 'evil,' gave the word 'bonechief' used by Chaucer and Trevisa as the contrary of 'mischief.' The allusion is to the shirt poisoned with the blood of the centaur Nessus, which was sent by Dejanira to Hercules as a love charm, but which clings to his body and eats into his flesh. **his**, 'her husband's,' this sing. antecedent is easily inferred from the pl. 'men' (l. 1034). A similar transition from the sing. to the pl. occurs in *P. L.* ix. 1183, "Thus it shall befall | Him, who to worth in *women* over-trusting, | Lets *her* will rule."

1040. Todd refers to Eur. *Orest.* 605, ἀεὶ γυναῖκες ἐμποδὼν ταῖς ξυμφοραῖς | ἔφυσαν ἀνδρῶν πρὸς τὸ δυστυχέστερον, "Women ever stand in the way of men's destiny on the side inclining to unhappiness."

1041. awry, 'astray,' in a moral sense; for this comparatively rare use of the word cf. Bp. Hall (in Richardson), "To draw the weak sinner awry"; Fairfax's *Tasso*, "Misled this knight awry." This and the next line form a rhymed couplet.

1043. which ruin ends; in prose, though we may speak of 'ruin ending a career,' we should rather say of 'deeds' that '*they* end *in* ruin.'

1044. pilot; in order to distinguish this word from 'steers-mate' in the next line, it may be taken to mean 'master of a ship,' as in *P. L.* i. 204, "The pilot of some small night-founder'd skiff." 'Pilot' is from Dutch *pijlen*, 'to sound water,' lit. 'with a pole' (*pijl*, Eng. 'pile'), and *loot*, 'lead'; so that 'pilot' originally meant 'sounding lead or line,' and hence the person using it, 'the leadsman.' For a similar *metonymy* cf. 'bow' and 'stroke' for *men* pulling the bow and stroke oars. **needs must wreck**, 'cannot avoid wrecking *himself* or *being* wrecked.' For this passive use, through an intermediate reflexive form understood, cf. *P. R.* ii. 228, "Rocks whereon greatest men have oftest wrecked." 'Wreck' (from A.S. *wrecan*, 'to drive,' whence the vb. 'to wreak (vengeance)' and the subst. 'wrack,' 'sea weeds driven ashore') is lit. 'what is driven ashore'; and, hence, any kind of breaking up or destruction (*e.g.* in the expr. 'rack and ruin'). The verb seems to have been used only twice by Milton in his poetry; it does not occur in the English Bible, where, instead, a ship is said to be 'broken' (2 *Chron.* xx. 37).

1045. **steers-mate**; the masc. 'steersman' would be out of place here.

1046. **of**, 'by.' Supply 'is he' (exclamatory) after 'Heaven.' Cf. Eur. *Orest.* 602, γάμοι δ' ὅσοις μὲν εὖ καθεστᾶσιν βροτῶν, μακάριος αἰών, "Happy his life, to whom marriage is well accorded."

1047. Cf. *Prov.* xxxi. 10, "Who can find a virtuous woman? For her price is far above rubies"; xii. 4, "A virtuous woman is a crown to her husband"; Eur. *Iph. in Aul.* 1158, 1162, 3, συμμαρτυρήσεις ὡς ἄμεμπτος ἦν γυνή ... σπάνιον δὲ θήρευμ' ἀνδρὶ τοιαύτην λαβεῖν | δάμαρτα; φλαύραν δ' οὐ σπάνις γυναῖκ' ἔχειν, "Thou shalt thyself attest | How irreproachable a wife I was, ... A wife like this | Is a rare prize; the worthless are not rare."

1048. 'That harmonizes with him in domestic goodness.' **combines**, 'unites, agrees, is in harmony with.' **good**, by *enallage* adj. for noun.

1050-1052. In these lines 'virtue' is assigned a higher place than 'domestic goodness.' The latter consists in making home happy under the common circumstances of every-day life: the former is called into action at the great crises of life, when this happiness is threatened by some extraordinary danger, some formidable temptation—for instance, those to which Delilah so easily succumbed.

1050. **opposition**, *sc.* 'to its exercise.'

1051. **remove**, *sc.* 'from its path,' 'overcome.'

1052. **acceptable**, Latin accent. **above**, *i.e.* 'in the sight of God.'

1053-1060. Three pairs of rhymes run through these lines. The lines contain the statement of Milton's opinion of the inferiority and subjection of women. This opinion is also stated in *P. L.* x. 149-156, where it is put into the mouth of the "Sovran Presence" himself ("... God set thee above her ... and her gifts | Were such as under government well seem'd | Unseemly to bear rule "). The Scripture ground for this is, among others, *Ephes.* v. 22, 23, "Wives submit yourselves unto your own husbands, as unto the Lord; for the husband is the head of the wife." Cf. Menander, *Fragm.* τὰ δευτεραῖα τὴν γυναῖκα δεῖ λέγειν, | τὴν δ' ἡγεμονίαν τῶν ὅλων τὸν ἄνδρ' ἔχειν. | ἡ δ' οἰκία ἐν ᾗ πάντα πρωτεύει γυνή, | οὐκ ἔστιν ἥτις πώποτ' οὐκ ἀπόλετο, "A wife ought to play the second part, and the husband ought to take the lead in everything. The house in which the wife has taken the lead, has ever gone to ruin.'

1055. **his female.** One would like to be sure that Milton does not use this unpleasant expression on purpose. **Gave ... in due awe.** 'Gave' is a *verbum praegnans*: the full constr. being 'Gave ... *to keep her* in due awe.' See l. 920, n.

1056. The constr. is 'nor *gave to him* (permission) to part *for* an hour from,' etc. In prose instead of 'nor gave' we should expect '*and forbad*'—the negation being transferred to the verb.

1057. **Smile she,** 'whether she smile.' **lour,** also spelt 'lower'; it is a variant of 'leer'; but the meanings of the two words are differentiated—'leer' being to 'glance slily,' 'lour' 'to glance frowningly.' No connection with adj. 'low' and its derivative 'lower.'

1058. **confusion,** 'ruin'; see l. 471, n.

1059. **swayed,** 'ruled'; used absolutely in the active in *P. L.* x. 375, "There let him victor sway."

1060. **dismayed,** 'paralyzed,' 'rendered powerless' (from A.S. and O.H.G. *magan*, 'to have power,' 'to be able,' whence Eng. 'may,' 'might'). The word is used in this strong sense by Spenser, *F. Q.* vi. 10-13, "When the bold Centaures made that bloudy fray | With the fierce Lapithes, which did them dismay."

1061-1064. These lines are an example of the *stichomuthia* of the Greek drama, *i.e.* carrying on the dialogue in single lines—a line to each interlocutor; see ll. 1061, 2, 1571, 2.

1061. **But had we.** We should now say, either "But we had best retire," or "But had we *not* best retire?" Johnson finds fault with this play upon the word 'storm,' as out of place. But it seems obvious that the Chorus had in mind their metaphor of the ship sailing under fair weather, used of Delilah (l. 714); they wish to contrast to this the storm of Harapha's approach.

1062. **contracted,** in the Lat. sense of 'brought together,' 'gathered' (*con*, 'together,' *traho*, 'to draw'): we similarly speak in Saxon English of a 'storm gathering.'

1064. **riddling days,** 'those days in which I could feel a pleasure in proposing and answering riddles.' Samson utters this in a tone of fretful impatience. Setting riddles was a common "parlor amusement" among Orientals at their social gatherings (Kitto, *Encycl.*). It is so still.

1066. **honeyed words.** In answer to Johnson's strange objection to this expression, Todd quotes, among others, from Wither's *Fidelia*, "his honied words," and Tasso's *Aminta*, "melate parole." The Classics, too, are full of this and similar expressions; cf. Hom. *Od.* xviii. 283. μειλιχίοις ἐπέεσσι; Moschus, *Idyll.* i. ὡς μέλι φωνά, "A voice like honey"; Theognis, *Eleg.* 365, γλώσσῃ δὲ τὸ μειλίχιον αἰὲν ἐπέστω, "Let honeyed words be ever on thy tongue"; so also Hom. *Il.* i. 249, τοῦ καὶ ἀπὸ γλώσσης μέλιτος γλυκίων ῥέεν αὐδή, "From whose persuasive lips | Sweeter than honey flowed the stream of speech"; *Ps.* cxix. 103, "How sweet are thy words unto my taste! yea, sweeter than honey to my mouth!"   **a rougher tongue**, *i.e.* 'one with a rougher tongue,' as may be inferred from 'him,' next line.

1068. Harapha. There is no giant of this name mentioned in the history of Samson's life; but in 2 *Sam.* xxi. 16, David and his warriors fight and overcome several giants who are each named, and said to be "of the sons of the *giant*"; this last word being rendered in the margin "*Rapha.*" From this marginal reading Milton invents the name of "Harapha."

1069. pile: the word is meant to indicate the *bulk* of Harapha; so Sil. Ital. *Pun.* xii. 143, has "Herculea moles," 'Herculean build.'

1070. wind, keeps up the comparison to a storm.

1071. less conjecture, 'am more at a loss to conjecture.'

1072. Scan thus:—"Thè súmpt | ùoùs Dál | ìlà | flóating | thís wáy."   **floating**, *sc.* 'like a ship.'

1073. habit. Harapha had come unarmed; see l. 1119 *sq.*

1074. Or peace or not; the constr. is '*whether he carries* peace or not.'   **alike ... comes**, 'his coming is a matter of equal indifference to me.' Contrast the cool contempt of Samson's tone here with the angry energy of his words and action when Delilah approached (l. 725).

1075. fraught, 'freight,' 'the business he comes charged with.' For this rare form cf. Marlowe, *Jew of Malta*, i. 1, "Come ashore and see the fraught discharg'd"; Shak. *Tit. Andr.* iv. 2. 71, "Lo, as the bark that hath discharg'd her fraught." The metaphor of the storm in the text, however, may well continue unaltered—'fraught' being the *thunder* with which the 'storm' (l. 1061) is charged.

1076-1177. *Every speech of Harapha contains an insolent taunt, and almost every one of them ends with a coarse personality; while every speech of Samson contains a challenge to the cowardly insulter. Harapha after a vaunting introduction of himself, sneeringly says that he is come to look at Samson and see if his 'appearance answers loud report.' Samson's reply is a curt challenge. Harapha answers he will not fight a blind adversary. Thereupon Samson renews his challenge, offering odds against himself. Harapha declines again on the ground that Samson's strength was due to magic art. The meanness of this insinuation will be understood when it is remembered that magic was an abomination in the eyes of the Hebrews. Samson solemnly declares that his strength was due not to magic, but to the living God, and now challenges both*

Harapha and his god, Dagon. Harapha's ready retort is that all that Samson's God has done for him has been to bring him to his present miserable condition. There is something most touching in Samson's reply: for while he submits meekly to this taunt as far as he himself is concerned, he displays, in the midst of his miseries, an unabated ardour of zeal for the glory of his God, and challenges Harapha a fourth time.

1076. **chance**, 'lot,' 'what has befallen thee,' in the Latin sense of *casus* (from *cado*, 'to fall,' 'to happen').

1077. **these**, pointing to the Chorus. **it**, 'thy chance.' Harapha wishes, or pretends to wish, that Samson was not blind, and had not lost his former strength, so that he might have been able to fight him on equal terms.

1080. **Og**; king of Basan, who attempted to oppose the passage of the Israelites through his territories (*Deut.* iii. 11). **Anak**; see l. 528, n. **Emims**. This was the name given by the Moabites to a race of giants that dwelt on the eastern borders of Canaan; they were "a people great and many, and tall as the Anakims," *Deut.* ii. 10.

1081. **Kiriathaim**; an old town east of the Jordan, called, when in the possession of the Moabites, Shaveh ('the plain of') Kiriathaim, *Gen.* xiv. 5.

1081, 1082. **Thou know'st ... art known.** The same silly vaunt is uttered by Satan, *P. L.* iv. 83, "Not to know me argues yourselves unknown." Harapha disparagingly says that Samson's name was obscure ("If thou at all art known"), and then contradicts himself immediately afterwards ("Much have I heard," etc.).

1085. **on the place**; we should now say 'at the place' or change the expression into 'on the *spot* where those encounters took place.'

1087. **camp**, 'the open field between two hostile armies (from Lat. *campus*, 'a field'): such a fight 'in camp' took place between David and Goliath (1 *Sam.* xvii.), and between the "twelve young men" of Abner and the twelve of Joab (2 *Sam.* ii. 14). The Greeks had its equivalent in their μονομαχία (*Hdt.* v. 1). Such contests were meant to decide the point in dispute between the two armies. They may have been fought at permanent encampments like the 'camp of Dan' (*Judges*, xiii. 25), or in temporary camps such as that pitched by the Philistines in Judah (*Judges*, xv. 9). Probably Harapha had in his mind this latter 'camp,' before which took place the slaughter of the 1000 Philistines,' which disaster his vanity makes him think he might retrieve (see l. 1095 *sq.*). **listed field**, 'enclosed space' (Fr. *champ clos*; such as Samson proposes in l. 1117) for a duel between warriors fighting for their own glory, and not as champions

of rival armies, as when they fought 'in camp. See l. 463, n.
Milton derives his idea from mediaeval chivalry, with its 'lists
of tournay,' and its laws of the duello.   See l. 1226, n.   There
was nothing of this, as far as I am able to ascertain, among the
Hebrews.

1088. **noise,** 'report.' Harapha uses the word slightingly of
Samson's fame.

1089. **survey If,** *i.e.* 'survey *and ascertain* if'; *verbum praegnans*;
see l. 920 n.

1091. **were,** 'would be.' **taste,** 'make trial of,' 'have practical
experience of,' through a fight; cf. *P. R.* ii. 131, "Have found
him, view'd him, tasted him."

1092. **single,** 'single out,' 'challenge to a single fight'; cf.
Shak. 3 *Henry VI.* ii. 4. 1, " Now, Clifford, I have singled thee
alone."

1093. **Gyves,** 'fetters'; see l. 1235. Cf. Shak. 1 *Henry IV.* iv.
2. 44, "March wide betwixt the legs, as if they had gyves on."
Tancred and Gismunda, v. 1, "The noble county Palurin, that
there lay chain'd in gyves" (where see note in Dodsley, ii. 218).
The word is almost always used in the pl.   It occurs as such in
Layamon's *Brut* (1205) probably for the first time, and borrowed
from the Welsh; so in *Piers Plowman,* "And schal never gyves
the (thee) greve." In the *Monk of Evesham* (1469) the word occurs
in the rare form of the sing. (*gyve*).

1096. **wish,** 'wish for.'

1097. **thrown,** 'thrown away,' as 'unclean' things like dead
bodies would be.

1098. **So had,** 'thus would have.'

1099. **Palestine,** *i.e.* ' Philistia,' the land of the Philistines, see
l. 144, n.

1102. **mortal duel,** 'the listed field' of l. 1087, see l. 1175, and
line 1226, n.   Milton commits a still bolder anachronism when
he uses the word in connection with the Son of God in his contest with Satan; *P. R.* i. 174, "Now entering his great duel";
so Drayton in his *David and Goliath* makes the latter to be
" expert in all to duels that belong."

1105. **in thy hand,** 'in thy power'; not to be confounded with
' *to* thy hand,' which would mean 'ready for thee.'

1107. Another little Euripidean trait; see l. 123, n.   Note
also the coarse personality of this remark, and of those in ll. 1136
sq. and 1167   The constr. of the line is faulty; the word 'need'
being a substantive when taken with 'hast,' but a verb when
taken with 'washing'; the two constructions thus confounded
are (1) 'thou *hadst* need (*i.e.* would'st need) much washing,' and
(2) 'thou hast need *of* much washing.' Cf. *Comus,* 394, " But

Beauty ... had need the guard of Dragon ... to save her blossom";
Shak. *Much Ado*, i. 1. 318, "What need the bridge much
broader than the flood?" See Abbott, § 297.

1109. **assassinated,** 'secretly betrayed'; cf. *Doct. and Disc. of
Divorce*, i. 12, "As for the custom that some parents and guard-
ians have of forcing marriages, it will be better to say nothing of
such a savage inhumanity, but only thus, that the law which
gives not all freedom of divorce to any creature endued with
reason, so assassinated, is next in cruelty." The subst. similarly
has the idea of 'secret action,' not necessarily 'of murder' in *P.
L.* xi. 219, "The Syrian king, who *to surprize* | One man, assassin-
like, had levied war | — *War unproclaimed.*" The history of the
word is given by Brachet :—"Assassin is the name of a well-
known sect in Palestine which flourished in the 13th century
—the *Haschischen* (drinkers of *haschisch*, an intoxicating drink,
a decoction of hemp). The Scheik Haschischin, known by the
name of the Old Man of the Mountain, roused his followers'
spirit by help of this drink, and sent them to stab his enemies,
especially the leading Crusaders." See the details of his procedure described in Marco Polo's *Travels* (Yule, i. 132, *sq.*). The
word is restricted by the French author Joinville (*Life of St.
Louis, circ.* 1310) to mean a member of this sect. In English it
is used by Dan Michel (*Ayenbite of Inwyt*, 1340) with reference
to the implicit *obedience* of a servant to his master, without any
suggestion of murder ; and so in modern French and Italian the
word has the signification (like that of the text) of a secret
attack not necessarily followed by murder.

1112. **with,** 'in.' **chamber-ambushes.** *Judges*, xvi. 8, "Now
there were men lying in wait abiding with her in the chamber."

1113. **Close-banded,** 'strictly leagued' (like 'assassins').

1116. **shifts,** 'evasions' ; the A.S. *scyftan* means 'to divide'
(cognate with Germ. *scheiden*, Eng. 'shear'). It is only in M.E.,
as in the *Ormulum* (1205) and in *Genesis* and *Exodus* (1230) that
the Scandinavian meaning of 'to change' in a neutral sense
first occurs. Cf. a change of linen, or a change of workmen, as a
'night shift' of miners ; in *Comus*, 273, "Extreme shift | How
to regain my sever'd company," it means a last or desperate
expedient.

1117, 1118. **sight ... rather flight.** This kind of a jingle on
words (*paronomasia*) is imitated by Milton from Hebrew usage ;
Keightley quotes passages in illustration from the Hebrew Scrip-
tures, and says it is of frequent occurrence in *Isaiah* ; see l. 1278.
flight. Samson with contemptuous sarcasm says that the narrow
enclosure will prevent Harapha from having the *advantage* of
running away from him.

1120. **brigandine,** 'scale armour,' 'coat of mail' ; cf. *Jer.* xlvi.

4, "Put on the brigandines." The word occurs in the form of
brigantaille in Gower, *Conf. Am.*, and of *bryganders* ('set with
gylt nayle') in Fabyan's *Chronicle*.   Lit. it means 'armour worn
by light troops or *brigands*' (from It. *briga*, 'strife,' whence Eng.
'brigade'); but the word 'brigand' next came to be applied to
robbers and then to pirates, whence 'brigandine' (in Fairfax's
Godfrey of Boulogne) and 'brigantine' (in Holland's *Plutarch*)
came to mean a light pirate-ship; afterwards contracted into
brig. **habergeon**, dim. of *hauberk*, 'armour for the neck' (from O.
H.G. *hals*, 'neck,' and *bergen*, 'to protect'). The word is used by
Chaucer in the *Rime of Sir Thopas*; it occurs as 'haburjon' in
his contemporary *John of Trevisa*, and as 'haburion' in Wyclif.

1121. **Vant-brace**, 'armour for the *fore-arm*' (Fr. *avant-bras*
from Lat. *ab*, *ante*, and *brachium*, 'arm'). The word occurs in
Shak. *Tr. and Cr.* i. 3. 297. **greaves**, 'armour for the legs.' O. Fr.
grève; cf. 1 *Sam.* xvii. 6, "And he had greaves of brass upon his
legs." **gauntlet**, 'iron gloves,' dim. from Fr. *gant*, 'glove.'

1122. **weaver's beam**. This was the description given of
Goliath's spear, 1 *Sam.* xvii. 7, "And the staff of his spear was
like a weaver's beam." **seven-times-folded**, 'made of seven folds'
(of metal or leather). So was the shield of Turnus (*Æn.* xii.
925, "Clipei extremos septemplicis orbes," "Both the outer
folds of his seven-fold shield"), and of Ajax (Ovid, *Met.* xii. 2,
"Clipei dominus septemplicis," "Lord of the seven-fold shield";
Hom. *Il.* vii. 222, σάκος αἰόλον ἑπταβόειον, "Seven-fold shield of
varied workmanship").

1123. **oaken staff**. So David "took his staff in his hand,"
when he went to meet Goliath (1 *Sam.* xvii. 40). In using the
epithet 'oaken,' Milton was thinking perhaps of the British
oak: the 'oak' of Scripture is a different tree, which is mentioned frequently for its shade, but only once for its strength
(*Amos*, ii. 9).

1124. **raise such outcries**, 'knock so rudely.' **clatter'd iron**,
'armour clattering under Samson's blows'; termination *-ed* for
-ing, see l. 119, n.   The passive form may be preserved in the
rendering 'battered.'

1125. **withhold ... from**, 'prevent ... from getting at.'

1132, 1133. **spells**, 'magic incantation'; from A.S. *spel*, 'story,'
'narrative' (whence 'gospel,' 'god-spel'); used at first in a good
sense, as in the *Ormulum* (1205), "And spellest hemm" (preach-
est to them); *Owl and Nightingale*, "thisse spelle" (story); but
occurring in the bad sense of 'magic' in Gower's *Conf. Amantis*
(1393).   'Spell' (of letters) is from the same root, and means lit.
'to *tell* the letters,' but was early confounded in meaning with
'spill'—'to point out the letters with a *spill* or splinter of wood.'
But 'spell,' 'a turn,' in the expression 'a spell of work,' is from

a different root. **black enchantments**; cf. the expr. 'black art.' The epithet 'black' in such connections means 'working evil'; thus a 'black witch' was one that worked mischief (Halliwell); so 'black Macbeth,' 'black and midnight hags,' in Shakspere. In M.E. and in O. Fr. the same association of ideas led to the spelling 'nigromancy' ('black divination') occurring in the *Romance of Alexander* and *Piers Plowman*, and as late as Berners' *Froissart* and Holinshed's *Chronicle*, instead of the proper spelling 'necromancy' ('divination of the dead').

1134. Armed ... charmed; see l. 1117, n. **strong**, predicative and *proleptic*, 'so that thou becamest strong.' There occurs another *anachronism* here in the allusion, pointed out by Todd, "to the oath taken before the judges of the combat by the champions—'I do swear that I have not upon me, nor on any of the arms I shall use, words, *charms*, or *enchantments*, to which I trust for help to conquer my enemy, but that *I do only trust in God*, in my right, and in the strength of my body.'" Cockburn, *History of Duels.* "Milton's Harapha is as much a Gothick giant as any in Amadis of Gaul." There is a similar reference to this oath in the *Dumb Knight*, i. 1, where Dodsley quotes to the same effect from Segar, *on Honor.* **which**, antecedent 'strength,' implied in the adj. 'strong.'

1138. chafed, 'angry'; contracted through Fr. *chauffer*, from Lat. *calefacere;* used in its literal sense of 'to warm' in Shak. *2 Henry VI.* iii. 2. 141, "Fain would I go to chafe his paly lips | With twenty thousand kisses." **ruffled porcupines:** cf. Shak. *Hamlet,* i. 5. 20. "And each particular hair stand on end, | Like quills upon the fretful porpentine."

1139. forbidden arts; the Jews were forbidden to consult wizards and familiar spirits under penalty of death, *Lev.* xx. 6; and such practices are branded as abominations, *Deut.* xviii. 9.

1140. Living God, an expression very frequent in Scripture, *e.g.* 1 *Tim.* iv. 10, "We trust in the living God"; see l. 1134, n.

1143. while I preserved, 'as long as I should preserve'; cf. Shak. *Temp.* iii. 2. 120, "But while thou livest, keep a good tongue in thy head."

1146. invocate, 'invoke'; so 'invocated,' l. 575. This unusual form occurs in Shak. *Rich. III.* i. 2. 8, "I invocate thy ghost"; and in Drayton's *Polyolbion* as an intransitive, "Some call on heaven, some invocate on hell."

1147. spread before him, 'lay the case before him in prayer'; cf. 2 *Kings*, xix. 14, "And Hezekiah went up into the house of the Lord and spread it (Sennacherib's letter) before the Lord."

1151. Avow, 'solemnly declare'; Fr. *avouer* (from Lat. *ad, votum*, 'a vow,' 'wish'); a different word from 'avouch,' which is the word 'vouch' (Lat. *voco*, 'to call') with the otiose prefix '*a*' on the analogy of 'avow.' **challenge**, 'defy'; used in *P. R.* iv. 260, in the older sense of 'claim' ("Whose poem Phoebus challeng'd for his own"). The use of the word in this sense occurs as far back as *Robert of Glou.* (1298, "To calangy by ryghte the kynedom "). A still older meaning. 'to accuse' (Lat. *calumniari*, 'to slander'), occurs in the *Ancren Riwle* (1210, "Hwar of kalenges tu me ") and survives down to Wyclif (1 *Peter*, iii. 15, "That thei ben confoundid, whiche chalengen falsly youre good conversacioun in Crist ").

1152-1155. Prof. Masson (*Life of Milton*, vi. 676) sees in this challenge an allusion to Milton's longing for another Salmasius to fight against.

1153. **the utmost**; see l. 484, n. **godhead**; cf. 'deity,' l. 464.

1157, 1158. Milton here uses two common Scriptural expressions : *e.g. Exod.* xxx. 33, "(He) shall even be cut off from his people "; 2 *Kings*, xxi. 14, "And deliver them into the hands of their enemies."

1161. **common prison**; see l. 6, n.

1162. **asses**; see l. 37, n. Dunster thought the reference here was to Apuleius's ass, some of whose experiences were undergone in a pistrinum, or pounding mill. It is not likely that with a Scriptural allusion ready at hand, Milton would have gone to the *Golden Ass* for one. **comrádes**, accented as in Fr. (*camarade*) and Sp. (*camarada*).

1164. **boisterous**, 'strong,' 'indicating strength'; cf. 'robustious,' l. 569; and *Doct. and Disc. of Divorce* (Addr. to Parl.), "Yet God forbid that truth should be truth, because they have a boisterous conceit of some pretences in the writer." The word had no '*r*' in its original form; cf. Wyclif, *Matt.* ix. 16, "No man putteth a clout of *buystous* clothe into an elde clothing" ('strong,' 'new,' in Gr. ἄγναφος, 'unbleached'); Chaucer, *Manciples Tale*, "I am a boistous man, right thus I say" ('outspoken'); Dunbar, *The Thrissil and the Rois* (1503), "And lat no bowgle (young bull) with his busteous hornis " ('strong '). The '*r*' is inserted in the Bible of 1551, *Wisd. of Sol.* xi. 10, "boisterous kynge" ('severe '), and in Surrey's *Virgil* (1553), "Boisterous winde," which expr. also occurs in *Matt.* xiv. 30 (Gr. ἰσχυρός). In all these examples, as in the text, the modern bad sense attaching to the word is absent.

1167. **barber's razor**; see l. 1107, n. **subdued**, there is a coarse double meaning here : 'subdue thee with a razor,' *i.e.*' shave off thy hair with it.'

1169. thine, 'thy countrymen.' Samson is too proud even to notice Harapha's indignities personally, and to say "from *thee*."

1172. **ear ... eye**. Milton again uses the graphic language of Scripture, *e.g. Ps.* xxxix. 12, "Give ear to my cry, O Lord ";

xvii. 1, "Give ear to my prayers, O Lord"; *Gen.* vi. 8, "Found grace in the eye of the Lord."

1175. mortal fight; see. l. 1102, n.

1178-1267. *Having exhausted his stock of vituperation upon Samson's personal appearance, Harapha now proceeds to attack his character. He calls him a murderer, a revolter, and a robber, and refers to events in his career in support of his allegation. Samson, who had taken no notice of the vituperation, is stung to the quick the moment his character is maligned. He, one by one, eagerly clears it from the three charges brought against it by Harapha, and concludes with another challenge, which the Philistine again declines. It illustrates how carefully Milton attends to the appropriateness of the sentiments of his characters, that while Harapha has hitherto declined Samson's challenges for the impudent reason that he is blind and filthy, he now declines it on the insolent ground that he is a convict. This is too much for Samson; he bursts forth, calls Harapha a boaster and coward to his face, and, seeing he is unworthy to be challenged to honourable fight, threatens unceremoniously to strike him with the bare hand. Harapha departs, muttering something that is an important link in the chain of the action. The Chorus is full of ominous forebodings as to the consequences of his malice, but by a skilful dramatic contrast, Samson is perfectly unconcerned—death, the worst thing his enemies can inflict, is the best he can desire, and his death will involve the death of his enemies.*

1178. Fair honour, ironical : 'fair indeed is the honour !' **God**, dative, supply 'to.'

1181. Tongue-doughty, 'whose courage lies in words not deeds' ; cf. Beau. and Fl. *The Little French Lawyer*, v. 1, "Tongue-valiant"; Æsch. *Agam.* 1370, θρασύστομος ; so *Sept. c. Theb.* 608; Soph. *Ajax*, 1142, ἀνὴρ γλώσσῃ θρασύς. **doughty**, from A.S. *dugan*, 'to avail,' 'be worth,' whence *dugtig*, 'excellent,' 'able,' *duguth*, 'excellence'; Prov. Eng. 'dow,' 'to be worth,' and, perhaps, the modern 'do' in 'how do you *do* ? ' 'this will *do*.' This word has run through a history the reverse of that of the word 'virtue,' inasmuch as from its earlier meaning of ' excellent' (cf. *Piers Plow.* "And al that Marc hath ymad, Mathu, Johan, and Lucas | Of thyne douhtieste dedes, don on our secte ") it passed into its present one of 'valiant.'

1181. prove me these, 'prove me *to be* these' ('to be *such* ').

1182. Judges, xiii. 1, "And the Lord delivered them (the children of Israel) into the hand of the Philistines forty years " ; see l. 251.

1183. they took thee ; see ll. 253 *sq.*

1184. league-breaker. The league referred to was a cessation of mutual hostilities, and in particular an abstinence on the part of the Philistines from hostile raids (see l. 257), on condition that the Israelites paid a tribute (*Josephus*, v. 8. 8).

1185-1188. *Judges*, xiv. 19, "And the spirit of the Lord came upon him, and he went down to Ashkelon, and slew thirty men of them, and took their spoil, and gave change of garments unto them which expounded the riddle." The riddle is that mentioned in l. 1016, and the 'change of garments' was the stakes agreed upon.

1190. powers, 'forces'; used again in this concrete sense in l. 251.

1191. The constr. here is harsh, whether we understand, a *zeugma*:—' did no violence to others nor *took* spoil *from them*'; or take 'spoil' as a verb—so that 'did' is, first, a principal and, then, an auxiliary verb:—' did no violence ... nor *did* spoil *them*.'

1192. Among, 'from among.'

1193. argued, see l. 514, n.

1195. politician, 'crafty,' 'intriguing.' Milton often uses this word and its cognates in a bad sense; cf. *P. R.* iii. 391, "And in my ear | Vented much policy"; ib. 400, "Or to need | Thy politic maxims" (both referring to Satan); *Reform in England*, "Aphorismers and politicasters stand hankering and politizing"; Shak. *Twelfth N.* iii. 2. 34, "I had as lief be a Brownist as a politician"; 1 *Henry IV.* i. 3. 24, "This vile politician, Bolingbroke"; Sir T. Browne, *Letter to a Friend*, 47, "The politick nature of vice."

1196. bridal friends, 'friends invited to the marriage feast.' **bridal.** The term. -*al* has been mistaken in this word for the adj. term. (as in 'mortal,' Lat. -*alis*). It is derived from A.S. *bryd*, 'bride,' and *ealu*, 'ale,' and originally meant 'a marriage-feast'; used in this sense in *Piers Plow.* ii. 43, "To morwe worth ymade the maydenes bruydale"; and Wyclif, *Luke*, xiv. 8, "Whanne thou art bodun to bridalis sitte not at the mete in the first place." The word afterwards became so well recognized as an adj. that Ben Jonson formed a new subst. 'bridaltee' from it. In modern English the expr. 'bridal-feast' is a tautology, and 'bridal-cake' is less correct than the older 'bride-cake.'

1197. await me, 'watch me,' 'lie in wait for me.' This is the literal meaning of the word, which is from O. Fr. *agaiter*, whence also Mod. Fr. *guetter*, 'to be on the watch for,' cf. *Piers Plow.* ii. 184, "I bydde thee awayte hem well, let none of hem escape"; Chaucer, *Freres Tale*, "The lyoun syt in his awayt alway | To slen the innocent if that he may"; *Acts*, ix. 24, "But their lying await was known to Saul." **thirty spies**, see l. 386, n.

1198. cruel death. *Judges*, xiv. 15, "They .. said unto Samson's wife, entice thy husband, that he may declare unto us the riddle, *lest we burn thee* and thy father's house with fire."

1199. secret, *i.e.* the *incident* on which the riddle was based. *Judges*, xiv. 8, 9, " And behold there was a swarm of bees and honey in the carcase of the lion " (slain by Samson, l. 128), "and he took thereof in his hand, and went on eating and came to his father and mother, and he gave them, and they did eat ; *but he told not them* that he had taken the honey out of the carcase of the lion." Samson's object in keeping the incident a secret was that to Jews, and especially to a Nazarite, contact with a dead body was defilement. Josephus omits all mention of the circumstance of Samson eating the honey himself ; no doubt from this consideration.

1201. set on, 'determined on.'

1202. chanced, 'chanced upon,' 'met by accident.' (From Lat. *cado* ' to fall ' : cf. the expr. ' fall in with a person.')

1203. used hostility, *sc.* ' on them (as on my enemies).'

1204. my underminers, 'secret plotters against me.' Cf. Shak. *All's Well*, i. 1. 131, "Bless our poor virginity from underminers and blowers-up." **In their coin,** *i.e.* ' with apparel taken from their own countrymen ' ; see l. 1185, n. (the meaning is *not* 'repay their undermining with undermining ').

1205. My nation, ' *You say* my nation ' ; see l. 782, n.

1206. force of conquest, 'power acquired through the sword.'

1207. Is well ejected, ' is rightly driven out,' ' there is nothing wrong in ejecting.'

1208. private person ; this can have either of two allied meanings ; (1) a person not acting in any public capacity, holding, as it were, no commission from the government of Israel (cf. l. 1212, and Shak. *Henry V*. iv. 1. 255, " What have kings that privates have not too?") ; or (2) an obscure person, Samson thus replying to Harapha's insinuation in l. 1082 ; cf. Beau. and Fl., *Wife for a Month*, ii. 2, "The poor slave that lies private has his liberty | As amply as his master in that tomb."

1210. Single, 'in my single person, unsupported by my countrymen.'

1211. I was, ' *I reply* I was.' **private,** adj. for subst., like Lat. *privatus*, 'one possessing no political authority.' **raised,** a common Scriptural expr., *e.g. Judges*, iii. 9, "The Lord raised a deliverer to Israel." There is a *zeugma* in the word :— ' *endowed* with strength, and *sent forth* with a command,' *i.e.* 'vested with authority,' ' commissioned.'

1214. sent, emphatic, 'destined,' 'heaven-sent.'

1215. for nought. either (1) 'as a person of no consequence,' 'as a nobody,' or (2) ' for no consideration,' ' wantonly.'

1218. had, would have. **my known offence,** 'which, therefore, you cannot ignore.' Harapha had tried to ignore the true cause of Samson's fall, by insinuating that it was due to the superior might of Dagon and the Philistines.

1220. **shifts,** nom. absol., see l. 1116, n. **appellant,** 'challenger,' a term borrowed from the mediæval duello, and therefore an *anachronism;* cf. Shak. 2 *Henry VI.* ii. 3. 49, "This is the day appointed for the combat, | And ready are the appellant and defendant." Fabyan, describing a grand tournament between ' certeyn gentylmen' of Scotland, and certain Englishmen in 1384, says "the erle marshall overthrewe his appellaunt, while Syr Wyllyam Darell refusyd his appellant, or they had ronne theyr full coursys."

1221. **maimed,** 'disabled.' The word is now used to mean ' crippled,' ' deprived of a limb ' (as in *P. L.* i. 459, *Mark,* ix. 43), as if it was derived from Lat. *mancus.* This derivation, however, is doubtful. In Cotgrave the Fr. word is *mehaing* (' a maime, or abatement of strength by hurts received '); Sir T. More also spells the word with an *h*—"Spoyled, meyhemed and slaine many a good virtuous man "; in Blackstone ' mayhem ' is defined as injury to a man's ' limbs,' which is explained to mean "*members which may be useful to him in fight.*" This is the sense in the text.

1222. **thrice,** according to the law of arms. In Shak. *Lear,* v. 3. 116, the Herald reads out the challenge for any of Edmund's enemies to appear "by the third sound of the trumpet," and Edgar enters at the third blast. In reality Samson has challenged Harapha more than thrice.

1223. **of small enforce,** 'acquiring little strength or endeavour.' ' Enforce,' verb for subst. The verb occurs in the sense of ' strengthen' in Chaucer, *Wife of Bathes Tale,* "And yet with sorwe thou enforcest thee" (hence the modern ' reinforce '), and in that of ' endeavour' in Wyclif, *Luke,* i. 1, "For sothe for manye men enforceden to ordeyne the tellyng of thingis."

1224. **slave enrolled.** There is no mention of such a class of slaves in Scripture, and I can only venture on the following suggestion :—From the context it was evident that Samson was of the class of those who were made slaves in punishment for a crime (what Justinian, *Inst.* i. 12, 3, and Grotius, *De Jure Belli et Pacis,* ii. 5. 3, call *servus poenae*). Such criminals among the Romans were compelled to work in the *ergastula* (' prison work-houses ') in chains, and were called *inscripti* or *inscripta ergastula* (' enrolled in the prison black-book '). Harapha, of course, by an anachronism, is made to pretend that Samson is such an ' enrolled ' criminal slave.

1225. **Due,** ' liable.'

1226. Another reference to the laws of single combat. Todd

quotes at length from Vincentio Saviolo showing that the privilege of trial by combat was denied to criminals and convicts, and whoever fought a duel with such was considered dishonoured thereby. **man of arms**, 'a man of honour,' 'one following the honourable profession of arms.'

1228. **descant on**, 'discuss from various points of view,' 'make remarks on.' Accent *déscant*, one of the few instances in Milton of throwing *back* the accent. Originally the term was a technical one in music, meaning the variations of a *part song* upon the simple melody or *plain song*. Hence Milton uses the word in *P. L.* iv. 603, of the song of the nightingale.

1229. **part**, 'depart,' like the Fr. *partir ;* so used again in l. 1481. **slight**, adv.

1230. **survey thee**, 'take thy measure,' 'lay hold of thee.' Samson, sarcastically using Harapha's own word, threatens to 'survey' him with his hand, as the latter had surveyed him with his eyes (l. 1089).

1231. **O Baal-zebub**, a Philistine god, the principal seat of whose worship was Ekron ; cf. 2 *Kings*, i. 16, where he is called the "god of Ekron."

1232. **render death**, 'inflict death in reply.' 'Render' is used in the Lat. sense of 'return' (*reddo*); cf. *Matt.* xxii. 21, "Render (ἀπόδοτε) therefore unto Cæsar the things which are Cæsar's." Observe that Harapha always 'talks big,' but never acts up to his vaunts.

1234. **bring up thy van**, 'advance,' lit. 'move forward thy vanguard.' Samson uses the language that perhaps he had often used when challenging large *bodies* of Philistines. He seems as if unaccustomed to challenge them *singly*.

1235. This is very truculent, but Samson's object in speaking thus is to show that he has now discovered Harapha to be a thorough coward, and therefore unworthy to fight with him in honourable duel. This is Samson's rejoinder to Harapha's declaration, in l. 1226, that *he* did not think Samson worthy to fight with him. Another instance of Milton's balance of sentiments.

1237. **baffled**, 'disgraced,' 'mocked.' A passage in Hall's *Chronicle* (quoted in Richardson) describes the manner in which a man convicted of perjury was disgraced among the Scots. The word for this was 'to baffull,' which Skeat connects with Scotch 'bauchle,' 'to treat contemptuously,' and traces to an Icelandic source. The older etymology referred it to the Fr. *bafouer*, 'to baffle.' In Spenser this is the kind of disgrace inflicted upon the boaster Braggadochio (*F.Q.* v. 3. 37); and in *F.Q.* vi. 7. 27, the manner of it is thus described :—"And after all for greater infamie | He by the heeles him hung upon a tree, | And *baffuld so*, that all which passed by | The picture of his punishment might see." In Beau. and Fl. *A King and no King*, iii. 2, Bessus, the coward, is similarly treated : " In this state I continued till they hung me up by the heels, and beat me with hazel sticks ... for the whole kingdom took notice of me for a baffled, whipped fellow." In the more general sense, as in the text, the word occurs in Shak. *Rich. II.* i. 1. 170, "I am disgraced, impeached and baffled here." Middleton and Dekker's *Roaring Girl*, i. 1, " Yet do you now thus baffle me to my face?" In Ben Jonson's *The Devil is an Ass* (Gifford, v. 127), the stage direction is "Baffles him, and exit."

1238. **bulk without spirit vast**, *i.e.* ' thee *who art* vast bulk without spirit,' *hyperbaton ;* ' without spirit' is to be understood as an adj. phrase equivalent to ' spiritless.'

1239. **structure**, cf. the expr. ' pile high-built,' l. 1069.

1240. So Hercules swung Antaeus, the Libyan giant and wrestler, in the air (but strangled him while aloft).

1241. **shattered**, *proleptic* constr. ' which would be shattered (by the fall) '; in prose the line would stand, ' *at* the risk of *shattering* thy sides.' **hazard**, of Arabic origin, *al zar*, ' the die '; orig. it meant a game of chance, played with dice, and is used by Chaucer to mean the vice of gambling. *Pardoners Tale*, " And now that I have spoke of Glotonie, | Now wol I you defenden (forbid) hasardrie."

1242. **Astaroth.** Commonly this Phœnician goddess is associated with the god Baal as symbolizing the productive powers of nature (*Judges*, x. 6). Milton, however, in making Harapha swear by her, identifies her with the Roman goddess Bellona, having in mind 1 *Sam.* xxxi. 10, where the Philistines hang up the armour of Saul after he is slain, in the "house of Ashtaroth," the action clearly indicating that she was looked upon as the goddess of war. This line gives the first hint of some calamity in store for Samson, but for the present we are made to fear nothing worse than ' irons ' (next line). This fear is gradually intensified by Milton with great skill, see l. 1252, n.

1243. **braveries**, ' vaunts ': for the history of the word, see l. 717, n. **loaden**, ' laden ' ; this form occurs again in *P. L.* ix. 576, " A goodly tree ... loaden with fruit."

1244. **His giantship ;** a mock title of honour on the analogy of ' his lordship.'

1245. **unconscionable**, ' enormous ' : lit. ' having no conscience,' ' no moderation ' ; used in the sense of ' too great for,' ' disproportioned,' in *Doct. and Disc. of Divorce*, i. 2, " Affliction of an unconscionable size to human strength." ' Conscionable ' is a carelessly-formed adj. from ' conscience '; since the term ' -able ' is joined to verbs, and as there is no verb in one word in English meaning ' to be conscientious,' no such **adj.** as this can properly be formed.

1246. **sultry,** ' hot,' ' angry.' The word here has less of its modern sense than in *Lyc.* 28, " What time the gray-fly winds his sultry horn "; from vb. *swelt, swelter,* die of heat. **chafe,** ' rage '; this word as a noun is rare; cf. Spenser, *F. Q.* vi. 5, 19, "That in his chauffe he digs the trampled ground."

1248. **divulge,** ' announce publicly, far and wide,' cf. *P. L.* viii. 583, "To them made common and divulged." Shak. *Merry Wives,* iii. 2. 43, " I will ... divulge Page himself for a secure and wilful Actaeon "; Hall's *Chronicle,* " The councel of Fraunce caused a common fame (although it were not trewe) to be divulged abrode." Lat. *vulgare* (vb.), *vulgus,* common people. **Five sons,** see l. 1068, n. **Four sons** are mentioned in 2 *Sam.* xxi. 15–22, but one of these is said in the English version to be " the brother of Goliath the Gittite," thus making up five.

1250. **I will ... to,** ' I will .. *go* to.' This *ellipsis* of the verb after ' will,' followed by a preposition of motion, is common in Elizabethan literature, cf. Shak. *Macb.* iii. 4. 133, " I will, to-morrow, | And betimes I will, to the weird sisters "; see ll. 920, 1250 ; and Abbott, § 405.

1252. Note how the catastrophe is gradually shadowed forth : the interest rises from mere inquietude to a breathless expectation of some great action. The mind quickly passes from the fear of more rigorous treatment threatened by Harapha (l. 1242) to the more awful terror of an unknown calamity. See ll. 1266-7, 1300, 1346-7, 1379, 1387-9, 1426, for the successive steps by which this transition is effected. This foreshadowing of coming events is in imitation of the practice of the Greek drama.

1253, 1254. **offered fight ... mention.** A Latin constr. for the ordinary English ' mention the offer of fight,' or ' mention *that* a fight had been offered,' cf. l. 1377, ' we present.'

1257. **than,** *sc.* ' what is.'

1258. **cannot well,** ' can hardly.'

1259. **intend advantage of,** ' intend to derive advantage from ' ; ' intend ' is again used with a substantive as an objective case in *P. L.* xii. 73, " This usurper ... to God his tower intends| Siege and defiance," iv. 898, "If he intends our stay | In that dark durance." This constr. is explained by the literal meaning of the word (Lat. *intendere animum*) ' to aim at,' ' to pay attention to,' as in Bacon, *Adv. of L.* ii. 20, 11. " Herodicus who did nothing all his life, but intend his health " ; Heywood, *Foure Prentices of London,* i. 1, " Whilst you intend the walls "; Beau. and Fl. *Spanish Curate,* iii. 4, *Ama.* " Why do you stop me ? " *Lean.* " That you may intend me."

1260. **work ... hands**, 'work which it would require many ordinary men to perform.' **my keeping**, 'the cost of my maintenance.'

1261. **owners.** Samson speaks of himself as a slave.

1263. **to rid**, the constr. is 'if he rids,' 'by ridding'; the meaning is 'to deliver,' cf. *Exod.* vi. 6, "I will rid you out of their (the Egyptians') bondage"; Shak. *Rom. and Jul.* v. 3. 241, "Some means to rid her from this second marriage."

1264. **to me**, *i.e.* '*is* to me.'

1265. **So.** The co-ordinate 'that' is omitted in the next line: 'It may so fall out, *that* it may draw their own ruin ...'

1266. **it;** *i.e.* the attempt to gain this end.

1267. **who**, antecedent 'they' implied in 'their.'

1268-1300. *The Chorus draws a picture of just men, long suffering under the oppression of the wicked, from which the deliverance is twofold : either through the might of a deliverer effecting the speedy overthrow of the oppressor, or through the patience of the sufferers enduring, till finally they win the crown of life—which is the reward of the righteous at their death. This they illustrate by referring to the "Saints," who were once so delivered through the might of Cromwell, and who now have to deliver themselves through patience, such as is shown in the blind and neglected Milton perhaps more than in any other Puritan of the Restoration times.*

1268. **comely**, 'becoming,' cf. *Ps.* xxxiii. 1, "For praise is comely for the upright." The more usual meaning of the word 'externally or physically graceful' is frequent in Canticles. **it**, antecedent follows, l. 1270, "when God," etc.

1270-1286. The allusion is to Cromwell overthrowing the monarchy. It is strange that the unmeasured terms in which Milton, here and elsewhere, speaks of the monarchy, both before and after the Commonwealth, did not raise the scruples in the mind of the Licenser, which a much less pronounced passage in *Paradise Lost* (i. 599) is said to have done. The allusion there however was to the *future*, regarding which the fears of the Royalists were more lively, than their consciences were sensitive regarding the past.

1272. **quell**, see l. 563, n.

1273. **brute**, 'relying upon sheer physical strength,' 'not based on moral right or intellectual superiority.'

1274. **Hardy**, 'bold,' Fr. *hardi*, cf. *P. L.* ii. 425, "None | So hardy as to proffer or accept | Alone the dreadful voyage": *hard*, as an attribute of matter, is a derived meaning.

1275. **pursue**, 'persecute'; cf. Wyclif, *John*, xv. 20, "If thei han pursued me, thei schulen pursue you also"; so the subst.

in 1 *Tim.* i. 13, " Me ... that first was a blasfeme and a pursuere and ful of wrongis."

1277. He, 'the deliverer,' l. 1270. **ammunition,** 'preparation for.' This comparatively late word was substituted in Howell's *Letters*, 1635, for the older 'munition.' The original meaning was 'fortification' (Lat. *moenia*, 'walls,' root MU, 'to bind '), in which sense Spenser uses 'munificence' ('munifience'), from the same root.

1278. feats ... defeats, for the jingle see l. 1117. n. ; and cf. *P. L.* i. 642, " Tempted our attempt." ' *Feat* ' is 'fact,' lit. 'what is done' : ' *defeat* ' is ' de-fact,' ' to un-do.'

1279. plain. This epithet is fitly applied to Cromwell. His speeches, unless they are set down to hypocrisy, and his words to Lely, the painter—" paint me as I am "—bear it out.

1283. expedition, ' speed '; cf. *P. L.* vi. 86. " The banded powers of Satan hasting on | With furious expedition "; Shak. *Rich. III.* iv. 3. 54, " Then fiery expedition be my wing." The same meaning is apparent in ' expedite,' ' expeditious.'

1284. lightning glance ; the use of a subst. as an adj. where usually a possessive case would be used is seen in the expressions " Hell-fire " (*P. L.* ii. 364), " Hell-hounds " (ii. 654), " Hell-gate " (ii. 725), " Heaven-gates " (i. 326), " Heaven-towers " (xii. 52).

1285. surprised, 'taken by surprize.'

1286. defence, ' power of defence.'

1287. Cf. Eur. *Phoen.* 393, δεῖ φέρειν τὰ τῶν θεῶν, " We should submit in patience to the dispensations of the gods."

1288. saints. This was the name by which the Republican Independents, in their fanatic pride, called themselves. The name is frequently applied in the New Testament, especially in the Epistles, to believers in Christ, *e.g.* in *Heb.* vi. 10, *Ephes.* i. 1, *Phil.* i. 1, *Col.* i. 2, etc. **fortitude,** ' endurance under oppression.' For the sentiment in ll. 1288-1291 cf. *P. L.* xii. 570, " Suffering for Truth's sake | Is fortitude to highest victory "; ix. 31, " The better fortitude | Of patience." The earlier meaning of the word was ' strength,' as in Shak. 1 *Henry VI.* ii. 1. 17, " Coward of France ... despairing of his own arm's fortitude."

1292. Either, ' both.' **these,** viz. ' might ' (l. 1271) and ' patience ' (l. 1287). **is in thy lot,** ' have fallen to thy lot,' namely ' might has fallen to thy lot *before*. and patience, *after*, the loss of thy eyesight.' It would be making the Chorus more sanguine than their speeches warrant, to suppose that they have any hopes of Samson exerting his strength for the deliverance of Israel. It is therefore not possible to take ' either ' to mean ' *one* of the two,' and ' is ' to mean ' is still ' (in the future).

1294. bereaved, see l. 48, n. ; and cf. Spenser, *F. Q.* ii. 3. 23,

"That quite bereav'd the rash beholder's sight." **sight bereaved,** a Latinism ; see l. 1253, n.

1295. **May chance**, 'chances.' The Chorus wishes to intimate as delicately as possible to Samson that power has departed from him, and patience alone is left to him. Hence this use of the potential for the indicative.

1296. **crown**, 'deliver.' Death is here looked upon as the victory of patience over oppression ; cf. *Rev.* ii. 10, "Be thou faithful unto death, and I will give thee a crown of life"; 2 *Tim.* iv. 7, 8, "I have fought a good fight; I have finished my course; I have kept the faith : henceforth is laid up for me a crown of righteousness."

1297. **Idol's day**, 'holiday in honour of an idol, Dagon.' **day of rest**, as the Sabbath, which is "God's day " to the Israelite.

1298. **Labouring**, 'exercising,' 'troubling.'

1299. **working day**, *sc.* 'labours,' *i.e.* 'keeps busy,' by a slight *zeugma.*

1301. **descry**, 'see,' 'make out.' The word is a doublet of 'describe,' and the two words are used interchangeably, *e.g.* in *P. L.* iv. 567, "I *described* (for 'descried ') his way | Bent all on speed"; Spenser, *F. Q.* iv. 1. 32, "His name was Blandamour that did *descrie* (for 'describe ') | His fickle mind full of inconstancie." The original meaning of both is seen in *Josh.* xvii. 5, "Ye shall therefore describe the land into seven parts," and in the expr. ' to describe a circle ' (Lat. *scribo,* 'to write,' 'mark '). From such uses two false etymologies of the word arose : one as if it was a doublet of 'discern ' (Lat. *dis cerno,* pt. *cretum,* 'to distinguish '), and was spelt ' discreve,' or ' discrie ' ; the other as if it was a doublet of ' decry.' This latter mistake occurs in *Comus,* 141, " And to the tell-tale sun descry | Our concealed solemnity " ; in Spenser, *F. Q.* vi. 7. 12, and in Foxe's *Martyrs.*

1301, 1302. **this way ... tending**, 'directing his steps hither,' like the Latin *huc tendens.*

1303. **sceptre**, in its original sense of ' staff,' ' rod,' such as was borne by *heralds* (cf. Hom. *Il.* vii. 277). **quaint**, used always by Milton in his poetry in its latest sense of ' strange,' ' curious.' The history of the word is as follows :—Its original meaning was ' known ' (Lat. *cognitus*), ' famous,' as in *Robert of Glou.* (1298), " Marius ... a quoynte man and bold," hence came the meaning of ' skilful,' *id.* " He ladde this kyndom swithe wel with quoyntise (' skill ') and wysdom." Next it acquired a bad meaning, 'cunning, *e.g. Metrical Homilies* (1330), *Tale of a Usurer,* "For thi did he quaintelye | Qwen he gert wormes ete this man " ; *The Plowman's Crede* (1394), " Dere brother, quath Peres, the devell is ful queynte " ; Chaucer, *Merchauntes Tale,* " O swete poison queinte " (' subtle '). Next comes a meaning of ' pretty,' ' elegant,' due to a supposed derivation from Lat. *comptus*, 'neat,' as in Shak. *Temp.* i. 2. 317, "My quaint Ariel"; *Much Ado*, iii. 4. 22, "But for a fine quaint graceful fashion, yours is worth ten on 't." From this the transition to 'odd' was easy.

1304. **amain**, 'with all the speed he may,' 'as fast as he can,' lit. 'with all his strength'; see l. 637, n. **speed**, nom. abs., 'his look indicating that he is on a message requiring speed.'

1306. The frequent ellipses in this and the preceding four lines give a hurried movement to the words, well depicting the idea of the hurrying messenger which they are meant to convey. Thus supply 'person' after 'some other,' 'he' before 'comes,' 'being' after 'speed,' 'to be' after 'now,' 'he is' before 'at hand'; see l. 1344.

1307. **voluble**, 'rapidly delivered'; cf. Cic. *pro Flacc.* 20. 48, "Homo volubilis quadam praecipiti celeritate dicendi," "A man voluble with a kind of headlong speed of speech." The word has the Latin accent and literal meaning in *P. L.* iv. 594, "This less volúbil earth" ('revolving less rapidly').

1308-1347. *The Officer summons Samson in the name of the Philistine lords to attend at their great assembly in order to amuse them with feats of strength. Samson refuses to go, the chief ground of his refusal being religious—the Jewish law forbids him to be present at idolatrous rites.*

1309. **manacles**; it is evident from l. 1235 that this word must be here taken to mean simply 'chains'; its proper meaning is 'handcuffs.' **remark him**, 'mark him out,' 'serve to distinguish him.' '*Re-*' has an intensive force here,—'clearly,' 'unmistakeably.'

1310. Milton makes the messenger deliver his message in the *indirect* narrative: in so doing he follows the practice of the Greek drama; cf. Æsch. *Agam.* 603 *sq.*; see ll. 1391-8, n.

1311. **is**, 'there is,' 'is celebrated.'

1312. **triumph**, 'pageant'; cf. *L'All.* 120, "Where throngs of knights and barons | In weeds of peace high triumphs hold." From Gr. θρίαμβος, 'a festal song in honour of Bacchus"; this among the Romans became *triumphus*, 'a procession on the entry of a victorious general into Rome'; this sense occurs in Chaucer's *Monkes Tale* (Zenobia): the mediæval sense of the word occurs in Palsgrave's *Dict.*, and is thus described in Bacon's *Essay on Masques and Triumphs* (xxxvii.), "The glories of them are chiefly in the chariots, wherein the challengers make their entry, especially if they be drawn with strange beasts, as lions, camels, and the like." The gorgeousness of these shows is alluded to also in Beau. and Fl. *The Noble Gentleman*, ii. 1 (Dyce, x. 133), "Why, sir, you'll stay till next triumph-day be past?" etc. The word has this sense frequently in Shakspere; *e.g. Rich. II.* v. 2. 52, "Hold

those justs and triumphs"; v. 3. 14, "Those triumphs held at Ox-
ford"; 3 *Hen. VI.* v. 7, 43, "Speed the time with stately triumphs,
mirthful comic shows "; so Ben Jonson, *Poetaster* (Gifford, ii.
455), "Your tabernacles, varlets, your globes and your triumphs"
(but see Gifford's note here) ; in his *Love's Triumph* the stage
direction is " The Triumph is first seen afar off, and led in by
Amphitrite." Such, too, is his *Neptune's Triumph.* In these
masques Ben Jonson imitated Petrarch whose *Trionfi* illustrate
the use of the word in both senses of ' procession ' and ' victory.'
He first describes *processions* of those who have been famous in love,
chastity, fame, etc., that pass in vision before his eyes, and then
applies the allegory to the *victory* of love over man, of chastity
over love, of death over both, of fame over death, and so on.
pomp, see l. 436, n.

1313. **human rate**, ' the proportion of strength granted to
ordinary human beings.' **rate**, ' allowance '; cf. Spenser, *F. Q.*
iv. 8, 19, " The one right feeble through the evill rate | Of food
which in her duresse she had found " ; cf. ' rations.'

1317. **Where**. ' to a place where.' **heartened**, lit. ' encouraged,'
i.e. ' cheered,' ' invigorated.' He means ' refreshments,' no doubt;
as in Beau. and Fl. *The Island Princess*, " And see his diet be so
light and little, he grow not *high-hearted* on 't." Cf. ' a hearty
meal.' The verb occurs in Palsgrave and in Spenser, *F. Q.* iv. 9,
34, "Till seeing them through suffrance harten'd more."

1318. **fits**, ' befits '; see l. 929.

1320. In allusion to the Second Commandment (*Exod.* xx. 4,
5 ; *Deut.* xvii. 2 *sq.*).

1323-1325. The allusion is to the *holiday sports* (see l. 1421, n.)
that had been abolished by the Puritans, but had been revived at
the Restoration. Public games were distasteful to the earnest
religious temperament of the Jews. Such allusions to these as
occur in Scripture are due to the introduction of Greek and
Roman sports against which the national feeling rebelled. See
Josephus, xv. 8. 1, for an outburst of this feeling when Herod set
up his Caesarean theatre. **sword-players**, ' fencing-masters,'
' professional fencers.' The word is used in Holland's Pliny for
' gladiators.' ' Play,' from Lat. *plaga*, ' a blow,' means ' fight ' :
the word is so used as a verb in 2 *Sam.* ii. 14, "Let the young
men now arise and play before us "; see l. 1087, n. There may
also be an allusion here to the *sword-dance*, popular in Anglo-
Saxon times, and mentioned by Strutt as having been performed
in Queen Anne's time, and even later.

1324. **gymnic artists**, ' tumblers,' says Todd : ' professional
gymnasts or athletes' more likely perhaps ; ' gymnic ' from Gr.
γυμνός, ' naked.' The illustrations accompanying Strutt's description of " wrestling for the cock " represent the competitors

as partially undressed, and the boys "tilting at the butt" are like athletes in Greek training schools, quite naked. None of the tumblers in Strutt's illustrations are 'gymnic.' **riders, runners,** 'those who contended in horse and foot races.' 'Races' are the only kind of games perhaps mentioned in the Old Testament; *Ps.* xix. 5, *Eccl.* ix. 11.

1325. **Jugglers,** 'tricksters'; from Lat. *joculator*, a jester; Fr. *jongleur*, orig. 'a minstrel,' who composed verses and sang them to his own accompaniment; as such the profession was honourable; thus Taillefer, jongleur to William, fought and sang at Senlac. Cf. Chaucer, *Rom. of the Rose*, " Minstreles and eke jogelours | That wel to sing did her paine." But the word early came to mean *any* sort of entertainer, and then one who entertains (as in the text) with tricks of sleight of hand. These meanings are seen in *Mandeville*, " And then comen jogulours and enchauntours that doen many mervailles " (before the great Cham). Chaucer, *Squires Tale*, " An apparence ymaad by some magyk | As jogelours playen at these festes grete"; *Freres Tale*, "A lousy jogelour can deceiven them." **antics,** 'buffoons,' 'clowns in a play.' This word has undergone changes similar to those of the adj.: thus (1) the original meaning was 'ancient' (from Lat. *antiquus*); Shak. *Cor.* ii. 3, "The dust on antic time"; Spenser, *F. Q.* i. 11, 27, " The antique world "; so the subst., according to Halliwell, was applied to ancient sculptures and paintings in churches: cf. the expr. " the antique," for 'ancient art.' (2) 'Old and quaint, 'after ancient models'; Shak. *Twelfth N.* ii. 3. 4, " That old and antic song "; *Il. Pens.* 158, " Antique pillars, massy proof "; *L'All.* 128, " Antique pageantry ": so the subst. meant 'curious devices'; thus Spenser (*F. Q.* ii. 3. 27) speaks of the " curious antickes " on Belphoebe's buskins. (3) 'Grotesque,' Shak. *Rom. and Jul.* i. 5. 58, "Cover'd with an antic face" (of a mask), so the subst. means 'a buffoon,' as in the text; cf. Sir T. Browne, *Religio Medici*, i. 41, " The world to me is but a dream or mockshow, and we all therein but pantalones and anticks." In Shak. *Rich. II.* iii. 2. 162, Death is called an antic, and in Holbein's *Dance of Death* (Pl. xi.) Death is drawn as an 'antic.' **Mummers,** 'masqueraders.' Brand (*Pop. Antiq.*) describes mumming as a sport at Christmas time, which consisted in men and women exchanging clothes, and going the round of their neighbours, and partaking of their Christmas cheer. They wore masks, illustrations of which are given in Strutt. Mumming " frequently was attended with an exhibition of gorgeous machinery, resembling the wonders of a modern pantomime " (Warton). Spenser, in *Mother Hubbard's Tale*, has " with mumming and with masking all around." The word is derived from Low Germ. *mumme*, 'a mask,' and is related to the interj. 'mum,' 'silence'! These strange fooleries had their origin in the ingrafting of the merriment of the heathen Saturnalia upon the Christian festival.

mimics, from Gr. μῖμος, was orig. 'an actor in a pantomine, resembling the vice in the old English moralities, that later passed into the *fool* of comedy. In these two words ('mummers and mimics') Milton alludes contemptuously to the *spectacular drama* of the Restoration, by classing them with the vulgar 'holiday sports.' The comedies and operas of Dryden, Tom Killigrew, Sir R. Howard, Sir C. Sedley, and Sir W. Davenant, may well have seemed to him no better than pantomimes, fit to be acted by 'mimics.' Davenant and Killigrew were, besides, the managers of two companies of these 'mimics'—the Duke's and the King's companies of actors. In Shak. *M. N. D.* iii. 2. 19, 'mimic' is used as here for 'actor'—"And forth my mimic comes," said of Bottom.

1326. **with shackles tired,** 'weary with dragging my chains.' It would be forcing the sense here to take 'tired' as an *archaism* for 'attired,' 'ornamented,' used ironically for 'loaded' with chains ; *tired* and *over-laboured* both mean a *feeling*.

1327. **over-laboured** ; cf. 'over-watched,' l. 405, n.

1329. **occasion** ; see l. 224, n. **of,** 'for.'

1331. **make a game of.** The article would be omitted in modern prose, as in 'make sport of.'

1333. **Regard thyself,** 'have a care for your safety,' 'mind what you do.' In a similar spirit the Chorus warns Prometheus, who replies with the same sternness as Samson.

1334. Supply the ellipsis thus : '*You ask me to regard* myself ! *I should rather regard* my conscience,' etc.

1335. **broken,** 'broken down,' 'dispirited.'

1337. **absurd,** 'preposterous'; the absurdity lies in the incongruity pointed out by Samson in the three following lines.

1338. **fool or jester** ; like the court fool or the fool among the morrice dancers, or those kept in private families for their entertainment. Sir T. Killigrew was called 'King Charles' Jester.'

1339. **heart-grief** ; cf. the '*cordolium*' of Plautus, *Cist.* i. 1. 67.

1341. **on me,** 'in my case.' The prep. 'on' seems to have been used here from the attraction of the words 'indignities' and 'contempt', the latent idea being of heaping indignities and contempt on Samson. I am not aware of any use of the verb 'join' for '*en*join.'

1342. **I will not come.** Samson's determination is shown by his refusal repeated at the end of every speech (see ll. 1321, 1332, and here).

1343. **in..posed ... with speed,** 'imposed *to be discharged* with speed,' *verbum praegnans* ; see l. 1055, n.

1344. Brooks *i.e.* ' *and it* brooks ' ; see l. 1306, n.

1345. So, ' even as I have signified it above.'

1346. sorry what, ' sorry *for* what ' ; for ellipsis of prep. see l. **1408. stoutness,** ' stubbornnesss,' ' pride ' ; like Lat. *stolidus*, Germ. *stolz*, with both of which it is connected by etymology ; cf. *L'Alleg.* 52, " While the cock ... stoutly struts his dames before " ; *Is.* ix. 9, " Pride and stoutness of heart " ; Shak. *Coriol.* iii. 2. 127, " Let | Thy mother feel thy pride, than fear | Thy dangerous stoutness " : cf. the expr. ' a stout resistance.'

1346, 1347. These lines, like ll. 1266, 7, foreshadow the catastrophe in its aspect of double disaster, both to Samson and to the Philistines.

1348-1389. *The Chorus tries to reason with Samson, but as unsuccessfully as the Officer had tried to coerce him. To them he replies that though he employs his strength at the mill to earn his bread honestly, he will not exert it at a festival to amuse the worshippers of Dagon ; that if he does obey the summons, it will be of his own free accord, and at the risk of offending God. Then follows a pause, after which Samson unexpectedly declares that he will obey the summons, for he feels an inward prompting that tells him this day will be signalized by some great act to be performed by him. These lines occupy an important place in the development of the action* (see Introd. p. xvii), *and the skill is admirable with which Milton manages the difficult transition from Samson's firm resolution not to go, to his sudden determination to do so.*

1348. matters, *i.e.* Samson's relation with his ' owners.'

1349. to the highth, ' to the utmost ' : the idea is from bending a flexible body, such as a bow, as far as it *will* bend.

1353. well, ' with patience.'

1355. Samson intimates here more clearly than he had in l. 569 that his supernatural strength has fully returned to him.

1357. so, ' in this unworthy manner.'

1360. Vaunting, ' displaying ' ; cf. Spenser, *F. Q.* iii. 2. 16, " What shape, what shield, what armes, what steed, what stedd | And what so else his person most may vaunt ? " From Lat. *vanitare*, through Fr. *vanter*, ' to be vain-glorious.' But in M.E. from a mistaken etymology from Fr. *avant* (Lat. *ab, ante*) ' in front,' the word was spelt ' avaunt ' both as a subst. and a verb, *e.g.* Chaucer, *Prol.* " He dorste make avaunt " ; *Wif of Bathes Tale,* " Of o thing I may avaunten me." The meaning in the text and in Spenser may be due to this supposed etymology.

1361, 1362. The constr. here is difficult. (1) With a comma after ' besides ' it is simply ' besides how vile, ... *would the act be; and* what act *can be* more execrably,' etc. (2) Without this comma it becomes a harsh Latinism for ' besides *being most vile*,

... what act *can* be more execrably,' etc. ; the Latin constr. of
an interrogative in a dependent sentence, ' Besides *how* vile it
was ' being equivalent to the English constr. of an indicative,
' Besides *that* it was *most* vile.' See l. 167, n.

1362. **unclean.** The use of this Scriptural word in *Leviticus* and
Numbers shows what loathing Samson feels for the Philistine idol ;
by this " unclean act " he would cease to be " holy unto God."

1367. **Of,** ' from,' ' at the hands of.' **civil power,** refers to
' corporal servitude,' l. 1336. Samson means that, although his
body is captive to the civil authorities of the Philistines, his soul
is yet free and serves his God.

1368. **Where ... not,** ' when acts are done unwillingly and under
compulsion.'

1369. **sentence,** ' opinion,' ' judgment.' Lat. *sententia ;* cf. *P.
L.* ii. 51, " My sentence is for open war " ; Chaucer, *Man of
Lawes Tale,* " Herkne what is the sentence of the wyse | ' Bet it
to dyen than have indigence ' " ; Bacon, *Essay,* lviii. " Salomon
giveth his sentence that all novelty is but oblivion." The meaning is now confined to the judgment pronounced from a tribunal
of law.

1370. **constrains me to,** ' constrains me *to go* to ' ; for similar
omissions of the verb before a prep. of motion, see ll. 920, 1250 ;
and before an adverb of motion, see l. 1445.

1371. **Not dragging,** ' unless he drags me.' **The Philistian
lords command ;** the constr. is ' you would perhaps urge that
the,' etc. Though the Chorus has not said so, the drift of their
remonstrance implies it ; see l. 1205.

1374. **prefer, Set ... behind,** ' esteem more ... esteem less.' The
opposition is brought out better in Latin—*antepono (deo hominem)
... postpono (deum homini).*

1375. **which,** ' which conduct.' **jealousy,** ' wrath,' used often
of God, like παραζήλωσις in the Septuagint and Greek Testament.

1376. **unrepented,** ' *if* unrepented,' ' if I do not repent of it.'

1377. Thyer notes that such a dispensation was once actually
asked for and granted. Naaman the Syrian, the leper, asked
for a dispensation for himself from Elisha, that he might attend
his heathen master to the temple of Rimmon ; 2 *Kings,* v. 18, 19.
dispense with, ' forgive,' ' excuse ' ; cf. l. 314. *P. L.* v. 571,
" Yet for thy good | This is dispens't" ; Gower, *Conf. Am.* " But
for he had golde enough to give, his sinne was dispensed with
golde " ; so in Tyndale the ecclesiastical authority can " dispense
with a marriage," *i.e.* grant a dispensation for it. **me, or thee,
Present,** a Latinism, ' for my or thy presence ' ; see ll. 1253,
1433.

1379. Another presage ; see l. 1252, n.

1380. **here,** ' in this matter.' **reach** ; see l. 62, n.

1381-1389. These lines constitute the *peripeteia* or turning point of the action ; see Introd. p. xvii.

1382. **rousing motions in me** ; ' some *intimate impulse* stirring me,' such promptings from above as Samson had felt before ; l. 223.

1384. No messenger is present, but as the Chorus had warned Samson to expect a second message (l. 1352), he speaks as though the man will return.

1387. **aught of presage,** a Latinism for 'any presage.' The sense is ' if there is such a thing as a presage in the mind,' ' if there is any truth in presages in the mind.' Todd quotes Eur. *Andr.* 1072, πρόμαντις θυμὸς ὥς τι προσδοκᾷ, '' My mind presages as expecting ill.''

1389. **By,** for ; or ' by ' may be retained by altering the constr. thus in prose, ' this day will be *marked* by,' or ' this day will be *made* remarkable by.' **the last,** ' *be* the last.'

1390-1426. *The Officer delivers his second message, threatening recourse to physical force, if Samson still continues obdurate. But Milton has been careful to make his hero form his resolution before this threat is intimated to him ; and so Samson goes with the Officer in accordance with that resolution, and not because of the threat. His reply to the Officer contains a sentiment whose irony becomes terribly apparent afterwards, but his words of farewell to the Chorus are full of that spirit of noble devotion to God and his country that shines so fair through the dark night of his calamities.*

1391. **this second message,** unlike the first (ll. 1110 *sq.*), is delivered in direct narrative, after the manner of the heralds in Homer, who repeat their message word for word as it has been delivered to them. The direct narrative makes the message all the more peremptory.

1394. **and** ; adversative, ' and *yet.*' **our sending and command,** a *hendiadys* for ' our command sending for thee' or ' our sending (message) commanding thy presence.'

1395. **Dispute thy coming,** 'argue whether thou shalt come or not,' ' refuse to come.'

1396. **engines,** 'means,' ' contrivances,' here an abstract noun : cf. Bacon, *Essays*, xvii. ''(astronomers) did feign eccentrics and epicycles and such engines of orbs to save the phenomena.'' An earlier sense of the word was ' craft,' ' subtlety,' as in Spenser, *F. Q.* iii. 10. 7, '' His fals engins fast he plyde '' ; Lydgate has '' Scleight or engyne, fors or felonye '' ; see note on ' gins,' l. 933. Lat. *ingenium,* inborn faculty, native genius.

1397. **hamper,** ' render powerless, or incapable of doing mischief.' The word is used only here in Milton's poetry, and only once by Shakspere (2 *Henry VI.* i. 3. 148, "Good king, look to 't in time ; | She'll hamper thee, and dandle thee like a baby "). In Browne's *Britannia's Pastorals* (1613), the word occurs as a subst. meaning 'fetters' :—"The swarthy smith spits in his buck-horne fist, | And bids his men bring out the five-fold twist, | His shackles, shacklockes, *hampers*, gives and chaines, | His linked bolts." The word is derived from an Icelandic stem, meaning 'to maim' ; thus in Chaucer's *Tr. and Cr.* ii. occurs the verb '*hamel*,' ("Algate a foote is hameled of thy sorrow ") ; the same meaning explains "hamper-legged," given in Halliwell ; in the old Forest Laws '*hameling* a dog' meant to mutilate its fore-feet ; in Lowland Scotch *hammle* and *hamp* mean 'to walk awkwardly,' 'to halt' ; and in Ulfilas, *Mark*, ix. 43, the Gothic word *hamfamma* is equivalent to 'maimed' in the A. V. The original sense therefore was to 'maim,' 'mutilate the limbs' ; hence 'to disable,' 'chain,' 'impede.' **as**, 'so that,' see Abbott, § 109. **Of force**, 'perforce.'

1399. **to try**, ' to test,' 'to put to trial.'

1400. **which**, *i.e.* 'my trying their art.' **pernicious**, 'fatal,' 'destructive,' from Lat. *per*, and *nex*, 'death.' Cf. *P. L.* i. 282, "Fallen such a pernicious height " ; vi. 849, "Shot forth pernicious fire | Among the accurst." (The word has an entirely different meaning and derivation in *P. L.* vi. 520, " Pernicious with one touch to fire " ; 'quickly lighted,' from Lat. *pernix*, 'swift').

1401. **too many**, *i.e.* ' *to be* too many.'

1402. **Because ... not**, 'as I shall not suffer them too,' 'that they may not.'

1404-1407. These words of Samson are full of irony directed against the Philistine lords, and full of dissimulation of his purpose as regards himself. He had declared to the Chorus (l. 1389) that he did *not* care for life when he changed his resolution, while he here pretends anxiety for its safety.

1404. **resistless**, 'irresistible' ; cf. *P. L.* ii. 62, "Resistless way " ; *P. R.* iv. 268, "Resistless eloquence." ' Resist' in this compound is a subst. ; cf. the analogous word 'timeless' (*Fair Infant*, 2), '-less' is '-lôs' (from 'lose '), without. In Marlowe, *Jew of Malta*, iii. 4, the word has a different meaning : "Whose billows beating the resistless banks " (' unable to resist,' ' defenceless ') : but in Dido, *Queen of Carthage*, iii. 2, 'unresisted' is used in the sense of ' resistless ' in the text : "Fate that has so many unresisted friends."

1406. **for a life**, ' for the sake of life.'

1408. **Yet this**, ' yet *of* this ' ; for the constr. see l. 424, n. **To comply**; the full constr. is ' yet *of* this be sure *that I go* to comply.' In sense this line immediately follows l. 1403.

1408, 1409. Dunster thought these words were spoken in an *aside* to the Chorus, since the Officer replies as if he had not heard them. But there is no reason either why Samson should hesitate to speak his mind openly on this subject to the Officer, or why the latter should notice declarations with which as a messenger he has no concern.

1410. thy resolution, namely, ' to come with me.' The Officer having gained the object he was sent for, does not trouble himself about anything else that Samson may have said after his words " I am content to go." **Doff**, ' put off ' ; compounded of ' do ' and ' off,' which occur as separate words as early as 890 (*circ.*) in the *Legend of the Holy Rood*, " He dydë of his purpuran " (purple robe) ; the compound form occurs in *Will. of Palerne*, 1350 ; its composition is lost sight of in *Morte d'Arthure* (1440), where it is used with a second ' off,' " Doffe of thy clothes " ; cf. *Nativity Ode*, 33, " Nature in awe to him hath doff't her gaudy trim " ; Spenser, *F. Q.* iii. 9. 21, " She (Britomart) also dofte her heavy habergeon " ; Shak. *Tr. and Cr.* v. 3. 31, " Doff thy harness, youth." Other compounds of ' do ' are ' don ' (' do on '), ' dout ' (' do out '), ' dup ' (' do up '), all occurring in *Hamlet*.

1412. To favour ... to set. Both the ' to's ' depend on ' win,' but the first is a prep. governing the subst. ' favour '; the second, the sign of the infinitive. I prefer this to making ' to favour ' an infinitive, and supplying ' thee ' after it. Cf. Shak. *Hamlet*, iv. 5. 189, " Hell itself she turns to favour and to prettiness."

1413. along, *s.c.* ' of me,' *i.e.* ' with me.' The M.E. ' *and-lang* ' (from ' *and* ' = Lat. *ante*, Gr. ἀντί, Germ. *ent-*, meaning ' over against ') is similarly used as a preposition with the gen., the literal meaning being ' over against in length.' The same prefix is found in ' answer.' The word is not to be confounded with ' endlong,' ' lengthwise.'

1418. Lords ... lordliest. The play on words is sarcastic ; the idea of ' high-handed oppressiveness ' contained in ' lordliest,' occurs in ' lordly,' l. 1353. **in their wine**, ' over their cups,' ' when drunk.' The same association of ideas occurs in *P. L.* i. 502, " The sons | Of Belial flown with insolence and wine." The allusion in ' lords ' is both to the temporal nobility and to the bishops, both of whom Milton, as a republican and puritan, despised.

1419. well-feasted priest. The selfishness and sensuality of the priests are alluded to in *Lyc.* 114-5, " Enow of such as for their bellies' sake | Creep, and intrude, and climb into the fold." The allusion is to the clergy of the Established Church. The word is used contemptuously again in l. 857, and *Forcers of Conscience* 20, with the same allusion. **Then**, ' in their wine. '

1420. aught, adv. ' in anything,' orig. a subst. compounded of

' a whit,' *i.e.* ' a wight ' (' man '), and therefore taking a prep. ' of ' after it. But the constr. in the text (without ' of ') is an old one ; cf. *Piers Plow.* v. 311. " Hastow *aughte* (*i.e.* ' at all ') in thi purs any hote spices ? " ; ib. 539, " Coudestow aughte wissen us the waye wher that wy dwelleth ? " Chaucer *Chanounes Yemennes Prol.* " Can he ought tell a miry tale or tweie ? " *Man of Lawes Tale,* " If that the childe's moder were aught (' by any chance ') she." This adverbial use of ' aught ' has passed away, but its compound ' *naught* ' has passed into the common adv. ' *not.*'

1421. **holy-days,** see l. 1323-1325, n. Todd refers to a passage in the treatise of Reformation, in which Milton attacks the proposal of the bishops " to encourage recreations and sports on Sundays and Holy-days " ; and quotes from Ben Jonson, *Sad Shepherd,* i. 4, " They call ours Pagan pastimes, that infect our blood with ease." So here Milton implies that holiday sports are of heathen origin. By a warrant of Charles I. 1633, these sports were expressly countenanced on Sundays after divine service. Next year was published the *Book of Sports,* under royal authority. The Puritan opposition to such sports, and especially to the May games, commenced under Elizabeth, but James I., like his successor, lent them his countenance by also issuing a *King's Book of Sports.*

1422. Cf. Hor. *Ars Poetica,* 224, " Spectator, functusque sacris et potus et exlex," " An audience, drunk and lawless, just after offering sacrifices."

1426. The sense is plain enough, but the grammar defective. Supplying neither ' happen ' nor ' hear ' from l. 1423 answers quite satisfactorily, though they make sense in some sort : (1) ' Whether the last of me *will happen* or no I,' ... (*i.e.* ' though I can warrant that this will not be a *dishonourable* event in my life, yet I cannot warrant whether or not it will be the last event of my life ') ; or (2) ' Whether *this is* the last *you may expect to hear* of me or no I,' ... (*i.e.* ' the last time you will receive news of me '). Perhaps the simplest constr. would be (3) ' Whether *this is* the last of me or no I,' ... without attempting to express more precisely the verb meant.

1427-1440. *The Chorus invoke a blessing on Samson, and utter one of those unconscious prophecies that characterize the Chorus in Greek dramas—they pray that the angel that once announced his Birth may now be present at—what turns out to be—his Death.*

1427. An Alexandrine without the pause after the third foot.

1430. **Great** ; *proleptic ;* ' so that it becomes great.'

1432. **Fast,** firm, steadfast. This is the original meaning of the word in A.S. from which its other uses are derived :—(1) ' to abstain from food,' lit. ' to observe abstinence firmly ' : this is a very early derivative : it occurs in Alfric's *Homilies* (975) ; (2)

'swift,' through the intermediate sense of 'continual' occurring as an adv. *fastlice* in Old Eng. *Homilies* (1150); (3) 'tied,' 'secured,' occurring in *Genesis* and *Exodus* (1250), through the intermediate sense of 'secure' occurring in Beowulf (7th cent.); (4) 'close,' 'near,' occurring in *William of Palerne* (1350) ('fast by-side'). Similarly peculiar uses of the word in expressions like 'fast asleep,' 'playing fast and loose,' 'a fast young man,' 'fast bind, fast find,' can be traced to one or another of the above meanings. **father's field.** *Judges*, xiii. 9, "And the angel of the Lord came again unto the woman as she sat in the field."

1433. after his message told, a Latinism for 'after telling his message,' or 'after the telling of his message'; see l. 1377.

1434. shield Of fire, cf. the 'pillar of fire' that interposed between the Israelites and the pursuing Pharaoh, *Exod.* xiii. 21; and the 'wall of fire' that is to protect Jerusalem, *Zech.* ii. 5.

1435, 1436. *Judges*, xiii. 25, "And the spirit of the Lord began to move him at times in the camp of Dan between Zorah and Eshtaol."

1439. seed, a very frequent expression in the Bible for 'children,' 'progeny.'

1442. erewhile, 'a (short) time before.' namely 'on the occasion of his first visit,' l. 337. Milton uses the older form 'whilere' in *Ode on Circumc.* 10.

1444. glad news, cf. 'glad office,' l. 924, and n.

1445-1507. *Manoah announces his hopes of ransoming Samson; but there are difficulties, and these serve to bring out the father's affection; for he declares his resolution to give up all his substance to secure his son's liberation. This, perhaps, is the reason why Milton does not make the work of ransoming Samson an accomplished fact. Manoah then draws a picture of his son's life such as it will be when he has ransomed him—a picture all the more touching, drawn as it is immediately before the shout is heard that announces Samson's death.*

1445. Peace. Heb. *shâlôm*, one of the ordinary forms of salutation among the Jews both at meeting (*Judges*, xix. 20) and at parting (1 *Sam.* i. 17): the word is used in the sense of 'welfare,' and is still current in the East in the form of '*es-selám aleykum.*' **hither,** 'to come hither,' verb of motion omitted, see l. 1370, n.

1447. parted, 'departed,' see l. 1229, n.

1448. To come; we should now say 'to go'; but 'come' is from the same root as 'go,' viz. GAM or GA, and both words like Gr. βαίνω from the same root, meant, originally, 'to step,' and were used of such motion either *to* or *from*. Thus the original sense 'to step,' 'to walk,' occurs in Wyclif, *Acts*, xiv. 7, "A man was sijk in the feet ... which never had *goen.*" Halliwell notes the use of 'come' for 'go' (as in the text) as an archaism; and in Shakspere the use of 'go' for 'come' is frequent: *e.g.* 2 *Henry IV.* ii. l. 191, "Come, go along with me, Master Gower"; *M. N. D.* i. l. 115, "Come, Egeus, you shall go with me." Similarly Gr. βαίνω means either 'to go' (βῆ δ' ἐπὶ νηός; βὰν δ' ἰέναι) or 'to come' (ὡς ἀκμαῖος, εἰ βαίη μόλοι), or even 'to stand,' 'to rest in a place' (χρυσέα κλῂς ἐπὶ γλώσσᾳ βέβηκε). So in Anglo-Saxon 'cuman' is used for 'gegàn' (Cynewulf's *Wanderer,* "Hwáer cwóm mearg, hwáer cwóm mago? hwaer cwóm maddumgifa?" "Where has gone the horse, where has gone the man, where has gone the giver of treasure?") and conversely 'gegán' for 'cumán' (*Judith,* "Hie tha beághrodene fétheláste forth onetton, oth hie glaedmode gegán haefdon tó thám weallgate," "They then adorned with rings hastened their steps forward, until, glad of mood, they had come to the rampartgate").

1449. **rings,** *sc.* 'with the news.'

1450. **no will,** *sc.* 'to go thither.'

1453. **To give ... me,** 'to impart to you,' 'to make you share with me.'

1454. **good success** ; 'success' originally meant 'event' (l. 737), 'result,' whether good or bad ; 'good' in the text is no more superfluous than 'bad' in *P. R.* iv. 1, "Perplexed and troubled at his bad success."

1455. **would much rejoice,** *i.e.* '*it* would,' etc. ; '*hope*' being the objective after 'rejoice.'

1456. **Say,** 'say on,' 'speak.' This absolute use of 'say' would not be correct in modern prose.

1457. **attempted,** 'tried to persuade,' cf. Shak. *Merch. of Ven.* iv. 1. 421, "Dear sir, of force, I must attempt you further." Mr. Oliphant notices the use of 'attempt' with an objective of the *person* in *Letters on the Suppression of Monasteries,* 1533. It is now commonly used with an objective of the *thing.*

1457-1471. Prof. Masson thinks there is an allusion in these lines to "the management needed for Milton's escape from punishment at the Restoration, and the variety of opinion in Parliament and at Court in his case." Milton's life had been in danger, and he had to lie in hiding ("abscondence" as Phillips calls it) for three months, until the Act of Indemnity was passed.

1458. **high,** 'main,' 'principal,' opposed to 'by' as in 'highways' and 'byways.'

1459. **prone,** 'prostrate.' This was the attitude of supplication among the Hebrews, see *Ruth,* ii. 10.

1460. **of,** partitive genitive, like Fr. *de.*

1462. set on spite, *i.e.* 'bent on *gratifying* their spite.'

1463. The reference is to the High Church Royalists. Milton never adopts half measures in his attacks on this party. In *Comus,* he alludes to them as the 'rout' of that magician who himself stood for Laud; in *Lycidas* they are called "blind mouths," in *P. L.* iv. they are "lewd hirelings," and here they are zealous idolaters; see l. 693. Among Milton's implacable enemies was "marginal" Prynne, the author of *Histriomastix.*

1464. The allusion is to the Presbyterians, who had joined the Royalists, and whose leaders, such as the Duke of Albemarle and Lord Sandwich, had been advanced to honour and office.

1465. Cf. Ovid, *Ars. Am.* iii. 653, "Munera, crede mihi, capiunt hominesque deosque," "Believe me, gifts win over both gods and men."

1466. This charge of avarice Milton had already brought against the Presbyterians in *Forcers of Conscience* (where he looks on them as Pluralists and Pharisees) and in *Sonnet* xiii. ("Hireling wolves whose gospel is their maw"). But it should be remembered that in the ranks of those whom Milton so deeply brands were men like Calamy and the saintly Baxter. **a third.** It is probable that Milton's escape was partly due to the indifferent attitude of the King himself and of Clarendon.

1468. had enough revenged, *sc.* 'themselves'; 'had taken sufficient revenge.'

1469. beneath their fears, 'too abject to be any longer formidable to them'; cf. the expr. 'beneath contempt.'

1470. Prof. Masson mentions among those who interested themselves in Milton's safety, the names of Andrew Marvell, the poet. and once Milton's assistant when he was Latin Secretary; Sir W. Davenant, who however was not in Parliament; Sir Thomas Clarges, and Sir William Morrice, both active promoters of the Indemnity Bill, and Mr. Annesley, afterwards Earl of Anglesey, an admirer of Milton's genius. **magnanimity;** in modern prose we should add 'itself' on the analogy of expressions like 'he is goodness itself,' etc. **to remit,** '*in agreeing* to remit,' *sc.* 'the punishment.'

1471. convenient; in Lat. sense, 'proper,' 'suitable'; cf. *Prov.* xxx. 8, "Feed me with food convenient for me"; *Eph.* v. 4, "Neither filthiness nor foolish talking nor jesting, which are not convenient."

1472. This and l. 1508 keep the reader alive to the catastrophe in course of being enacted outside the scene. **shout,** namely that raised at Samson's entry into the theatre at Gaza, l. 1624. **tore the sky**; so the fallen angels "Upsent | A shout that tore hell's concave," *P. L.* i. 542.

1477. **compass**, 'effect,' cf. *P. L.* iii. 342, "Adore him who to compass all this dies."

1478. **numbered down**, 'counted,' cf. *Luke*, xii. 7, "But even the very hairs of your head are all numbered"; so Wyclif uses 'noumbrid' in the same passage.

1479. **richest**, as he actually was perhaps; Josephus (*Antiq.* v. 8. 1) styles Manoah "without dispute the principal person of his country."

1480. **And**; grammar strictly requires '*than that* he should be left,' or '*while* he is left.' 'And' has been so used in l. 149. This constr. still exists as a common Irish provincialism, and Carleton's *Irish Peasantry* is full of it (*e.g.* "Oh Shane Fadh, acushla machree!" Says my poor mother in Irish, "You're going to lave us, avourneen, for ever, *and* we to hear your light foot and sweet voice no more." "Come, come," says my uncle, "I'll have none of this : what a hubbub you make, *and* your son going to be well married to such a purty colleen of a wife").

1481. **fixt**, 'fixed in purpose,' 'determined.' **part**, see l. 1229, n.

1482. **redemption**, the fuller Latin form of the contracted French 'ransom.' **patrimony**, this evidently from l. 1486, means not only his inherited, but *all* his property.

1484. Another play on words : 'If only my son is with me, that shall be riches enough to me.' **Not wanting him**, 'not deprived of his society.' **shall want nothing**, 'shall have no wants,' 'shall have every want gratified.'

1485-1486. **lay up ... lay out.** Johnson found fault with this jingle on words, but see l. 1117, n.

1487. **wont**, '*are* wont'; for this use of the word as an active verb, cf. Spenser, *F. Q.* iii. 12. 20, "The craftsman wonts it beautify;" *Shepheard's Calendar*, *December*, 115, "I that whilome wont to frame my pipe | Unto the shifting of the shepherd's foote." 'Wont' is properly 'woned,' past pt. of M. E. 'won' (A. S. *wunean*, 'to dwell'); but even before Spenser's time the word had come to be regarded as a verb, and a new past pt. 'wonted,' was formed from it, and occurs in Udall's *Apophthegms* (1542).

1489. **than thy age**, 'than thee, aged as thou art.' Samson himself has alluded to his premature old age, l. 938. **eyesight lost** ; a Latinism for 'loss of eyesight.'

1493. **locks**, objective to 'view,' understood.

1494. Todd quotes Ovid, *Met.* viii. 8, "Cui ... crinis inhaerebat, magni fiducia regni," "On whose head there grew a hair, the strength and safety of a great kingdom."

1495. **I persuade me** ; see l. 586, n. **had not**, 'would not have.' Masson's text reads 'hath,' in which case the construction is a contracted one for 'had not as he hath.'

1497. Garrisoned. The metaphor, unusual otherwise, is suggested naturally enough in the case of Samson, whose hair was his stronghold or fortress. A similar figure is applied to the golden hair of Nisus ; see Ovid, quoted in l. 1494, n.

1498. were not, 'were it not' : see l. 1455.

1499. Sophoclean irony again : the great service was performed, but it involved consequences the least expected by Manoah.

1500. Not to sit idle ; strict grammar would require the constr. to be 'not that he should sit idle,' depending on 'were not his purpose' above. This double negative with the subjunctive is equivalent to one negative with the indicative, 'it was his purpose that he should not sit idle.'

1501. about him ; join with 'useless.' The reference is to his flowing locks falling round about his shoulders.

1502, 1503. This is the logic of affection. The fond father whose hopes are highest just before the fatal announcement that is to destroy them, devoutly reasons that God who had already worked so many miracles on his son's behalf, may work yet another, and restore him his eyesight. **to his strength,** 'to help his strength,' 'co-operate with it.'

1505. Of his delivery ; *hyperbaton ;* join with 'hopes' above. The sober Chorus sympathizes with the more rational hopes of Manoah, but refrain from noticing the fond belief he has just expressed. There is the same unconsciousness here as in Manoah's speech.

1506. agreeable to, 'such as is natural to,' 'in accordance with.'

1507. as next ; 'as those whose interest in Samson is only second to yours, being his friends and countrymen.'

1508-1540. *These lines set forth the state of distraction and doubt and foreboding, that forms the transition from the recent hopes of Manoah and the Chorus to the bitter disappointment about to follow.*

1508. O. what a noise ! namely that caused by the fall of the house with " burst of thunder," l. 1655.

1509. Mercy of Heaven ; elliptical for '*May the* mercy of heaven *guard us*,' or words to that effect.

1512. whole inhabitation, 'the entire body of inhabitants.' The same use of the abstract for the concrete occurs in *Acts*, xvii. 26 (*Bible* of 1551), "And hath assigned before ... the endes of their inhabytacyon." **perished,** 'had perished' or 'were perishing.''

1513. are in, 'are indicated by.' Todd refers to Eur. *El.* 752, Οὖν

H

οἶδα πλὴν ἕν, φόνιον οἰμωγὴν κλύω, "This only know I, death is in that noise."

1514. **Ruin**, in the Latin sense of ' a fall,' *sc.* ' of a building '; hence its modern concrete meaning of a ' fallen building ' itself. Literally the word means a ' rushing down,' as in *P. L.* vi. 193, *P. L.* iv. 413, " Water with fire in ruin reconciled "; hence ' a hurling down,' as in *P. L.* i. 46, ii. 995. **at the utmost point**, ' utter '; cf. Fr. *à toute outrance*, It. *al ultimo segno* (Todd).

1516, 1517. How naturally is this the first thought to spring up in a father's bosom ! The Chorus, less distracted than Manoah, guesses nearer the truth.

1519. **dismal**, ' disastrous ' in a stronger sense than its modern one of ' gloomy.' The Romans had their *dies religiosi* (days of ill-omen), or *dies vitiosi* (unlucky days), or *dies atri* (black days), on which no business, religious or secular, was to be transacted ; these days, in the middle ages, came to be called *dies mali*, each month having two such days assigned to it ; this *dies malus* became in O.Fr. *di mal*, in English *dismal* (noun) ; thus Chaucer (*Boke of the Dutchesse*) has " in the dismal " (in perplexity) ; this noun next became an adjective ; thus Holland translated Livy's *de diebus religiosis* by " about the dismal days," and Spenser (*F. Q.* ii. 8. 51) has " Paynim this is thy dismal day," (destined day of death) ; later, in Foote's *Liar* (1761) there is " in the dismals " (in the dumps). The present meaning of "gloomy " may be a reversion to another mediaeval name, *dies Ægyptiaci*, derived from the three days of the plague of *darkness* of Moses's days.

1521. **Best keep together**, *i.e.* ' *we had* best keep *ourselves* together,' or as in Elizabethan English ' *we were* best,' etc. Both constructions were originally impersonal, ' we were better ' being equivalent to ' it were (would be) better for us,' as is shown by still older form, ' us hadde ben better,' occurring in the *Tale of Gamelyn*. The change from ' be ' to ' have ' can be traced in the similar constr. ' him leófre *waes* ' (Alfred's *Proverbs*, lit. ' to them (it) liefer (dearer, preferable, better) was ') passing into ' they *hadden* leovere ' (*Romance* of *Alexander*). The change in both cases was probably due to false analogy : the Lat. *mihi est* (lit. ' there *is* to me ') being equivalent to the ordinary English ' I *have* '; the impersonal ' them was leovere ' was similarly taken to be equivalent to ' they hadden leovere.' The transition from the older constr. with ' be ' to the later one with ' have ' gave rise to a curious confusion of the two : thus in a poem of 1380 occurs ' thou *haddyst* be better have gold.'

1521-1522. As the Chorus, following the practice of the Greek drama, have to continu ' on the stage till the end, these lines afford a reason for their not running out, as would be but natural, to see what the matter was.

1526. need...to fear; the sign of the infinitive is here expressed after 'need,' probably to prevent 'fear' from being mistaken for ' substantive after ' much.'

1527-1535. These nine lines and l. 1537 were added by Milton subsequently. The effect of the addition is to bring out the dramatic reaction of feeling noted below, and to prolong the suspense before the messenger enters and clears all up.

1527-1528. The Chorus, in that sudden revulsion of feeling that the occurrence of the unexpected brings about, now begin wildly to entertain that very hope upon which, when but lately expressed by Manoah, they had looked with sober mistrust; while the latter, driven by the same reaction from fervent hope to chill despair, now considers that to be presumptuous which he had but just believed to be probable. In this outburst of wild hope before an impending but unforeseen calamity, Milton imitates Sophocles; cf. the Choruses in *Ajax*, 693 *sq.*, *Antig.* 1115 *sq.*, both, as in the text, spoken just before the entry of the messenger. So also in *Œd. Tyr.* 1086 *sq.*, and *Trach.* 205 *sq.*

1529. dealing dole; another perfectly serious *paronomasia*, after the Hebrew manner noted before. Indeed such punning on such an occasion is kept in countenance by examples much nearer home; *e.g.* in Gaunt's punning lament over himself in Shak. *Rich. II.* ii. l. 73 *sq.* The double meaning in 'dole' is (1) 'share' (A. S. *dael;* whence Eng. 'deal,' cf. Germ. *theil*), the constr. being in this case a cognate accusative, and the sense being sarcastic, ' dealing out (to them their) share (of blows); (2) ' grief ' (Fr. *deuil* from Low Lat. (*cor-*) *dolium* ' (heart-) grief '), the sense in this case being ' spreading grief.' The original meaning of (1) was ' a share of *almsgiving* '; this sense and that of ' grief ' both occur in Chaucer's *Romaunt of the Rose.* There is a comic pun on these two meanings of the word in *Ralph Roister Doister*, iii. 3, " And I will crie halfepenie doale for your worshyp. | Come forth, sirs, heare the dolefull newes I shall you tell." Shakspere too uses the word in both senses, *e.g.* 1 *Henry IV.* i. 1. 169, "The dole of blows," and *Merry Wives,* iii. 4. 68, " Happy man be his dole." This last, a form of blessing, is very common; cf. Ray's *Proverbs, Damon and Pythias* (Dodsley, i. 190).

1533. of old, ' in olden times '; adv. phrase to be joined with ' wrought ' and contrasted in sense with ' now.'

1535. subscribe, ' assent '; cf. Shak. 2 *Henry VI.* iii. 1. 38, " I will subscribe and say, I wronged the duke." Supply ' to what you say ' after ' subscribe,' and ' in it ' after ' tempts belief.'

1536. notice, ' news,' ' information '; frequent in Shakspere **in**

this sense; cf. *Meas. for Meas.* iv. 5. 7, "Go call at Flavius' house
and tell him where I stay : give the like notice to Valentinus."

1537. **Of** ; supply ' notice ' from above, the Chorus taking up
and continuing Manoah's speech. The stiffness of the construction is explained, no doubt, by the fact that this line was a
subsequent addition. The way this addition arose was thus :—
Line 1536 was originally a part of the speech of the Chorus,
following immediately upon l. 1526, and itself followed by ll.
1538-40. On the insertion of the new lines noted above, l. 1536
fell to Manoah, leaving the Chorus to begin their speech with l.
1538. Now a speech in English cannot very well begin with
' For,' although if Milton had chosen to adopt a Graecism (cf.
the frequent commencement of speeches in Greek plays with
γάρ), he could have made the Chorus begin with ' For evil news.'
He, however, evidently preferred the insertion of a new line.

1538. **post**, adv. ' post haste ' ; a person was said to ride ' post '
when fresh relays of horses were *posted* or stationed at intervals
on the route. **baits**, ' travels slowly ' ; ' to bait ' is to stop on the
way to feed the horses (' bait,' lit. ' a bite ').

1539. **to our wish**, ' in accordance with our wish ' ; Fr. *à
souhait.*

1540. A Hebrew is with propriety made the messenger. A
Philistine's patriotism would make him reluctant to narrate
with truth the disaster that had befallen his gods and country,
and even if truthful, he would lack that *feeling* with which the
Hebrew tells the story of his countryman's terrible revenge and
glorious death.

1541-1659. *The Messenger enters dazed and perturbed at the
dreadful sight he has just witnessed. His first hurried utterances
are most skilfully managed by Milton so as to revive Manoah's
hopes once again, before they are dashed for ever (ll. 1558-67 and
l. 1572). Manoah is most eager in his inquiries, whereas the
calmer Chorus never speaks until they have heard all that the
Messenger has to say. In the midst of his crushing grief Manoah
does not forget honour : he wishes to know how his son died,
whether in a manner worthy of himself. Satisfied on this point,
he then, and only then, asks for details of the catastrophe, which
the Messenger proceeds to give in a long uninterrupted narrative.*

1541. **fly** ; this word is frequently used transitively for the
intransitive ' flee.' in the sense of ' escape ': that in such cases
' flee ' is the proper word can be shown by turning the sentence
into the past tense : thus ' fly the sight' becomes ' fled (not
' flew ') the sight.' The two verbs were originally distinct,—
fleógan, pt. fleág, ' to fly ' ; and fleóhan, pt. fleáh, ' to flee,'—
but the confusion began very early. Thus in the A.S. poem of
the *Battle of Maldon* ' fleogan ' is used to mean ' fly ' (" Hé lét

him thá of handum leófne fleógan hafoc with thaes holtes," "He then allowed him to fly from off his hands the favourite falcon towards the wood " ;) and then some lines below, to mean 'flee' ("Gylpwordum spraec, thaet hé nolde fleógan fótmaél landes," "He spoke in boastful words that he would not flee a foot of ground.") This indiscriminate use continues throughout M.E., helped by the variety of spelling in the d⌣⌣⌣⌣. Later, we find in Gawain Douglas's translation of the *Æneid* (1513), and in Ascham's *Toxophilus*, 'flee' (a relict of the Northern dialect) used for 'fly,' and, on the other hand, in Foxe's *Documents* (1546) 'fly' used for 'flee' ('fly the realm '). This last use occurs in the text and is still common.—The entry of a Messenger with loud exclamations when he has some dire calamity to announce, occurs in Æsch. *Pers.* 251 *sq.*

1543. **erst,** 'lately'; see l. 339, n. **and yet behold.** The sight is yet vivid before the horrified imagination of the man, after it has passed away from before his eyes.

1544. **pursues,** implying that he wishes, but in vain, to forget the painful sight.

1545. **providence,** a dissyllable. **instínct,** Latin accent.

1546. **and scarce consulted,** *i.e.* 'almost unconsciously'; he did not deliberately direct his steps towards the place where Manoah and the Chorus were.

1549. **knew remaining,** a Graecism, οἶδα μένοντας, for ' knew *to be* remaining'; participle instead of infinitive after verb of knowing.

1550, 1551. **As ... So,** a Latinism, *tum ... quum,* for 'although ... yet.' **event** ; see l. 737, n. **too much,** ' deeply'; the 'too ' implies that the concern was *painful,* was something which he wished were *less*.

1552. **loud,** ' heard far and wide.' **and here,** *i.e.* 'and *came or arrived* here'; omission of the verb of motion, '(*arrived*) *with rueful cry,*' *i.e.* a rueful cry announced the accident.

1553. **hear not,** ' have not heard,' *i.e.* 'you do not tell us.' Manoah is impatient to hear the cause of the crash and uproar.

1554. **No preface needs** ; passive in sense and impersonal ; ' there is needed no preface'; cf. *P. L.* iv. 235, "Whereof here needs no account "; ix. 215, "Where most needs "; x. 80, "Attendance none shall need." **preface,** *i.e.* words of preparation to soften the blow if the news is the worst they fear. Manoah impatiently urges the Messenger to tell the worst at once.

1555. **It,** *i.e.* 'what the accident was.' **would ... forth,** 'would involuntarily break from my lips.' **I recover,** *i.e.* 'I stop to recover.'

1556. distract, 'distracted'; Fr. *distrait*, frequent in Shakspere; cf. *Twelfth N.* v. 1. 287, "He's much distract"; *Jul. Caes.* iv. 3. 155, "With this she fell distract." In words like 'distract,' 'exempt' (l 103), 'except' (*P. L.* ii. 300), 'succinct' (*P. L.* vi. 643), the '*t*' is the true participial term., so that the forms 'distract*ed*,' etc., have really a double termination like Lat. '*-tatus*' in frequentative verbs. **to ... utter,** 'to make sure that my words convey what I mean.' The messenger not only wishes to give an intelligible account of what has happened, but is apprehensive of the effect it will have upon old Manoah, as his speech, l. 1562, indicates.

1557. sum, 'main fact'; Lat. *summum,* 'the last or most important thing'; cf. *P. R.* i. 283, "And last, the sum of all, my Father's voice"; *P. L.* vi. 673, "The sum of things" (afterwards called 'the main'); viii. 522, "The sum of earthly bliss"; xii. 575, "The sum of wisdom." **circumstance,** 'the accompanying details,' used collectively, as in Hooker, *Eccl. Pol.* iv. 1. 3, "To what purpose all this circumstance."

1560. not saddest, 'not the saddest that can happen.'

1562. Cf. Shak. *Two Gen. of Ver.* iii. 1. 220, "I have fed upon this woe already | And now excess of it will make me surfeit." Todd refers to Petrarch, *Sonet.* 104, "Pascomi di dolor," "I feed on grief." The Messenger asks Manoah to indulge first in such grief as humanity may prompt him to feel even for enemies, and implies that a greater grief is in store, which he refrains from communicating at the same time, lest both be more than he can endure.

1563. Relate by whom, 'say at whose hands'; join with "overwhelmed and fallen," l. 1558. For 'by,' see l. 1580. Short speeches by different speakers here, as in Greek plays (*e.g.* Soph. *Œd. Tyr.* 626 *sq.* ; *Œd. Col.* 327 *sq.*), make up a line (hypermetric in the present case) :—"Reláte | by whóm. | By Sám | son. Thát | still lèss | ens."

1565, 1566. refrain ... To utter. This use of 'refrain' with an infinitive clause for object may be traced to its use as a regular transitive, as in *P. L.* vi. 360, "Refrained his tongue."

1567. irruption, 'a breaking in upon,' a Latin use of the word, cf. Seneca, *Ep.* cxvii. "Calamitates quae ad me irruperunt," "The misfortunes that have burst upon me "; cf. the expr. 'to break the news abruptly.'

1568. too deep, *sc.* 'into thy heart.'

1569. them, 'the news,' which like Fr. *nouvelles* is strictly a pl., as Milton makes it here. He uses the singular, however, in l. 1538, and in *P. R.* i. 64, "This ill news." The sing. had been used by Lyly (*Euphues,* 1579), "other newes is none," and is common in Shakspere.

1570. Note the dramatic effect of this announcement. Todd refers to Soph. *Elect.* 673, τέθνηκ' 'Ορέστης. This line constitutes the "*Discovery*" of the Action.

1571. **defeated**, 'undone,' 'destroyed'; see l. 1278, n.

1573. This metaphor would naturally come to Manoah's mind. The idea here is the same as that in ll. 156 *sq.* Manoah had failed to ransom Samson's body from the prison of the Philistines, but death had done this, and more—it had ransomed his soul from the prison of the body.

1574. **windy**, 'empty,' cf. *Is.* xxvi. 18, "We have as it were brought forth wind, we have not wrought any deliverance in the earth"; so Homer uses μεταμώνιος and ἀνεμώλιος for 'vain' (lit. 'windy'). The context shows that there is besides a particular reference to Plato's ἀνεμαῖον, 'windy,' 'vain,' used in the *Theaetetus* as opposed to γόνιμον (151), 'fertile,' and as equivalent to ψεῦδος (161), 'false,' and οὐκ ἄξια τροφῆς (210), 'not worth rearing.' The explanation of this is to be found in Aristotle's ὑπηνέμια ᾠά, 'wind eggs'—τίκτουσιν ᾠὰ ... ἐξ ὧν οὐ γίγνεται νεοττὸς οὐδεὶς ἀλλ' ὑπηνέμια πάντα τὰ τοιαῦτά ἐστιν, "They lay eggs...from which no chicks are hatched, but which are all windy," *Hist. An.* vi. 2, 10.

1576, 1577. Newton refers to Shak. *Henry VIII.* iii. 2. 355, for the same metaphor, and to *Love's L. Lost*, i. 1. 100, "Byron is like an envious sneaping frost | That bites the first-born infants of the spring." **bloom**, 'flower'; cf. mod. Germ. *blume*, and M.E. *Metrical Psalter*, 1300 *circ.*, "Als blome of felde sal he welyen ("wither") awai." **lagging rear of**, *i.e.* 'late departing.'

1578. It is noticeable that Manoah does *not* give way to grief in spite of what he says here: the two lines, 1590-1, can hardly be looked upon as the expression of uncontrollable sorrow. See Introd. p. xxx, and ll. 1708-9, n.

1579. **death**, *i.e.* 'the *manner* of one's death.' **crown**, '*final* glory'; so **shame** must be taken to mean '*last* disgrace,' in order to complete the antithesis.

1582. **of**, 'by.'

1584. The Messenger's words, together with Manoah's up to "cause," make one line. So also is l. 1586 made up.

1587. **At once**, 'at the same time.' The sense is 'because he could not destroy (his enemies) without destroying himself.'

1590. Thus at last "*poetic justice*" is fulfilled. Samson's error and the beginning of his misfortunes were due to his having been "over-weak against himself"—he now expiates that error, and ends those misfortunes by being "overstrong against himself."

1594. **Eye-witness**, 'having been an eye-witness,' in apposition with 'thou.'

1596. Occasions, the unusual use of the pl. here, perhaps, serves to impart a notion of indefiniteness exactly as it does to its equivalent 'circumstances' ; '*some* occasion or another.' See l. 244 for another sense.

1599. Little, *sc.* 'of the business I had come upon.'

1600. was rumoured ; supply 'it,' see l. 1641. In M.E., as in modern Italian, the impersonal pronoun is often omitted when the true nominative follows as a sentence introduced by the conj. 'that.'

1603. minded, 'purposed.' 'resolved' ; cf. *Ruth,* i. 18, "When she saw that she was steadfastly minded to go with her" ; Baret's *Alvearie,* "To mind or purpose ; *in animo habere.*"

1604. at ; by *synesis* for 'from' ; 'not to be absent' being equivalent in sense to 'to be present.'

1606-1611. In the description of the theatre, Milton has effected a compromise between the arrangement of a Greek and Roman theatre, and that given in the book of *Judges* of the Philistine theatre at Gaza.

1606. Half round ; this was the shape of the Roman theatre, that of the Greeks being a segment larger than a semicircle. **two** : this number is stated by Josephus, *Antiq.* v. 8, 12, and can be inferred from *Judges,* xvi. 25. **vaulted high,** 'supporting lofty arches.' There is no mention of the arch in the Hebrew Bible, and the English rendering 'arches' in *Ezek.* xl. 16, is not correct. Landor, therefore pointed out the expression in the text as an instance of anachronism. Modern research, such as those of Rosellini and Wilkinson, has, however, established the fact that arches were known in ancient Egypt and employed in domestic architecture, though absent in their temples. Hence it is inferred that the Jews *may* have introduced the arch from Egypt into Canaan.

1607, 1608. each degree of sort, 'each grade of person of rank,' 'every grade of *the quality,*' as enumerated in l. 1653. **sort,** from Lat. *sors,* originally meant 'destiny,' as in Chaucer, *Prol. to Knightes Tale,* "Were it by a venture or sort or cas." Hence the derived meanings of (1) 'manner' in the phrase 'in sort' (corresponding to Fr. *de sorte que*) found in Spenser : (2) 'company.' Elizabethan literature swarms with instances of this use of the word, *e.g.* "a goodly sort," "a sort of shepheard groomes" (Spenser), "a sort of wolves," "a sort of tatter'd rebels" (Beau. and Fl.), "a sort of flatterers" (Marlowe), "a sort of ravens" (Dekker), "unchosen and unarmed sort" (*Ferrex and Porrex*). (3) 'rank,' lit. 'lot in life,' as in the text : cf. *Acts,* xvii. 5, "certain lewd fellows of the *baser sort,*"(where Wyclif has "comyn puple," and the Gr. Test. τῶν ἀγοραίων ; Ben Jonson, *Every Man in his*

Humour, i. 3, "A gentleman of your sort, parts, carriage, and estimation."

1609. **The other side**, *i.e.* 'the side corresponding to the diameter of the circle'; this side had no wall, so that the common people assembled outside could see Samson's performance from behind his back.

1610. **banks**, 'benches,' the words are doublets like 'kirk' and 'church,' 'dyke' and 'ditch.' Milton here does not follow the Scripture account which states that "there were *upon the roof* about three thousand men and women that beheld while Samson made sport" (*Judges*, xvi. 27).

1611. **obscurely**, 'unnoticed.' Being a Hebrew, the man would naturally wish not to attract attention.

1612. **grew high**, *zeugma* : 'the feast waxed merrier, and day advanced towards noon.'

1613. **high cheer**, 'goodly entertainment.'

1616. **livery**; lit. anything *delivered* to a servant,' such as (formerly) an allowance for the keep of a horse, or (as now) a suit of clothes. Though the word occurs in Chaucer, and in Cavendish's *Life of Wolsey*, Spenser thought it necessary to explain its meaning in his *View of the Present State of Ireland*. Milton uses the word without any of its present prosaic association in *Comus*, "Liveried angels," *L'All.* "Clouds in thousand liveries dight," and *P. L.* iv. "Sober livery" of twilight.

1617. **timbrel**, a musical instrument of percussion, also called a 'tabret' or 'tambourine.'

1619. **cataphracts**, Gr. κατάφρακτος ; cavalry in which both man and horse were protected (φράσσω) by coats of mail. The word is so explained by Servius in a note to Virg. *Aen.* xi. 770, and is used by Polybius, Plutarch, and Livy for 'mailed horses.' Dacian cavalry are represented as 'cataphracts' on Trajan's Column, and Major Denham (*Travels*) states that the Begharmi lancers of Central Africa were cased, both man and horse, in iron mail.

1621. **Rifted**, from subst. 'rift,' which is again from the verb 'to rive,' meaning 'to tear,' 'to split.' **clamouring with praise**, 'clamorously praising.' For the rare use of 'clamour' as a transitive cf. South's *Sermons*, "to clamour the sun and stars out of their courses"; Shak. *Winter's Tale*, iv. 4. 250, "Clamour your tongues"; this last, however, being a doubtful passage. The word is used contemptuously in the text like Lat. *clamito*.

1622. **thrall**, see l. 370, n.

1623, 1624. **undaunted, where ... place**; *hyperbaton* for 'undaunted came to the place where.' **set before him**, 'appointed for him to perform.'

1626. **still**, 'without hesitation,' from the original sense of 'always'; see l. 963, n.

1627. **All**, to be joined with 'what,' l. 1623, as the object of 'performed.' **stupendious**, so spelt again in *P. L.* x. 351, and in both places having the Latin sense of 'amazing' (*stupeo*, 'to be astonished'). Richardson quotes from other 17th century writers where the *i* is also inserted. So 'tremendous' was once spelt 'tremend*u*ous,' and is now pronounced 'terrimend(g)*i*ous' as a vulgarism.

1628. **antagonist.** Samson now figures in his capacity of *Agonist* (see note on Title). This capacity must not be confounded with that of *Protagonist* (πρωταγωνιστής or 'chief actor') of the play, which Samson also fulfils.

1630. **his guide**, see ll. 1-11, n.

1631. **we**, *i.e.* 'I and those others who stood further off.'

1632. *Judges*, xvi. 26, "And Samson said unto the lad that held him by the hand, Suffer me that I feel the pillars whereupon the house standeth, that I may lean upon them."

1634. **arched roof**, see l. 1606, n. Todd notices that Milton is fond of the arch; cf. *Nativ. Ode*, 19, and *P. L.* i. 726, "arched roof," *Il Pens.* 157, "high embowed roof."

1635. **which**, Latin constr. for '*and* (when he felt) *them.*'

1637. **eyes fast fixed**, *i.e.* 'in that attitude in which he would be if he had eyes, and fixed his gaze on the ground.' Cf. Hom. *Il.* iii. 217, κατὰ χθονὸς ὄμματα πήξας, "Fixing his eyes upon the ground."

1641. **as reason was**, 'as *there* was (good) reason'; Milton often omits the impersonal 'there': see l. 1721, and cf. *P. L.* vi. 126, "Most reason is"; viii. 443, "Good reason was"; *P. R.* vi. 526, "Good reason then."

1642. **beheld**, participial adj. agreeing with 'which' contained in 'what,' l. 1640.

1645. **amaze**: verb used as noun; so once in the pl. in Shak. *Love's L. Lost*, ii. 1. 246, "His face's own margent did quote such amazes." **strike**, there is a double meaning in the word, and a dreadful irony in one of its significations.

1646-1659. These lines constitute the *Catastrophe* or *Lusis* of the action (see Introd. p. xvii.). They also constitute its τὸ φοβερόν or the circumstance that rouses the feeling of terror in the spectator. According to Aristotle's distinction (*Poet.* ii. 14) it may be inferred to be of the highest order, the dreadful deed being perpetrated not on an enemy, not even on those near and dear to us, but—what is more terrible than either of these—upon the perpetrator himself.

1648. when, *hyperbaton* for 'As when mountains tremble with,' etc. The reference is to an earthquake, such as accompanies a volcanic eruption. The simile is also used in *P. L.* vi. 195, *sq.* **pent,** 'pent up,' 'confined,' within the bowels of the earth, and seeking forcible exit; cf. Shak. *Venus and Ad.* 1046, " As when the wind, imprisoned in the ground | Struggling for passage, earth's foundation shakes." **massy,** a hybrid, the Saxon termination *-y* (A.S. *-ig*) being joined to the Romance word 'mass.' Spenser, Shakspere, and Milton all use this form, and none of them seems to have used the later form *massive*, which occurs in Congreve, perhaps for the first time, being probably a post-restoration word, from Fr. *massif*.

1653. These constitute the 'degrees of sort,' l. 1607.

1654. *Hendiadys* for 'the choice flower of their nobility.'

1655. round, ' neighbouring.'

1657. inevitably. This word is significant. It distinguishes the suicide of Samson, on the one hand, from that of Ajax, the sensitive Greek, who preferred a 'glorious death' by suicide to living a life of disgrace; and, on the other hand, from that of Cato, the Roman Stoic, who committed suicide because he looked upon it as a 'rational means' of terminating life. Samson's prayer for death (l. 650) shows that he did not presume to take the matter into his own hands, and his present action towards himself is unavoidably bound up with that other towards his enemies, to which he felt himself called by divine inspiration (l. 1381 *sq.*). It is to be noted also that in Jewish law there was no direct prohibition of this act, and in those cases in which it was committed (such as those of Saul, Ahithophel, and Zimri) no opinion, either in condemnation or approval of the deed, is expressed.

1660-1707. *The Chorus now break the long silence, in which respect for the father had held them while he was eagerly making his anxious inquiries, and, in the Commos or Lament, declare that Samson had at last fulfilled the work to which he had been consecrated, and that his death was not willingly self-inflicted, but the work of dire necessity. The First Semichorus draws a picture of the Philistines caught red-handed and destroyed in the midst of their idolatry and feasting and just after they had unconsciously importuned to his task the heaven-appointed instrument of their destruction. Then the Second Semichorus draws, in a series of glorious similes, the contrasted picture of this instrument of God, despised and neglected, but unexpectedly reviving and dealing terrible vengeance on his enemies, and leaving behind him a fame that will live for ever.*

1660. dearly bought, *sc.* ' with his own life.'

1661. Living or dying, ' *whether* living or dying,' *i.e.* ' both in life and in death.'

1664. Cf. Hom. *Od.* vii. 60, ἀλλ' ὁ μὲν ὤλεσε λαὸν ἀτάσθαλον, ὤλετο δ' αὐτός, "He brought destruction upon the arrogant race (of giants), and perished himself."

1665. **tangled,** Milton uses this form again in *P. R.* ii. 162, "Tangl'd in amorous nets."

1666. Cf. Æsch. *Prom. Vinct.* 105, τὸ τῆς Ἀνάγκης ἔστ' ἀδήριτον σθένος, "Unconquerable is the force of necessity." Eur. *Hel.* 514, δεινῆς Ἀνάγκης οὐδὲν ἰσχύειν πλέον, "Nothing is stronger than dire necessity." So Plato, *Legg.* v. 10. These Hebrews here speak in the language, though not in the spirit, of the Greek chorus. Milton has elsewhere contrasted free-will with necessity (*P. L.* iii. 110 *sq.*, v. 526 *sq.*), and providence (or, as it is there called, *fate*) with necessity (*P. L.* vii. 171 *sq.*). In the text, while the expression 'not willingly' points to the first of these contrasts, Milton would hardly make his Hebrews say in the spirit of the Greek chorus that necessity has on this occasion overruled the Providence of God. This, however, is what the Greek dramatists mean when speaking of fate and the fates, whom Æschylus (*Agam.* 994, *Prom. Vinct.* 524) represents as stronger than Zeus. Milton's idea seems to approach closer to the Stoic doctrine which identifies fate with Providence, and teaches that it is able to turn evil into good by making it subserve its own far-reaching purposes. **whose law,** 'the law of necessity,' or the law of nature, as modern science would call it, which acts uniformly, no matter whether its action affects the good or the bad ; it is opposed to the law of freedom, by which the moral nature of man is enabled to rise superior to its surroundings. Samson had won this moral freedom through the chastening and purification his soul had undergone in adversity, but this could not save him from the operation of the unalterable decree of fate, or, as the scientist would say, of the physical laws of nature. It is in this contrast that the pathos of the tragedy lies. It is noticeable, too, that while Milton preserves the form of the traditional doctrine of the Greek drama in his use of the word 'necessity,' he gives that doctrine an entirely new meaning that brings it into better harmony with Hebrew and Christian ideas on the point.

1667. **in number more.** *Judges,* xvi. 30, "So that the dead which he slew at his death were more than they which he slew in his life."

1668. **all thy life had,** *i.e.* 'thou in all thy life *hadst.*'

1669. **Semichorus,** Gr. ἡμιχόριον. The Chorus now divides itself into two, one half taking for the subject of its ode the fate of the Philistines, the other half, the triumph of Samson. **sublime,** 'exalted,' 'raised in spirit'; lit. 'high,' 'raised aloft,' as in *P. L.* vi. 771, "He on the wings of cherub rode sublime."

1670. Drunk with idolatry, 'insensible, in the midst of their idolatry, of the offence they have given to God, and supinely unconscious of the impending calamity'; cf. *Is.* xxix. 9, "They are drunken but not with wine; they stagger, but not with strong drink." Although 'drunk' is repeated in the text, the constr. is substantially a *zeugma*; cf. *P. L.* i. 502.

1671. fat regorged; the constr. is either (1) an exceedingly bold *zeugma*—'drunk (*i.e.* surfeited) with the regorged fat,' or (2) an *anacoluthon* for 'and while *they* regorged the fat.' **regorged**, *i.e.* 'eaten (or 'ate') to excess'; *re*- being intensive, 'repeatedly,' 'excessively.'

1672. Chaunting. This spelling (used again in *Il Pens.* 63, 'chauntress') is due to the influence of French pronunciation. Spenser is full of words spelt with *au*, which properly should have only *a*. The same phenomenon of orthography or rather heterography was common in the spelling of Indian proper names in English, before the introduction of the Hunterian system. **preferring**, see l. 464, n.

1673. living Dread. The expression is compounded of the epithet 'living,' so commonly applied in Scripture to God, and of 'dread' from a passage in *Isaiah* (viii. 13, "Sanctify the Lord of hosts himself .. let him be your dread "). The word was used as a title; thus Spenser calls Elizabeth "his dearest dread " (*F. Q.* Introd. i.), and Una the " deare dread " of the Elfin knight (*F. Q.* i. 6. 2). So as an adj.; thus Henry V. is called "most dredde lord " (Rymer's *Documents*); James I. is called "most dread sovereign " in the Dedication of the *A. V.* (This form, without the *ed*, appears in Chaucer's *Clerkes Tale*, "bilovid and drad.")

1674. In Silo. The Ark of the Covenant, which stood in the Holy of Holies in the Tabernacle, and was the symbol of the presence of God among his worshippers, remained in Siloh from the latter days of Joshua (xviii. 1) to the time of Samuel, judge of Israel after Samson (1 *Sam.* iv. 3 *sq.*). **bright**; the reference is to the "Glory of the Lord" that dwelt in the sanctuary. In the *Targums* this is called the *Shekineh*, lit. 'a dwelling'; hence, 'the outward manifestation of divine glory.'

1675. spirit of phrenzy. Milton perhaps was thinking of the Latin saying *Quem Deus vult perdere, prius dementat*, "Whom God wishes to destroy He first drives mad," or the Greek proverb, quoted in a note to the fragments of Euripides, ὅταν δὲ Δαίμων ἀνδρὶ πορσύνῃ κακὰ | τὸν νοῦν ἔβλαψε πρῶτον, "God first deprives of reason the man for whom He contrives evil." Todd quotes a similar sentiment from the *Scholia* on Soph. *Antig.*

1676. Who, *i.e.* 'the Spirit,' which is here personified like the Greek Furies and Erinyes.

1679. set on, 'intent on.'

1680. Unweetingly, 'unknowingly.' The archaic adj. 'un-weeting' also occurs in Milton, and the verb 'weet' is common in Spenser, from root VID, 'see,' 'know.' **importuned,** see l. 775, n.

1681. Speedy ; adj. for adv., cf. the expr. 'come quick.'

1682. fond, see l. 228, n.

1683. into, 'under' in prose.

1685. or to sense reprobate, 'or *left* to *a* reprobate sense,' 'abandoned to wicked thoughts,' cf. *Rom.* i. 28, "God gave them over to a reprobate mind to do those things which are not convenient." 'Reprobate' is used always by Milton in his poetry, as once by Shakspere in the dramas (*L.L.L.* i. 2. 64, "Reprobate thought") as an adj., which it originally was (Lat. *reprobatus,* 'reproved,' 'censured,' hence 'deserving reproof').

1686. blindness internal. These words strikingly bring out the contrast between Samson and his Philistine enemies ; cf. *Ephes.* iv. 18, "Being alienated from the life of God ... because of the blindness of their heart" ; *Lucretius,* ii. 13, "O miseras hominum mentes ! O pectora caeca," "O miserable souls of men, O blind hearts !" Ovid, *Met.* vi. 472, "Pro superi, quantum mortalia pectora caecae | Noctis habent," "O ye gods above, how blind a night fills the hearts of men !" Todd refers to Guarini, *Pastor Fido,* "O cecità de le terrene menti," "O blindness of earthly souls !"

1687. The Second Semichorus take up the idea in the last line and complete the picture of the contrast.

1688. thought, *sc.* 'to be' or 'to have been.' **extinguished,** 'rendered powerless,' the metaphor is expanded below.

1689. inward eyes. What he here represents as vouchsafed to Samson, Milton prays in *Paradise Lost* (iii. 51-54) might be granted to him. Cf. *Ephes.* i. 18, "The eyes of your understanding being enlightened." Todd quotes from Henry More, Milton's friend, "But corporal life doth so obnubilate | Our inward eyes that they be nothing bright"; cf. also Guarini, *Pastor Fido,* "Aprir nel cieco senso occhi lincei," "To open piercing eyes within blind sense."

1690. fiery virtue, 'impetuous strength,' 'ardent courage '; cf. *P. L.* ix. 694, "Your dauntless virtue." The same metaphor, but with a different application, occurs in Chaucer, Prol. *Reeves Tale,* "Yet in our ashen cold is fire yreke "; (raked together) cf. Gray, *Elegy,* "And in our ashes live their wonted fires."

1692. Prof. Masson has been the first to give the correct meaning of this passage. On account of the 'but' in l. 1695, other readings, such as 'and not,' 'nor' instead of 'and,' had been proposed in this line, but there is no need to alter the original reading, 'and.' The idea sought to be conveyed here in simile is that of one despised by his enemies, suddenly becoming formidable to them. But *one* simile not being adequate for this purpose, two, or rather three, have been used by Milton. The Philistines from their lofty seats looking down upon Samson groping his way to perform the feats set before him, with feelings of present security from a once dreaded enemy, are likened to "villatic fowl" looking down from the safety of their roosting-place upon the serpent crawling at evening dusk beneath. Suddenly there comes danger and destruction from a quarter least expected, and the downrush of the crashing house is likened to the swoop of an eagle from the sky overhead. That the destruction so dealt is not the work of a cruel wrong-doer, but proceeds from the just anger of an offended God, is set forth in a third simile, in which the eagle is not the rapacious bird of prey, but the messenger of Jupiter's wrath, charged with his thunderbolt. **evening**, 'that sallies forth in the evening.' **dragon**, 'serpent,' as in *Nat. Ode*, 168, "the old Dragon"; *P. L.* x. 529, "Satan ... now dragon grown ... huge python." Cf. *Rev.* xii. 9, "And the great Dragon ... that old serpent." So in Homer, *Il.* ii. 308, the dragon sent by Jupiter is a serpent. Pliny, under the name of Draco, evidently describes the habits of the boa constrictor (*Hist. Nat.* viii. 11. 12; xxix. 20, etc.). The word is derived from Gr. δέρκομαι, 'to see,' and this idea, absent in the text, occurs in *Comus* (395, "dragon watch") and in the description of the dragon watching the Gardens of the Hesperides. Another idea, swiftness of flight, commonly associated with the dragon, is also absent here, but occurs in *Il Pens.* Spenser, *F. Q.* i. 11; Shak. *M. N. D.* iii. 2. 379; Ben Jonson, *Catiline*, iii. 3; Beau. and Fl. *The Honest Man's Fortune*, iii. 3. Lastly, there are the fire-breathing dragons of romance.

1693. **Assailant.** So the dragon in the *Iliad* attacks a sparrow's nest. **perched roosts**, *i.e.* 'roosts furnished with perches.' 'Perch' for birds (Lat. *pertica*) is lit. 'a rod,' and the same word as 'perch' in linear measure. 'Roost'; Skeat discards the etymology from 'to rest,' and suggests that the word is derived from the same root as 'roof,' and rafters under a roof are meant. **nests**, *sc.* for hatching young ones.

1694. **in order ranged**, the reference is to the seats in the theatre, arranged in rows.

1695. **tame villatic fowl**; the two epithets are used with a contemptuous reference to the besotted Philistines. 'Villatic,' 'belonging to the farm-house'; 'barn-door fowl' are meant; cf. Plin. *H. N.* xxiii. 17, "Villaticas alites"; Varr. *R. R.* iii. 9. 3, "Villaticae gallinae."

1696. **cloudless thunder**, 'thunder from a cloudless sky,' and therefore all the more terrible, because unexpected. Such thunder among the ancients was an ominous portent. Thus it presaged Caesar's death and the battle of Philippi (Virg. *Georg.* i. 487), and was once a warning to an Epicurean loose-liver (Hor. *Od.* i. 3. 4). **bolted**, ' shot like a bolt or arrow.' Milton uses the same metaphor in *Reason of Church Government* with reference to Samson's locks : "They sternly shook thunder with ruin upon the heads of those his evil counsellors, but not without great affliction to himself." Jortin points out that the simile of the eagle or vulture is used of Ajax as the terror of his enemies by Sophocles, *Ajax*, 167 *sq.*

1697. **given for**, ' given *up* for,' ' despaired of as.'

1699. **self-begotten bird**, ' the Phoenix.' Another *Anachronism ;* the phoenix being the product of the Greek imagination, though placed in the east. Johnson censures the introduction of this simile. But the phoenix had long been in use as a figure in Christian literature. Sir T. Browne refers to Tertullian, Ambrose, Cyril and other Christian writers as using it as a type of the Resurrection. On a poem, the ' *Carmen de Phoenice* ' of Lactantius, was based the A.S. Phoenix of Cynewulf, which is also an allegory on Christian life and death. **self-begotten,** see l. 1703, n.

1700. **Arabian woods.** Milton derives the unusual idea of *woods* in Arabia no doubt from Pliny, *Hist. Nat.* xiii. 9) who says that this bird died with the date-palm, Gr. φοῖνιξ), and Ovid, (*Met.* xv. 296 *sq.*), who says that it builds its nests in the *branches* of the palm. Shakespeare improves upon this in *Temp.* iii. 3. 23, " There is one tree, the phoenix throne, one phoenix | At this time reigning there ;" and in the *Phoenix and the Turtle*, " Let the bird of loudest lay | On the sole Arabian tree." **embost**, ' hidden,' *sc.* ' in the woods ' ; from O. Fr. *embusquer*, It. *imboscare* (*bosco*, ' a bush ') ; Milton also uses the form ' imbosk ' in his prose works ; cf. Spenser *F. Q.* iii. 12. 17, " As a dismayed deare in chace embost ; " so, in the cognate sense of ' enclosed ' in *F. Q.* i. 3. 24, " In mighty armes embost," and metaphorically in iv. 4140, " he lig in ease embost." The word has various meanings in Shakspere (see Schmidt's *Lex.*), and an entirely different sense in *P. L.* xii. 180 ; see Dodsley's note to *Albumazar*, v. 2 (vii. 200).

1701. **no second knows**, cf. *P. L.* v. 272, " A phoenix ... that *sole* bird " ; Ovid, *Amor.* ii. 6. 54, " Et vivat phoenix, unica semper avis " ; Shak. *Henry VIII.* v. 5. 41, " But as when the bird of wonder dies, the *maiden* phoenix." In the *Phoenix and the Turtle*, however (where Shak. again makes the phoenix a female), he gives her a mate, the turtle-dove, and " Single nature's double name | Neither two nor one was called." **nor third ;** this is, strictly speaking, unnecessary, but serves to emphasize the word ' second ' above.

1702. holocaust, 'a whole burnt-offering,' from Gr. ὅλος, 'whole,' καίω, 'to burn,' cf. *Ps.* li. 19 ; used in the Septuagint ; in Tyndale's *N. T.* the word stands for any burnt-offering.

1703. her. The phoenix is a male with the ancients ; Milton, like Shakspere (see l. 1701, n.), makes it a female. **ashy womb.** Modern poets differ somewhat from the account given by the ancients, who describe the new phoenix as arising out of the dead *body* (and not the *ashes*) of its parent (*e.g.* Hdt. ii. 73, ἐπεάν οἱ ἀποθάνῃ ὁ πατήρ, "After its father dies" ; Ovid. *Met.* xv. 402, "Corpore de patrio," "From the body of its father " ; Plin. *H. N.* x. 2, "Ex ossibus deinde et medullis," "From the bones and marrow (of the dead bird) " ; Tac. *Ann.* vi. 28) ; and, as carrying it on its wings from Arabia to the city of the sun (Heliopolis) in Egypt, for cremation, enclosed in a hollow " egg " or ball of myrrh. Milton follows this account in *P. L.* v. 273 *sq.*, but here, like Shakspere, Dryden and Byron, he makes the old bird burn itself. This notion had its origin perhaps in Ovid, *Met.* xv. 400. **teemed,** ' brought forth into life,' ' born ' (again).

1704. Revives ; the constr. is ' Virtue, like that bird ... teemed, revives ' ; so that the simile ends at this last word.

1706. her, *i.e.* ' of virtue,' which here stands for a ' person of virtue' ; the gender is due to the Latin gender (*virtus*, f.), and to the supposed sex of the phoenix, with which virtue is compared. Cf. Hom. *Od.* xxiv. 196, τῷ οἱ κλέος οὔποτ' ὀλεῖται | ἧς ἀρετῆς, "Wherefore the fame of her virtue shall never die." Tyrtaeus, *Eleg.* ii. 9. 31, οὐδέ ποτε κλέος ἐσθλὸν ἀπόλλυται οὐδ' ὄνομ' αὐτοῦ, | ἀλλ' ὑπὸ γῆς περ ἐὼν γίγνεται ἀθάνατος, "Never does his fair fame or his name perish, but though he be in the grave, he yet becomes an immortal."

1707. secular bird, *i.e.* ' *as* a secular bird.' Pliny is particular in noting that the phoenix, according to the senator Manilius, lives 509 years : Herodotus mentions 500 years, and so Ovid, *Met.* xv. 395, " Haec ubi quinque suae complerit saecula vitae." A *saeculum* among the Romans was a period of a century. **ages of lives,** *i.e.* ' *during* ages,' etc., ' for generations of men.' *The perpetuity of fame,* which is the moral Milton draws here from the story of the phoenix, is also drawn by Shakspere from the same story, *Henry VIII.* v. 5. 47.

1708-1758. *After a long silence, during which we may well imagine that an internal struggle has been going on, Manoah speaks. He sees no cause for lamentation, no reason "to give the reins to grief," but he finds a source of consolation in the noble manner of his son's death, and what has happened is "well and fair." —With this, the active, practical nature of the old man turns him* *resolutely away to the work of finding the body, and preparing to pay the last honours due to the dead. The Chorus, whose meditative bent of mind contrasts strongly with Manoah's nature, stays behind, to draw the solemn moral—" all is best "—and to reveal the frame of mind in which events have left it—" calm of mind, all passion spent "—thus too showing in their last words that the end of the tragedy as set forth in Milton's Introduction has likewise been fulfilled.*

1708. Come, come. Note the impatience with which Manoah breaks upon the lament of the Chorus. So Hecuba checks her grief when she hears of the noble death of her daughter Polyxena, who gave herself up to be slain as a sacrifice upon the tomb of Achilles (Eur. *Hec.* 591 *sq.*).

1709. quit himself, 'acquitted himself,' 'discharged his duty'; see l. 509, n.

1710. Like Samson, *i.e.* 'as Samson, the consecrated servant of God, was expected to do.' **Heroicly,** this is the proper adverb from the adj. '*heroic*'; the form '*heroically*' is the adv. from an adj. with a redundant or double termination, '*-ic-al.*'

1713. sons of Caphtor, 'the Philistines'; see l. 251, n.

1715. freedom. This freedom was accomplished soon after in the days of Samuel. This is a prophecy in Manoah's mouth, but it might be put as one into Milton's as well. The Revolution effected the freedom of England from Stuart misgovernment. **let but them,** the prose order is 'let them but,' *i.e.* 'if they only.'

1716. occasion; see l. 224, n. **this,** is emphatic. The Israelites had neglected former opportunities ; see l. 241 *sq.*

1717. Cf. Eur. *Rhes.* 758, θανεῖν γὰρ εὐκλεῶς μέν, εἰ θανεῖν χρεών ... τοῖς ζῶσι δ' ὄγκος καὶ δόμων εὐδοξία, "To die with glory, if a man must die, | ...to the living, to his house | Is triumph, is renown." Tyrtaeus, *Eleg.* ii. 9. 23, αὐτὸς δ' ἐν προμάχοισι πεσὼν φίλον ὤλεσε θυμὸν | ἄστυ τε καὶ λαοὺς καὶ πατέρ' ἐνκλεΐσας, "Himself, falling amidst the foremost warriors, loses his own life, but to his city and his people and his father he brings fame."

1718. which, 'what,' 'a circumstance that.' **happiest yet;** the prose constr. would have a comparative, 'happier still.' **all this,** *i.e.* '*he has done* all this.'

1721. Nothing is here, '*there* is nothing (no cause) here '; see l. 1641, n.

1722. knock the breast, in prose 'knock the breast *for.*' This was a sign of mourning among the Hebrews ; see *Luke,* xxiii. 48. **no contempt,** 'no contemptible action,' 'nothing deserving contempt.'

1723. nothing but, 'nothing *that is not*,' 'nothing but *what is*.' See Abbott, § 123. This constr. seems better than taking 'but' as a preposition meaning 'except' governing 'well and fair' as substantives.

1724. quiet us, 'calm the violence of our grief.'

1725. go find, 'go *to* find.' The sign of the infinitive is often omitted after verbs of motion; cf. Shak. *Hamlet*, ii. 1. 101, "I will go seek the king." See Abbott, § 349. Conversely, when the prep. 'to' is expressed, the verb of motion is often omitted; see l. 1250.

1726. from the stream, by *hyperbaton*, to be placed *after* 'with lavers,' next line.

1727. lavers pure, 'vessels for washing, full of pure water.'

1728. with what speed, *sc.* 'I can'; 'with all possible speed.' **the while,** 'meanwhile,' adv. qualifying 'will send.'

1729. to say us nay, 'to refuse,' *sc.* 'to accede to my wish that my kindred should come to take away Samson's body.' The expression '*to say nay*' is old, and occurs in *Havelock the Dane* (1280); cf. Shak. *Rich. III.* iii. 1. 119, "You'll say a beggar nay." The phrase seems to have survived the doing away of the distinction between 'nay' and 'no' (as set forth in Sir T. More's attack on Tyndale's translation of the *N. T.*), for Shakspere uses the forms "by yea and no," "the very yea and the no is."

1730. *Judges*, xvi. 31, "Then his brethren and all the house of his father came down and took him, and brought him up, and buried him between Zorah and Eshtaol, in the burying-place of Manoah his father."

1732. silent. Although loud lamentations were characteristic of Jewish mourning, there are passages in Scripture pointing to silence as one of its features also. Thus Job's friends sit on the ground seven days and seven nights with him, "and none spake a word unto him." In *Ezek.* xxiv. 17, "covering the lips" is one of the signs of mourning. The loud wailing was chiefly done by hired mourners, while silence for a time was observed by the relatives and friends. **obsequy.** This singular is unusual; it occurs in Spenser, *F. Q.* ii. 1. 60, "But ere they did their utmost obsequy"; in Fabyan, *Chron. Pref.* "They (ij tapers and ij candilstykks) do be sett at my grave and to brenne the tyme of the hole obsequy"; and in Daniel, *Civil Wars*, is mentioned the "solemn obsequy" of Richard II. Usually in English the pl. is used like the Lat. *obsequiae*. It is possible that by using the sing. Milton here means to give the word the meaning of 'train' (lit. 'a following'), and then as is not unusual with him repeats the idea immediately afterwards in "funeral train." The funeral ceremonies properly so called would not be performed on Philistine ground, very likely.

1734, 1735. shade Of laurel, *hendiadys* for 'shady laurel.'

1735. branching palm; the palm has no branches, but Milton twice repeats this epithet, *P. L.* iv. 39, vi. 885, by which of course is meant the tufted crown of leaves.

1736. trophies; see l. 1470, n. The hanging up of trophies at the tomb of a hero is a custom of chivalry. Although among the heathen Canaanites it was a custom to hang up trophies in the temples of their gods (1 *Sam.* xxxi. 10), such a proceeding would be obnoxious to the Jews; see Josephus, *Antiq.* xv. 8. 1. **enrolled.** 'recorded'; see l. 653, n.

1737. legend. 'biographical narrative,' lit. 'something to be read' (Lat. *legendus*), *e.g.* the inscription on the edge of a coin. The meaning in the text occurs in the titles of books, *e.g.* of the *Lives of the Saints*, or *The Golden Legend* (Lat. *Legenda Aurea*). *The Legend of Charlemagne,* Barbour's *Legendes of the Saints*, Chaucer's *Legende of Good Women*, and even Drayton's *Legends*, which are lives of historical personages, like Rollo, Gaveston, etc. In *Piers Plowman* occurs the expression 'the legende of life' for 'the book of life.' A passage in Hooker's *Eccl. Polity*, v. 20, and another in Bacon's *Essays*, show how the *Golden Legend* came to be discredited from the supposed fables and exaggerations introduced into it, until the word 'legend' acquired its present meaning. The word '*geste*' (properly 'deeds,' 'history,' *e.g.* 'a geste of Robin Hood') has undergone a similar degeneration into 'jeste' ('a joke'). **song.** Such were the songs of deliverance and victory sung by Moses (*Exod.* xv.), and by Deborah and Barak (*Judges*, v.), and by David (*Ps.* xviii., lxviii.). Such, too, were the Epinician Odes of Pindar.

1738. The object evidently was to do honour to Samson's memory, with athletic and martial exercises; like those performed at the funeral itself of Patroclus (Hom. *Il.* xxiii.). Alexander the Great on reaching Ilium offered libations at the tomb of Achilles, and "ran round it with his friends naked" (an act apparently symbolic of athletic exercises), Plutarch, *Alex.*

1740. adventures high. Todd says this also is a term of chivalry and romance, and quotes from *Don Quixote* and Hawes' *Pastime of Pleasure.*

1742. Flowers. To scatter flowers on tombs was a custom among the ancients. Thus the Thessalians adorned the tomb of Achilles with amaranthus and lilies; cf. Virg. *Aen.* vi. 884. Electra on approaching Agamemnon's tomb sees περιστεφῆ κύκλῳ | πάντων ὅσ' ἐστίν ἀνθέων θήκην πατρός, "The sepulchre, | Wherein he lies inurned, with wreaths of flowers, | Glowing in all their various dyes, hung round." Soph. *El.* 896. The custom, however, does not seem to have existed among the Jews. St. Ambrose and St. Jerome mention it as prevalent among the early Christians (Brand, *Pop. Antiq.*). **Only bewailing,** 'finding but *one* cause of lamentation' in the history of his life, but otherwise finding in it nothing but cause for national pride and glory.

1744. Manoah here departs.

1745. **All is best,** 'all is *for the* best.' The *Alcestis, Andromache, Bacchae, Helena,* and *Medea* of Euripides, all conclude with the same sentiment in the same words, but without that touch of Christian (or Hebrew) resignation conveyed by the words "all is best"; πολλαὶ μορφαὶ τῶν δαιμονίων, | πολλὰ δ᾽ ἀέλπτως κραίνουσι θεοί, καὶ τὰ δοκηθέντ᾽ οὐκ ἐτελέσθη, | τῶν δ᾽ ἀδοκήτων πόρον ηὗρε θεός, "With various hand the gods dispense our fates; | Now showering various blessings, which our hopes | Dared not aspire to ; now controlling ills | We deemed inevitable : thus the god | To these hath given an end exceeding thought." Cf. also Plato, *Rep.* x. 12, οὕτως ἄρα ὑποληπτέον περί τοῦ δικαίου ἀνδρός, ἐάν τ᾽ ἐν πενίᾳ γίγνεται ἐάν τ᾽ ἐν νόσοις ἤ τινι ἄλλῳ τῶν δοκούντων κακῶν, ὡς τούτῳ ταῦτα εἰς ἀγαθόν τι τελευτήσει ζῶντι ἢ καὶ ἀποθανόντι, "Hence in the case of the just man, we must assume that, whether poverty be his lot, or sickness, or any other reputed evil, all will work for his final advantage, either in this life, or in the next." In the Greek drama the last words are almost always spoken by the Chorus. Exceptions occur in the *Prometheus* of Aeschylus and the *Trachiniae* of Sophocles. **though oft we doubt**; as the Chorus had done in ll. 667-704.

1746. **dispose,** ' dispensation,' ' disposal ' ; verb for noun.

1748. Cf. Shak. *Meas. for Meas.* iv. 6. 7, " 'Tis a physic that's bitter to sweet end."

1749. **hide his face** ; an expression common in Scripture for the displeasure of God ; *e.g. Ps.* xxx. 7, "Thou didst hide thy face, and I was troubled."

1751. **in place** ; 'in this place,' ' on this occasion,' or perhaps in the *proper* place,' ' opportunely,' like Gr. ἐν καιρῷ, and opposed to ' out of place.' The phrase occurs very often in Spenser in various shades of meaning ; *e.g. F. Q.* i. 2. 38, " Then was she faire alone, when none was fair in place " ; i. 3. 37, " Deare sir, whatever that thou be in place " ; i. 5. 36, "They all beholding worldly wight in place" ; i. 10. 65, " And many bloody battles fought in place "

1753. **them,** ' themselves.'

1755. **acquist,** 'acquisition.' Todd quotes from Howell's *Letters,* Fanshaw's trans. of the *Lusiad,* and other contemporary writings to illustrate the use of this word. Richardson quotes from Hale, *Origination of Mankind.* "His (man's) acquests are like the acquests of a servant," and Bacon, *Of a War with Spain,* "To aspire to monarchy and new acquests." Cf. also Sir T. Browne, *Christian Morals,* ii. 4, "Let not mere acquests in minor parts of learning gain thy pre-existimation." This word, and 'intent' above, are substantives formed from the Latin past pt. *acquisitum, intentum.*

1758. **And calm of mind,** 'and *with* calm of mind.' **passion,** nom. abs. This beautiful conclusion has a double application. It refers to the fulfilment of the object of the tragedy by purging the mind of passion, and to the condition of Milton's own mind after he had fought the good fight of religion and freedom.

INDEX TO NOTES.

PRINTED IN GREAT BRITAIN BY
UNWIN BROTHERS LTD., WOKING AND LONDON